MULTIPLE NATURE-CULTURES, DIVERSE ANTHROPOLOGIES

Studies in Social Analysis
General Editor: Martin Holbraad
University College London

Focusing on analysis as a meeting ground of the empirical and the conceptual, this series provides a platform for exploring anthropological approaches to social analysis while seeking to open new avenues of communication between anthropology and the humanities, as well as other social sciences.

MULTIPLE NATURE-CULTURES, DIVERSE ANTHROPOLOGIES

Edited by

Casper Bruun Jensen and Atsuro Morita

berghahn
NEW YORK · OXFORD
www.berghahnbooks.com

First published in 2019 by

Berghahn Books

www.berghahnbooks.com

© 2019 Berghahn Books

Originally published as a special issue of *Social Analysis*, volume 61, issue 2.

Library of Congress Cataloging-in-Publication Data

Names: Jensen, Casper Bruun, editor. | Morita, Atsuro, editor.
Title: Multiple Nature-Cultures, Diverse Anthropologies / Edited by Casper
    Bruun Jensen and Atsuro Morita.
Description: First edition. | New York : Berghahn Books, 2019. | Series:
    Studies in Social Analysis ; Volume 9 | "Originally published as a
    special issue of Social Analysis, volume 61, issue 2" — Title page
    verso. | Includes bibliographical references and index.
Identifiers: LCCN 2019022985 (print) | LCCN 2019022986 (ebook) | ISBN
    9781789205381 (hardback) | ISBN 9781789205398 (paperback) | ISBN
    9781789205404 (ebook)
Subjects: LCSH: Nature—Effect of human beings on. | Naturalism.
Classification: LCC GF75 .M85 2019 (print) | LCC GF75 (ebook) | DDC
    304.—dc23
LC record available at https://lccn.loc.gov/2019022985
LC ebook record available at https://lccn.loc.gov/2019022986

British Library Cataloguing in Publication Data

A catalogue record for this book is available from the British Library.

CONTENTS

ILLUSTRATIONS

INTRODUCTION
Minor Traditions, *Shizen* Equivocations, and Sophisticated Conjunctions

Casper Bruun Jensen and Atsuro Morita

This volume was prompted by the 50th Anniversary Conference of the Japanese Society of Cultural Anthropology (JASCA), held in Chiba, Japan, in May 2014, in conjunction with the International Union of Anthropological and Ethnological Sciences (IUAES).[1] The conference's theme, "The Future with/of Anthropologies," offered an occasion to reappraise the state of the art of contemporary anthropologies and to reflect on where they might be headed. The book examines the interrelations between the possible existence of multiple nature-cultures (or alternatives to that distinction) and the definite existence of diverse anthropological traditions. In different ways, the contributors reflect on the entanglements of a variety of analytical traditions and ways of engaging with different forms of nature-culture. Doing so, they offer various perspectives on how future anthropologies might respond to the long shadows cast by the Western nature-culture distinction.

Notes for this section begin on page 12.

Even in the West, the dichotomy between nature and culture is far from straightforward. As Marilyn Strathern (1980: 177) noted decades ago: "No single meaning can in fact be given to nature or culture in western thought; there is no consistent dichotomy, only a matrix of contrasts." Once one turns to the nature-culture complex from non-Western anthropological perspectives, the 'matrix of contrasts' becomes even more tangled (Viveiros de Castro 1998; Wagner 1981). After reviewing some recent arguments about the existence of multiple nature-cultures, we proceed to consider how these discussions overlap with, and are diffracted by, the existence of diverse anthropologies. For illustration, we dwell on the complexity of nature and culture in the context of Japanese anthropology. This focus allows us to pinpoint some key issues that arise when one examines (partial) connections between diverse anthropologies and multiple nature-cultures.

Do 'They' Have Nature and Culture?

Several decades of work in feminism, anthropology, and ecology have criticized the Western cultural inclination to 'dominate' nature (e.g., Merchant 1983). Increasingly, however, the dichotomy of nature and culture has itself come under fire. Most significantly, this has occurred as part of the simultaneously unfolding 'ontological turns' in anthropology (e.g., Holbraad et al. 2013) and in science and technology studies (STS) (e.g., Jensen 2012; Mol 2002; Pickering 1995). While societies generally distinguish between human and non-human domains, these differences do not usually map onto the Western contrast between nature and culture (Strathern 1980). Yet the conceptual importance of that distinction remains central to much anthropology.

One consequence of assuming a separation between nature and culture is that ethnographic material will appear to elicit relationships between them. Fields such as ecological and environmental anthropology advertise by their very names the promise of 'bridging' domains (see also Latour 2004). However, the dichotomy is also operative in political and economic anthropology, where nature figures as the ground upon which the dramas of culture unfold. Another consequence is that people's activities can be characterized either in terms of their cultural treatment of natural environments or in terms of environmental influences on society and culture. For example, if indigenous people treat plants, trees, and landscapes with certain forms of 'respect', this can be described as living harmoniously 'with nature' (e.g., Bird-David 1999). Such forms of analysis pave the way for broader claims about the differences between indigenous holism and Western nature-culture dualism.

Scholars like Strathern (1980) and Eduardo Viveiros de Castro (1998) have carried out a long struggle to escape the parochialism of seeing all the world's peoples reflected in a Western image. Famously, they developed forms of anthropology that took the practices and cosmologies of people not simply as ethnographic 'information' that could be theoretically processed using the standard anthropological repertoires, but as conceptual starting points for widening, redefining, or challenging them. Below, we consider what such a challenge looked like during the initial appearance of 'nature' in Japan. First, however, we situate the discussion in relation to Bruno Latour's diagnosis of modernity.

Have 'We' Ever Been Modern?

In *We Have Never Been Modern*, Bruno Latour (1993) famously argued that Western modernity is premised on a strict separation between nature and culture. Since this separation can never be maintained in practice, not even in the 'modern' West, however, he argued that in reality no one has ever been modern. Latour was by no means inattentive to the strenuous attempts to shore up the nature-culture distinction. But in his diagnosis, these efforts simply cover over the multiple ways in which 'moderns' continuously undo, mix up, or hybridize their categories.

Whether one turns to commerce, politics, technology, or society, one finds 'nature within' (from the minerals of our infrastructures to the animals harnessed to sustain human livelihoods). Reversely, whether one turns to natural parks, ocean beds, or the Antarctic, one finds 'culture within' (from laws and regulations to tourism and resource extraction). In short, one can examine neither natural nor cultural 'domains' for long without coming face to face with a multitude of entities that cross the line and act in a sphere where they are not supposed to belong. Although the modern world claims to be dual, it is thus, in fact, a multiplicity.

In a parallel effort, Andrew Pickering's (1995) *The Mangle of Practice* dispensed with the nature-culture distinction and put in its place a 'dance of agency' in which an open set of elements engaged in unpredictable encounters. Much of Pickering's later work has pointed to the dangers of modern approaches that are capable of imagining nature only as a set of entities to be rationally controlled (see, e.g., Pickering and Guzik 2008). Increasingly, Pickering has sought out minor traditions in support of an imagination of co-existence based on flows of becoming. Such minor traditions might also be elicited in the form of diverse anthropologies.

Diverse Anthropologies and Minor Traditions

It goes without saying that anthropology takes multiple forms. There are also various conventional ways of categorizing this diversity, including by substance and theme, temporality and development, or national tradition. In the American context, Franz Boas famously developed the four-field approach. In this classification, anthropology was viewed as a set of domains, each with its own set of problems and concerns. Later developments, however, made this classification appear ever more tenuous.

Gender studies questioned the distinction between nature and nurture, between sex and gender, and between the physical-biological and the sociological-cultural (e.g., Ortner 1972). Multispecies anthropology pointed to the mutual shaping of people and their animal companions and raised questions of shared communication and forms of cross-species 'kinship' (Haraway 2006). At the same time, science and technology studies offered analyses of the conceptual instability and variability of the distinction between nature and culture, both in general (Latour 1993) and within particular forms of scientific inquiry (Knorr Cetina 1999). Each of these developments suggests that any substantive typology of general anthropological domains must be viewed with considerable skepticism.

Another way of characterizing the diversity of anthropologies proceeds by correlating time and theoretical development. Genealogical rather than thematic, this kind of story line narrates changes from evolutionary approaches to functionalism, structuralism, and symbolic and political anthropology, ending with an explosion of approaches after the 1970s, the debris of which has not yet settled and probably never will.

Finally, the idea of national traditions is regularly invoked. Thus, French anthropology is said to be inclined toward abstraction, as exemplified by structuralism, while English anthropology has a penchant for empiricism, American anthropology in the tradition of Boas is culturalist, and German approaches have romantic traits (Barth et al. 2005). Notably, this way of accounting for anthropological diversity centers on the traditions of a few countries. Rarely is it imagined that other anthropologies could exist, or perhaps even *do* exist, which rely on premises that are at variance with those that emerged in the Euro-American centers (but see Ribeiro and Escobar 2006).

In their study of Franz Kafka, Gilles Deleuze and Félix Guattari (1986: 16) argued that 'minor writing', rather than describing what is written in a small or otherwise insignificant language, characterizes "that which a minority constructs within a major language." Following this line of thought, we might be on the lookout for minor anthropologies with conceptual and descriptive styles that are different from those of the major traditions, without, for that matter, being radically detached from or incommensurable with them. The question, as Deleuze and Guattari suggested, is rather how such traditions create their distinctiveness from a marginal position 'within'.

While minor traditions are inflected by major ones, it is worth noting that the influence is not one-way, since the latter have also been shaped by encounters with initially foreign intellectual environments. Thus, Boas traveled from Germany to the US and brought along the idea of *Kultur*, which had such a formative effect on American cultural anthropology. Lévi-Strauss's encounter with the Americas in the 1940s led to the development of French structuralism while also being formative for Brazilian anthropology. Around the same time, the French sociology of Durkheim and Mauss were exported not only to the UK but also to Japan (Aruga 2000; Kuper 1996). In one sense, these exchanges can be seen as a sort of gradual convergence of sets of previously unrelated interests. Yet behind the façade of shared disciplinary projects, radical differences in style and interest persist. This is where we might search for minor anthropologies.

In Japan, as we shall see, the precursor of present-day anthropology emerged at the point of convergence between folklore studies (*minzokugaku*), known for its extremely descriptive style, and French social theory (Aruga 1939, 2000).

In time, this initial convergence led to new forms of diversity. Particular styles of description and analysis were recreated in encounters with dominant traditions, but they did not so much lose distinctiveness as gain it in a different form. Diversity was never abolished.

Shizen Equivocations: Nature Goes to Japan

Until the post-Meiji period, the notions of nature and culture were foreign to Japan. Even after they were introduced, the terms appeared disconnected. To this day, their immanent relationship, which appears so obvious to Westerners, often remains obscure, even to Japanese social scientists (Yanabu 1977). Around 1900, after nearly 50 years of discussion, *shizen* (自然, Chinese *ziran*) was established as the proper translation of 'nature' (see also Satsuka 2015: 19–20, 175–189). The problem was how to create an equivalence between 'nature' and the existing Chinese concept. In Chinese thought, things have propensities to develop and change as part of complex configurations (Jullien 1995). In order to retain harmony in the universe, it is important to abstain from intervening in these unfolding processes. Classic works, such as those by Lao-zi, used *ziran* to describe these immanent forces, and the term was thus specifically contrasted with any order created by human activity. When nature arrived on the Japanese scene, this use was well established among both state-sponsored Confucian political theorists and critics of feudalism (Maruyama 1974).

In Japanese, *shizen* is conventionally contrasted with *sakui* (作為), an action or artifice that is changed according to human will. Superficially, the contrast resembles the dichotomy between nature and culture. According to the translator and literary critic Yanabu Akira (1977), the decision to translate nature as *shizen* hinged on just this similarity. However, within the semantic field other contrasts gave the concept a very different inflection. For one thing, *shizen* was used as an adjective or adverb, not as a noun (*shizen-na* and *shizen-ni* roughly mean 'spontaneous' or 'spontaneously'). Moreover, the term referred neither to a general domain nor to a collection of entities (Saegusa 1968). For example, *shizen* could be used to characterize not only non-human processes but also human states. Being in a state of *shizen* (*shizen-tai*) means having a relaxed mind or body. In traditional, vernacular Japanese, and in stark contrast with the Western idea of a passive nature, the meaning of *shizen* can thus be roughly translated as 'spontaneous becoming'. Here is a key difference, for whereas nature, seen as a resource for human ingenuity, 'matches' with culture, *shizen* and its opposite *sakui* are mutually incompatible: wherever there is human effort, there is by definition no *shizen*.

In the early twentieth century, *shizen* gradually became a noun that could be used to denote things in the universe. Eventually, as noted, it became the common neologism for nature (Saegusa 1968). However, the original meaning has not vanished. The situation can be illuminated by the notion of 'equivocation', which Viveiros de Castro (2004) uses to denote situations in which people disagree without knowing that they do so, either because they use the same word for radically different purposes, or because they assume that their different words 'really' mean the same thing.

While Viveiros de Castro is mainly concerned with ethnographic encounters between Westerners and non-Westerners, the case of *shizen* indicates that such equivocations can be internalized in words and concepts. Along these lines, Yanabu has argued that even when *shizen* is used 'formally', for example, in literature or social science, the 'contradiction' between nature and *shizen* is often felt as a strange kind of gap between words and content, which is nevertheless rarely raised to the point of conscious reflection. Unbeknownst to most speakers, we might say, the concept contains an internal equivocation. We examine below the role that this equivocation has played in the emergence of certain minor traditions within Japanese social science.

The Minor and the Major

If Japan offers an interesting case for examining the relation between diverse anthropologies and multiple nature-cultures, it is, among other reasons, because the country offers a sort of reversal of Western anthropology. Whereas Western anthropologists aim to unlearn the nature-culture distinction through encounters with non-Western Others, Japanese anthropologists had to gradually learn the distinction in situations where the 'alterity' came from 'the West'.

As Julia Thomas (2001) has argued, the new concept of nature integrated diverse notions and imaginaries about land, climate, and livelihood in a way that turned the Japanese landscape into the basis for national identity. Commentators have argued that Japanese nature was part of nationalist projects from the early twentieth century (Ivy 1995; Sakai 1997), the same period in which the new meaning of *shizen* took form. Since scholars were involved in this naturalization of nationalism, the formation of new major traditions within the Japanese social sciences was based on correlating the new nature with a nativist politics. Yet not all intellectual developments were subsumed by the majority tradition. *Shizen* equivocations also facilitated the emergence of minor traditions.

Yanagita Kunio, the founder of Japanese folklore studies (*minzokugaku*), deliberately resisted the introduction of social science methods. His popular *The Legends of Tono*, published in 1910, emphasized the close ties between traditional lifestyles, rural landscapes, and spirituality. This work profoundly influenced the Japanese nostalgic imagination and prepared the grounds for a naturalized view of national identity. Yanagita also established the particular descriptive style of Japanese folklore studies, which freely traces connections among entities including people, spirits, and land. Yanagita's ([1930] 1993) *The Social History of the Meiji and Taisho Era*, for example, covers extremely variable topics, from the color of new garments to the cultivation of cotton and morning glory. It was entirely indifferent to distinctions between nature and culture.

As sociology and anthropology gradually 'modernized' under Western influence, Yanagita's unruly style was destined to recede to a minor position. A few years after the publication of *Social History*, Aruga Kizaemon, Yanagita's younger collaborator, adopted the social theory of Durkheim and Mauss to systematically analyze the structure of Japanese rural societies. This break with folklore studies marked the beginning of the domain of the social as an object of Japanese ethnography (Aruga 1939, 2000).

Even so, Yanagita's *Social History* continues to influence Japanese social science to this day. Although it fails to conform to the format and expectations of modern social science, and despite having hardly any recognizable analytical structure, it is still used in introductory courses to sociology and anthropology. This persistent popularity, we think, is indicative of the co-existence of certain discrepant predispositions in Japanese social science. On the one hand, Japanese scholars have long sought to modernize their disciplines by adopting Western approaches and theories. On the other hand, 'tradition' continues to provide a kind of implicit aesthetics, which focuses on the elicitation of tiny details and encourages roaming freely across empirical terrain.

Indeed, this aesthetico-descriptive style was deployed by later generations, including by the historian Amino Yoshihiko, for purposes that were different in equal measure both from Yanagita's original writings and from interpreters who aimed to shore up Japanese nationalism with evidence from folklore. Since the 1980s, Amino (e.g., 2012) has written numerous books that challenge the mainstream view of national identity by describing the empirical diversity of farmers, nomads, outcasts, and outlaws. Influential far beyond the confines of Japanese history, Amino's body of work has given rise to something like a paradigm shift in the social sciences.

It is telling that Yanagita was an avid reader of *L'Année Sociologique* and developed his style of folklore in conversation with, and as a deliberate alternative to, the cutting edge social theory of the time (Aruga 2000). Adopting a strategy resembling Gregory Bateson's (1972) 'complementary schismogenesis', which designated a contrastive and non-competitive mode of response, Yanagita dealt with the intrusions of French social theory not by articulating counter-theory but by creating the descriptive aesthetics of *minzokugaku*. However, this was not the only path taken.

In the 1950s, Japanese social science was under reconstruction as part of the general US-directed effort to modernize higher education. One outcome was the emergence of the now famous Kyoto School of ecological anthropology, for which the founder of Japanese primatology Imanishi Kinji—famous and controversial due to his studies of kinship and social structure among primates—was an important inspiration. Faced with American modernization theory and the post-war revival of Marxism, Imanishi's student Umesao Tadao ([1957] 2003) developed an ecological approach to human history. He saw the development of human societies as analogous to ecological succession, whereby the vegetation of a given space 'naturally' develops, for example, from grasslands to shrublands to forest. Excepting exogenous disturbance, succession was thus a unilateral process, the endpoint of which would be a highly stable climax vegetation.

On this theoretical premise, Umesao argued that both European and Japanese modernization was based on a kind of spontaneous development, which he called 'autogenic succession'. In contrast, China and the Middle East were inhibited from modernizing because of external disturbances, such as invasions by pastoral people. For Umesao, these processes evidenced multilateral development paths that could simultaneously be contrasted with Marxism and forms of modernization theory that assumed linear progress. Umesao's hypothesis aroused much controversy. In tandem with the decline of Marxism after the 1970s, however, his correlations of societies and their environments became very popular in Japanese public debate. Meanwhile, the influence of the Kyoto School's socio-ecological approach also increased within anthropology. Exemplifying Bateson's (1972) 'symmetrical schismogenesis', Umesao sought competition with foreign social theory. Rather than deploying a contrastive mode of response, like Yanagita, he escalated rivalry by adopting what Bateson would call similar 'norms of behavior'. Yet what is most interesting about Umesao's socio-ecological approach for our purposes relates to the *shizen* equivocation.

As noted, Japanese intellectuals tend to interpret 'nature' in line with the traditional Chinese sense of *shizen* as emergent dynamism. Famously, the 1880s Japanese introduction to Darwin's writings explained natural selection not as a selection by 'nature' but as an operation of immanent force (Yanabu 1977). Similarly, Umesao's concept of autogenic succession was premised on the idea that ecological transformation unfolds immanently within an ecosystem. Thus, even as the Kyoto School developed a specialized vocabulary, inspired by Western ecology and in direct competition with it, its core concepts embed Chinese traces of nature as spontaneous becoming. Autogenic succession is, in effect, a modern inheritor of the *shizen* equivocation.

In different ways, folklore studies and socio-ecology were both responses to the transformations wrought by the introduction into Japanese social thought of Western nature. Both were interwoven with the politics and policies of nationalist nature and, thus, with major national traditions. Yet both also became involved in complex processes of alignment with and differentiation from imported major traditions, becoming minor in the process. As for 'nature', even as it gradually became integral to Japanese anthropology, it has never been able to take over the semantic field.

Japanese (Non-)Modernity

James Ferguson (1997: 169) has observed that anthropology is obsessed with locality—ideally, locality that is "muddy, tropical, disease-infested." Places "that have not experienced development" are regularly seen as the "most anthropological" (ibid.). Behind this thriving cliché lies the notion that people in those locales are barely influenced by Western conceptions and modes of life, which is just why they offer ideal pedagogical sites for unlearning modernity. In this light, Japan appears as a singularly poor anthropological location: it is far too modern and hardly disease-infested at all. Indeed, since the Meiji 'restoration', Japanese society has often been perceived, both from within and from without, as the ultimate modernizer.

It is also common to characterize Japan in terms of proliferating hybrids and mixtures (Clammer 2001). Yet if Japan is at once unabashedly hybrid *and* modern, this runs counter to Latour's (1993: 30) argument that 'the modern' is characterized by "a total separation between nature and culture." Paradoxically, Japan appears fully modern although, from Latour's perspective, it lacks the distinguishing feature of modernity (Jensen and Blok 2013).

Above we have hinted at some explanations of this peculiar situation. Instead of modernity replacing tradition, the case of Japanese social science shows minor traditions burrowing through—and operating from within—major (imported) ones. Instead of purifications and hybridizations of modern nature and culture, Japanese (non-)modernity is infused with *shizen* equivocations. The entry of Western traditions in Japan, then, did not just eradicate minor traditions, it also helped to create them (see also Jensen and Morita 2012; Kasuga and Jensen 2012). The introduction of novel concepts such as 'nature' and the 'social' (imported with French social theory) generated conceptual frictions (Tsing 2005) that, in turn, led to the formation of new equivocal terms (e.g., *shizen*) and also to challenges to Western social theory in what only seemed to be its own language.

Meanwhile, the aesthetic affiliated with Yanagita's folklore ran as an undercurrent, at once offering to mainstream social science a target against which it could define itself and a descriptive style and aesthetic vision that continue to influence it. This situation is illustrative, then, not only of ethnographic diversity but also of diverse forms of anthropology, whose distinctions cannot be mapped onto substantive, temporal, or national classifications because they cut across them.

Over the last century, thematic orientations, conceptual genealogies, and national disciplinary traditions have become entangled in increasingly complex ways. The occasional intersections but otherwise parallel lives of major and minor anthropologies have contributed to the emergence of new approaches in particular locations and to the reassertion of the significance of older ones (in updated form) in others. Indeed, the entanglements of major and minor anthropologies might be characterized in terms of co-existing swirls of time and space (cf. Serres and Latour 1995). Or, as Strathern (1992) might say, perhaps we are living in an era where there is simultaneously more novelty and more tradition.

Sophisticated Conjunctions

The present moment testifies to a relativization, if not a collapse, of both nature and culture. It is no longer clear that there is 'one' of either. Indeed, it is no longer certain that nature and culture constitute encompassing domains at all (Strathern 1992: 215n41). It is as if nature and culture have either exploded or imploded. One response to this situation takes the form of calls to move beyond the two cultures of humanities and science (Snow 1959) to new forms of interdisciplinary integration of the cultural and the natural (Nowotny et al. 2001). The premise of interdisciplinarity is that forms of knowledge can be enhanced by integration and combination, for example, by developing shared problems or cross-cutting themes. Thus, the natural sciences can add knowledge of nature to the knowledge of culture produced by the social sciences, and vice versa.

Our examination of diverse anthropologies and of the nature-cultures they elicit reveals the limitations of this approach. Natural scientists are themselves already busily engaged in imagining and producing both nature and culture. Conversely, as we have highlighted, anthropology also deploys varied conceptions of nature. Whether we look to different countries and peoples or examine different anthropological traditions, we invariably find patterns of many cultures and many natures. Rather than an interdisciplinary puzzle, to which each discipline contributes a few pieces of knowledge that somehow miraculously add up, this is an image in which each discipline produces many whole worlds, the incongruence of which can be confidently assumed.

In this situation, no one is able decide in general which kind of nature or culture should matter and why. Nor does anyone have access to any neutral ground from which to determine whether and how different worlds should be brought into dialogue. Given that nature-cultures proliferate in all directions, the aspiration to 'integrate' disciplinary knowledge appears fundamentally flawed. Yet this does not mean that diverse anthropologies and their multiple nature-cultures are doomed to live parallel lives. As Barbara Smith (2012) has suggested, scholars are able to produce 'sophisticated conjunctions' of knowledge if they remain scrupulously attuned to, and reflexive about, their different conceptual orientations and assumptions. Nor are such conjunctions achievable only by university researchers, for as Strathern (2004: 551) has observed, ongoing societal transformation has itself become "a factor in the production of knowledge and its interventions form one of the platforms for the applications of knowledge."

There is thus a recursive and co-evolving relation between the kinds of natures and cultures propagated by intellectual discourse and the realities that they describe (Jensen and Winthereik 2013). Looking backward, what appear to be distinctive traditions and styles turn out to be products of moving ideas and people (Clifford 1992; Mohácsi and Morita 2013). The 'traditional' Chinese concept of *ziran*, too, is the result of a long history of East Asian exchanges (Amino 2012; Hamashita 2008; Morita 2013). Looking ahead there are also many new opportunities for lateral movements across practices, disciplines, settings, and problems, as well as novel ways of connecting what might seem to be disparate concerns (Maurer 2005).

The Contributions

With the present book, we seek to bring such opportunities and movements to light. Obviously, we are unable to deal with anthropological diversity and its multiple ways of tackling nature-culture in its entirety. We have simply gathered a range of scholars from very different traditions who come to terms with, or find ways around, nature-culture complexes. In illuminating the multiplicity of nature-cultures, they are also creating sophisticated conjunctions.

Beginning in the West, Strathern's contribution, "Naturalism and the Invention of Identity," focuses on the ways in which early modern Europeans, particularly John Locke, came to separate out natural and cultural relations and on the consequence of this separation for later understandings of kinship. Thus, her article traces the relation between this complex history and the emergence of the common Western distinction between nature and culture.

Moving between Western physics and Fijian religious movements, Naoki Kasuga's article, "Between Two Truths: Time in Physics and Fiji," works through a set of contrasts between their ways of imagining time. This analytical contrivance provides Kasuga with an opportunity to pose hard ontological questions back to physicists and Fijians—and also to anthropologists involved in the 'ontological turn'.

The next three articles unfold within Western science, the supposed realm of naturalism. In "Natures of Naturalism: Reaching Bedrock in Climate Science," Martin Skrydstrup draws on an ethnography of research in Greenland to examine the different inflections that climate scientists give to naturalism in the course of their work. Taking us to the Amazon, Antonia Walford's "Raw Data: Making Relations Matter," finds the very notion of raw data as bits of extracted pure nature oxymoronic. Rather than raw, nature is full of relations from the get-go, and they must be carefully removed from data to make it amenable to scientific analysis.

As suggested by its title, Heather Anne Swanson's article, "Methods for Multispecies Anthropology," examines the potential of experimenting with methods across disciplinary boundaries. Focusing on salmon fish ear bones, Swanson argues that anthropologically unconventional methods, such as otolith analysis, might enrich anthropology while contributing to an emergent minor anthropology that centers on entangled multispecies histories.

Continuing the focus on human-animal relations, Kazuyoshi Sugawara's article, "A Theory of 'Animal Borders,'" illustrates how the classical tradition of Kyoto School anthropology is being transformed in the twenty-first century. Drawing scholars like Dan Sperber, George Lakoff, and Maurice Merleau-Ponty into conversation with G|ui foragers of the Central Kalahari Desert, Sugawara offers a novel perspective on how relations and borders are established between people and animals.

Our own contribution, "Delta Ontologies: Infrastructural Transformations in the Chao Phraya Delta, Thailand," examines a history of entwined relations between technical infrastructures, traveling scientist-entrepreneurs, and galactic polities. This interplay has generated two contrasting yet intercalated delta ontologies—one terrestrial, the other amphibious.

Finally, Andrew Pickering's article, "The Ontological Turn: Taking Different Worlds Seriously," engages in the daunting task of figuring out what it means to inhabit different worlds. Differentiating his ontological approach from anthropological ones, Pickering develops the notion of 'islands of stability' to characterize how particular material and performative tracks make it possible to get wildly different 'grips' on reality.

Acknowledgments

This work was supported by JSPS KAKENHI Grant No. 24251017 and 15K12957, Open Research Area for the Social Sciences (ORA) co-funded by JSPS, ESRC, NWO, and ANR, and the Institute for Research in Humanities, Kyoto University.

Casper Bruun Jensen is Project Associate Professor in the Department of Anthropology, Osaka University. He is the author of *Ontologies for Developing Things: Making Health Care Futures Through Technology* (2010) and *Monitoring Movements in Development Aid: Recursive Partnerships and Infrastructures* (2013, with Brit Ross Winthereik). He is also the editor of *Deleuzian Intersections: Science, Technology, Anthropology* (2009, with Kjetil Rödje) and *Infrastructures and Social Complexity: A Companion* (2016, with Penny Harvey and Atsuro Morita).

Atsuro Morita is an Associate Professor of Anthropology at Osaka University. He has done ethnographic research on technology development in Thailand, focusing on how ideas, artifacts, and people travel in and out of Thailand. Together with Casper Bruun Jensen, he currently convenes the Japanese team of the Delta's Dealing with Uncertainty project. He is the author of *Engineering in the Wild* (Sekaishiso-sha, in Japanese) and editor of *Infrastructures and Social Complexity: A Companion* (2016, with Penny Harvey and Casper Bruun Jensen).

Notes

1. The original participants were Geoffrey Bowker, Casper Bruun Jensen, Naoki Kasuga, Eduardo Kohn, Atsuro Morita, Andrew Pickering, Hugh Raffles, Marilyn Strathern, and Kazuyoshi Sugawara.

References

Amino, Yoshihiko. 2012. *Rethinking Japanese History*. Ann Arbor: University of Michigan Press.
Aruga Kizaemon. 1939. *Daikazoku Seido to Nago Seido: Nambu Ninohe-gun Ishigami-mura ni okeru* [The institutions of large household and 'Nago' in Ishigami Village in Nambu Ninohe District]. Tokyo: Attic Museum.
Aruga Kizaemon. 2000. "Aruga Kizaemon Saigo no Kowa" [The last lecture by Aruga Kizaemon]. In *Aruga Kizaemon Kenkyu* [Aruga Kizaemon studies], ed. Ryukichi Kitagawa, 3–84. Tokyo: Toshindo.
Barth, Fredrik, Andre Gingrich, Robert Parkin, and Sydel Silverman. 2005. *One Discipline, Four Ways: British, German, French, and American Anthropology*. Chicago: University of Chicago Press.

Bateson, Gregory. 1972. *Steps to an Ecology of Mind.* New York: Ballentine Books.

Bird-David, Nurit. 1999. "'Animism' Revisited: Personhood, Environment, and Relational Epistemology." *Current Anthropology* 40 (S1): S67–S91.

Clammer, John. 2001. *Japan and Its Others: Globalization, Difference and the Critique of Modernity.* Melbourne: Trans Pacific Press.

Clifford, James. 1992. "Traveling Cultures." In *Cultural Studies,* ed. Lawrence Grossberg, Cary Nelson, and Paula Treichler, 96–117. New York: Routledge.

Deleuze, Gilles, and Félix Guattari. 1986. *Kafka: Toward a Minor Literature.* Trans. Dana Polan. Minneapolis: University of Minnesota Press.

Ferguson, James. 1997. "Anthropology and Its Evil Twin: 'Development' in the Constitution of a Discipline." In *International Development and the Social Sciences: Essays on the History and Politics of Knowledge,* ed. Frederick Cooper and Randall M. Packard, 150–175. Berkeley: University of California Press.

Hamashita, Takeshi. 2008. *China, East Asia and the Global Economy: Regional and Historical Perspectives.* Ed. Linda Grove and Mark Selden. London: Routledge.

Haraway, Donna. 2006. "Encounters with Companion Species: Entangling Dogs, Baboons, Philosophers, and Biologists." *Configurations* 14 (1–2): 97–114.

Holbraad, Martin, Morten Axel Pedersen, and Eduardo Viveiros de Castro. 2014. "The Politics of Ontology: Anthropological Positions." *Cultural Anthropology,* 13 January. https://culanth.org/fieldsights/462-the-politics-of-ontology-anthropological-positions (accessed 6 March 2017).

Ivy, Marilyn. 1995. *Discourses of the Vanishing: Modernity, Phantasm, Japan.* Chicago: University of Chicago Press.

Jensen, Casper Bruun. 2012. "Anthropology as a Following Science: Humanity and Sociality in Continuous Variation." *NatureCulture* 1 (1): 1–24.

Jensen, Casper Bruun, and Anders Blok. 2013. "Techno-animism in Japan: Shinto Cosmograms, Actor-Network Theory, and the Enabling Powers of Non-human Agencies." *Theory, Culture & Society* 30 (2): 84–115.

Jensen, Casper Bruun, and Atsuro Morita. 2012. "Anthropology as Critique of Reality: A Japanese Turn." *HAU: Journal of Ethnographic Theory* 2 (2): 358–370.

Jensen, Casper Bruun, and Brit Ross Winthereik. 2013. *Monitoring Movements in Development Aid: Recursive Partnerships and Infrastructures.* Cambridge, MA: MIT Press.

Jullien, François. 1995. *The Propensity of Things: Toward a History of Efficacy in China.* Trans. Janet Lloyd. New York: Zone Books.

Kasuga, Naoki, and Casper Bruun Jensen. 2012. "An Interview with Naoki Kasuga." *HAU: Journal of Ethnographic Theory* 2 (2): 389–397.

Knorr Cetina, Karin. 1999. *Epistemic Cultures: How the Sciences Make Knowledge.* Cambridge, MA: Harvard University Press.

Kuper, Adam. 1996. *Anthropology and Anthropologists: The Modern British School.* 3rd ed. London: Routledge.

Latour, Bruno. 1993. *We Have Never Been Modern.* Trans. Catherine Porter. Cambridge, MA: Harvard University Press.

Latour, Bruno. 2004. *Politics of Nature: How to Bring the Sciences into Democracy.* Trans. Catherine Porter. Cambridge, MA: Harvard University Press.

Maruyama Masao. 1974. *Studies in the Intellectual History of Tokugawa Japan.* Trans. Mikiso Hane. Princeton, NJ: Princeton University Press.

Maurer, Bill. 2005. *Mutual Life, Limited: Islamic Banking, Alternative Currencies, Lateral Reason.* Princeton, NJ: Princeton University Press.

Merchant, Carolyn. 1983. *The Death of Nature: Women, Ecology, and the Scientific Revolution.* San Francisco: HarperSanFrancisco.

Mohácsi, Gergely, and Atsuro Morita. 2013. "Traveling Comparisons: Ethnographic Reflections on Science and Technology." *East Asian Science, Technology and Society* 7 (2): 175–183.

Mol, Annemarie. 2002. *The Body Multiple: Ontology in Medical Practice*. Durham, NC: Duke University Press.

Morita, Atsuro. 2013. "Traveling Engineers, Machines, and Comparisons: Intersecting Imaginations and Journeys in the Thai Local Engineering Industry." *East Asian Science, Technology and Society* 7 (2): 221–241.

Nowotny, Helga, Peter Scott, and Michael Gibbons. 2001. *Re-Thinking Science: Knowledge and the Public in an Age of Uncertainty*. Cambridge: Polity Press.

Ortner, Sherry B. 1972. "Is Female to Male as Nature Is to Culture?" *Feminist Studies* 1 (2): 5–31.

Pickering, Andrew. 1995. *The Mangle of Practice: Time, Agency, and Science*. Chicago: University of Chicago Press.

Pickering, Andrew, and Keith Guzik, eds. 2008. *The Mangle in Practice: Science, Society and Becoming*. Durham, NC: Duke University Press.

Ribeiro, Gustavo Lins, and Arturo Escobar, eds. 2006. *World Anthropologies: Disciplinary Transformations within Systems of Power*. New York: Berg.

Saegusa Hiroto. 1968. "Shizen." In *Sekai Dai Hyakkajiten* [Great encyclopedia], vol. 10, ed. Tatsuo Hayashi, 229–231. Tokyo: Heibonsha.

Sakai, Naoki. 1997. *Translation and Subjectivity: On "Japan" and Cultural Nationalism*. Minneapolis: University of Minnesota Press.

Satsuka, Shiho. 2015. *Nature in Translation: Japanese Tourism Encounters the Canadian Rockies*. Durham, NC: Duke University Press.

Serres, Michel, with Bruno Latour. 1995. *Conversations on Science, Culture, and Time*. Trans. Roxanne Lapidus. Ann Arbor: University of Michigan Press.

Smith, Barbara H. 2012. "Terms of Engagement: The Humanities vis-à-vis the Sciences." Keynote talk for the conference "Science and Method in the Humanities," Rutgers University, 2 March.

Snow, C. P. 1959. *The Two Cultures*. Cambridge: Cambridge University Press.

Strathern, Marilyn. 1980. "No Nature, No Culture: The Hagen Case." In *Nature, Culture and Gender*, ed. Carol P. MacCormack and Marilyn Strathern, 174–222. Cambridge: Cambridge University Press.

Strathern, Marilyn. 1992. *After Nature: English Kinship in the Late Twentieth Century*. Cambridge: Cambridge University Press.

Strathern, Marilyn. 2004. "Laudable Aims and Problematic Consequences, or: The 'Flow' of Knowledge Is Not Neutral." *Economy and Society* 33 (4): 550–561.

Thomas, Julia A. 2001. *Reconfiguring Modernity: Concepts of Nature in Japanese Political Ideology*. Berkeley: University of California Press.

Tsing, Anna L. 2005. *Friction: An Ethnography of Global Connection*. Princeton, NJ: Princeton University Press.

Umesao Tadao. (1957) 2003. *An Ecological View of History: Japanese Civilization in the World Context*. Trans. Beth Cary. Melbourne: Trans Pacific Press.

Viveiros de Castro, Eduardo. 1998. "Cosmological Deixis and Amerindian Perspectivism." *Journal of the Royal Anthropological Institute* 4 (3): 469–488.

Viveiros de Castro, Eduardo. 2004. "Perspectival Anthropology and the Method of Controlled Equivocation." *Tipití* 2 (1): 3–22.

Wagner, Roy. 1981. *The Invention of Culture*. Chicago: University of Chicago Press.

Yanabu Akira. 1977. *Hon-yaku no Shiso* [Thought of translation]. Tokyo: Heibonsha.

Yanagita Kunio. (1930) 1993. *Meiji Taisho-shi: Seso-hen* [The social history of the Meiji and Taisho era]. Tokyo: Kodansha.

Chapter 1

NATURALISM AND THE INVENTION OF IDENTITY

Marilyn Strathern

> Our bodies must be understood as holobionts, whose anatomical, physiological, immunological, and developmental functions evolved in shared relationships of different species. (Gilbert et al. 2012: 334)

Not so long ago, an article on symbiosis appeared in the *Quarterly Review of Biology* (Gilbert et al. 2012) outlining the essential interactions between species entailed in the contribution of microbes to forming and sustaining life.[1] Given that its authors are historians and philosophers of biology, perhaps it is not surprising that they began with reference to the early modern period in Europe and a discussion of concepts of individuality. They argued (after Charles Taylor) that the general notion of the autonomous individual agent, as understood then, framed the study of life forms later known as biology. Today, they wrote

Notes for this chapter begin on page 26.

of organisms, "all classical conceptions of individuality are called into question by evidence of all-pervading symbiosis" (ibid.: 327).

In their tracing of non-individual-based notions, from organic systems or ecologies to the vocabulary of symbionts and holobionts, Gilbert et al. (2012) drew both on behavioral concepts, such as interaction or communication, and on a broader, more abstract conceptualization of 'relations', 'relationships'. That is where I would lay my own question. If Euro-Americans are to continue trying to shake off—it seems a never-ending task—restrictive notions of individuality, I wonder if they do not need alternative ways of thinking about relations as well. This is not least because in much conventional parlance relations presuppose already existing entities. So when our authors talk of "inter-active relationships among species" (ibid.: 326), the terms of the relation become, epistemically speaking, individualized. Of course, the problem has been taken up in numerous locations outside biology.[2] Yet perhaps we have not said everything that we need to say about relations. The concept may turn out to be at once key for comprehending symbiosis and a linguistic impediment to describing it.

This chapter considers some issues in the way that relations, epistemic and otherwise, have been imagined by Euro-Americans and what these self-acknowledged moderns (after Latour 2013b) may have been hiding from themselves. If it requires venturing into the kinds of subject matter that concern historians and philosophers, without being able to take advantage of their perspectives, it will become apparent that what is offered here is not meant to compete with them. An interest in evolving notions of biology, and of nature at large, it is argued, might spare a glance at people's ways of thinking about reproduction and at changing configurations of kinship.

Internal and External Relations

From work in Amazonia that has now become a *locus classicus* of debates about European cosmology, Viveiros de Castro (2004: 472) lays out one of its fundamentals, a contrast between relational and non-relational substantives: "Kinship terms are relational pointers; they belong to the class of nouns that define something in terms of its relations to something else ... Concepts like fish or tree, on the other hand, are proper, self-contained substantives: they are applied to an object by virtue of its intrinsic properties." Self-contained substantives appear in stark contrast to those of Amerindian perspectivism, where entities "named by substantives like *fish, snake, hammock,* or *beer* are somehow *used* [emphasis added] as if they were relational pointers, something halfway between a noun and a pronoun ... [Speaking generally,] [y]ou are a father only because there is another person whose father you are. Fatherhood is a relation, while fishiness is a[n] intrinsic property of fish. In Amerindian perspectivism, however, something is a fish only by virtue of someone else whose fish it is" (ibid.: 472–473).

Viveiros de Castro (2004: 473) invites us to imagine that all Amerindian substances are of this sort: "Suppose that, as siblings are those who have the same parents, conspecifics are those that have the same fish, the same snake, the same hammock, and so forth. No wonder, then, that animals are so often conceived, in Amazonia, as affinely related to humans. Blood is to humans as manioc beer is to jaguars in exactly the way that my sister is the wife of my brother-in-law." There might be an analogical inflection to Euro-American sibling and in-law relations, but not to the way they think of blood or beer. And here Viveiros de Castro's argument prompts a further thought. For Euro-American moderns, the relativity of kinship does not seem all-pervasive. While kin terminology remains an exemplar of relative thinking, since the terms imply relations, when the terms are thought of with respect to their referents—kinspersons—they are often used as if they too were "proper, self-contained substantives." That is, indeed, just how they might think of blood or beer. In the way they treat one another, kinsfolk are not regularly sustained as relatives through, for example, analogies with other relatives. Rather, as Schneider pointed out long ago for American kinship, they have first to be sustained as (individual) persons, as a mother, uncle, cousin, each with his or her own intrinsic mode of behavior or quality of relating.

We can gloss the Euro-American position by generalizing a contrast made by both Morita (2014) and Jensen (2012), namely, between internal and external relations.[3] Kin terms point to internal relations (a relation is implied in the term), while it is external relations that link kinspersons as more or less self-contained beings. The distinction is found in modern philosophy where it has its own complex trajectory, but from which I retain a simple difference between the relativity of internal relations (relations and *relata* being mutually defining) and the contingency of external relations. External relations are contingent on the character or quality of what is being related. In this Euro-American cosmology, classificatory schemes commonly define entities in relation to one another according to their intrinsic properties that enable the classifier to commensurate—bring into a single relation[4]—the sameness/difference of each with respect to the other. The (external) relation between them keeps the separateness of the terms in play. Tautology is evident: externality resides in the prior distinctiveness of the 'different' entities being related—in short, in perceptions of the fishiness of fish or of the fatherly qualities of the father.

Attributing such thinking to a distinct cosmology is stimulated by Descola's (2013) *Beyond Nature and Culture*. What he calls 'naturalism' is one of four experiential regimes[5] by which people identify and make relations with what is around them, 'identification' and 'relating' being, in his thesis, basic modalities in the structuring of individual and collective experiences. A preliminary distinction between internal and external relations is crucial: "Relationships are thus here understood not in a logical or mathematical sense (i.e., as intellectual operations that make it possible to establish an internal link between two concepts) but rather as the external links between beings and things that are detectable in typical behavior patterns and may be partially translatable into concrete social norms" (ibid.: 113). While identification involves a relation insofar as "it is based on judgments of inherence and attribution" of specific properties (ibid.), that relation remains intrinsic to the object identified, and when Descola talks of relations, his concern is with "the connections that this object has with something other than itself" (ibid.: 114).

Now whether or not such conceptions of 'identification' and 'relating' make sense as part of the naturalist cosmology, within which anthropology has itself flourished, it seems that there have been times when kinship and its reproductive potential have sat rather uneasily athwart them. In fact, the anthropologist might want to know why kin relations in some regimes are the very exemplars of cosmology, while in this one they are repeatedly pushed to one side.

A High Point in the Naturalist Tradition

The European concept of biology took popular hold in nineteenth-century England. Experiments in plant and animal husbandry had led to a scientific literature on the effects of selective breeding, and "debates about the value of creating healthy stock by introducing new hybrid strains, or the opposite— increasing quality and quantity by 'breeding in and in'—became more widely known" (Davidoff 2012: 239). That similar effects could be observed in human populations came to color concerns about heredity and the substance of connections between kin. If the capacious concept of nature expanded to embrace biology, it also emphasized reproduction as a physiological phenomenon.

For diverse reasons and variably according to social strata, in the same century marriage between close kin became widespread across Europe (Sabean 2007a, 2007b).[6] High rates of cousin marriage reflected repeated unions between families, both within and across the generations, and the English bourgeois were no exception. An anthropological study (Kuper 2009) pinpoints what was often expressed as desirable intimacy, the closeness of natal family members being assimilated to the closeness of affinally related ones. It is of this period that literary scholars "noted that the legitimate desire for a cousin sometimes appears [in works of the time] as a stand-in for forbidden attraction to a brother or sister" (Davidoff 2012: 239). Forbidden though it might be, the extravagant sentiment that close family members could display for one another underlined a mutual resemblance with conjugal relations. In public, there was vigorous debate on whether the incest taboo was "a law of nature" or whether marriage restrictions were rather "the fruit of civilization" (Kuper 2009: 101). By contrast with other controversies,[7] the protagonists "appealed to science, not theology" (ibid.: 83) and argued over the physiological effects of close unions as they showed in their offspring. Anthropologists came on the scene at this point, talking about primitive kinship and the evolution of society.

Suppose we approached this as though we were in a naturalist world where entities can be defined by intrinsic properties, the classification of substances—including reproductive material—being ordered through their external relations with one another. When Descola (2013: 239) says that naturalism privileges terms over relations, he means to point to what is generally taken for granted as a sense of the prior existence of things. That would not of course say anything about the precariousness of ordering and its relational effects

(Law 1994: 23), only that outside philosophical and critical reflection, moderns are effective in hiding it (the precariousness). Arguably, it is just such precariousness that kinship arrangements sometimes revealed. A supposedly natural order of kinship might rest on a schema of external relations, yet could the latter's externalizing and differentiating effect be rendered ambiguous, to the point of ambiguity being an object of attention, by over-insistence on it? Take practices of familial closeness. Relationally speaking, there was nothing to supplement knowledge of the appropriate ('natural') ways of acting.[8] Brother and sister, husband and wife: there are no internal relations here to hold kinspersons in place, through, for example, deliberate analogic referencing, only the appropriate behavior ascribed to (the nature of) each person. As suggested earlier, every kin designation may be internally relational (a 'brother' implying a brother or sister), but in being occupied by persons, the kinship positions do not control or govern each other as the terms to an internal relation do.[9] Instead, it seems, kinspersons relied on discriminating between different registers of intimacy and closeness.

There were many problems attributed to kin relations at the time, but not this one. Only with hindsight do kinship and its reproductive potential appear to be a problem with respect to one of the major preoccupations of the Enlightenment that the bourgeois of nineteenth-century England inherited: nature as at once a positive and a negative force in human affairs. The problem of kinship was hidden, both through its often remarked relegation to domestic affairs and through the eclipse of older understandings by the very concept of nature as such. Now biologized, as it came to be in concerns voiced over reproduction in marriage, nature was reinvented in the significance it carried for the behavior of kinspersons toward one another. Among other things, this stimulated the embryonic field called anthropology and what became its debates over 'nature-culture'.

Inventions: Identity and Relations

The debates did not of course begin then. But they might have taken a different shape if it had not been for certain early modern developments in ideas about relations, both epistemic and interpersonal. Vilaça (2013: 364) offers an arresting correlation between the birth of the notion of the individual and the identification of nature and culture as discrete domains.[10] An obvious entailment of imagining that there is a relation between nature and culture, and that it is an external one, is to keep separate the terms (nature, culture) of what may otherwise be—and in the eyes of many should only be—imagined as an internal relation of mutual implication. This is where anthropologists have focused much remedial work.[11] My own concern is with a tangential observation: when 'individuals' and the 'identity' of phenomena become prominent, as they did among other things in the attention given them by scholarly inquiry, so too do (external) 'relations' (colloquially put, as though there were at once more individuals and more relations around). For external relations at once hold things apart and hold them in place, that is, sustain their identities. If we were to seek examples, then what we know of certain early modern trends in relations of kinship is highly suggestive. On the one hand appeared new[12] ways of talking about persons without talking about kin positions as such; on the other hand one's relatives, like one's family's connections, could be thought of as extensions or additions beyond and external to the self. Out of a vast field of possibilities, I touch on two moments: the invention of 'identity' and the changing character of reproductive substance.

It is to the scientific and philosophical innovations of the European seventeenth century that we owe the concept 'identity'.[13] It became applied to the self-sameness of persons quite as much as of things, something of an irony in that for philosophers who drew examples from familiar experience one's self was the most unstable of entities. They argued over whether a person, understood as a self, could be a permanent subject, given all the variations in time, place, states of consciousness, and so forth, of which people were aware in themselves. The issue neither began nor ended with early modern writers, but they provided a new vocabulary for it. This put questions about persons into a wider field of inquiry concerning the identity of things.

Personal identity or the self, one well-known English philosopher, John Locke (1632–1704),[14] declared in 1690, "is not determined by identity or diversity of substance, which it cannot be sure of, but only by identity of consciousness" or understanding (see Locke [1690] 1975: chap. 27:23, 345). The purpose in quoting Locke is to point to what was under debate, that is, "the riddle of identity" (Porter 2000: 166). It was a question of discerning the intrinsic qualities by which the self could be defined. Porter reports of others who found the same instability in consciousness that Locke did in substance (flesh, matter), arguing, for example, that perception was discontinuous and divisible.[15] Taylor (1989: 171–172)—the political scientist and twentieth-century guide for the philosophers of biology concerned with individuality—reflects on Locke's "unprecedentedly radical form of self-objectification ... [enabling us] to see ourselves as objects of far-reaching reformation ... To take this stance is to identify oneself with the power to objectify and remake, and by this act to distance oneself from all the particular features which are objects of potential change [such as substance] ... This power reposes in consciousness." In the 'person', then, the seventeenth-century philosopher is dealing with a thinking, intelligent being. When by contrast he comes to talk of the permanent sameness of 'man' (the individual living organism, or human being in later parlance),[16] the identity of man is not differently conceived from that of plants or animals: "For in them the variation of great parcels of matter alters not the identity ... [A] plant which has ... an organization of parts in one coherent body, partaking of one common life, ... continues to be the same plant as long as it partakes of the same life" (Locke [1690] 1975: chap. 27:3–4, 330–331).[17] Apropos the objectification to which Taylor refers, different questions are being asked of plants, animals, and man, on the one hand, and of the person, on the other. For although, Locke says, we "know that, in the ordinary way of speaking, the same person, and the same man, stand for one and the same thing" (ibid.: chap. 27:15, 251), thought on the issue reveals a radical divergence between the way in which the identity of persons and the identity of man are formed.

Dare we ask what kind of 'biology' this is? The discussion about personal identity and living organisms makes no mention of kinship, despite it being quite prominent elsewhere. Locke drew on kinship in order to provide concrete examples of an otherwise abstract conception, namely, relations, but not when it came to person as self or to man as human being. He neither depicted persons and selves as kinspersons nor pondered on the procreation and nurture of man as a reproductive being.[18] Neither figure was categorically held in place by its kinship with others; instead, 'person' had quasi-theological/moral characteristics ('consciousness'), while 'man' had natural ones ('life', 'an organization of parts'). Given that kin ties were useful ways to illustrate relations, thus entwined the absence of one implied the absence of the other. Conversely, kinship could have been the link that brought relations to mind, or relations could have done so for kinship. As it was, the discussion about the identity of persons or the identity of human beings was held separate from a discussion about the formation of relations.[19] And if understanding relations is not an intrinsic part of understanding either, are we to conclude that kinship too, being entwined with questions about relations as it is, finds itself extraneous to the dual concepts of person or man? Whether between persons or between men, that would make kin relations a matter of 'external' linkage. The reader is invited to imagine a being whose relations—including those of kinship—lie outside its essential nature.

Yet apropos the anachronistic speculation, asking what kind of 'biology' was being imagined for an inquiry into the characteristics of persons and human beings, perhaps the option of drawing on 'kinship' (what? whose?) was never open. For that would be to discount the influence of certain ideas about kinspersons, families, and interpersonal connections that were also traveling along the same route as, and enrolled the self-same concepts of, identities external to one another.

Rehearsing the Familiar

Standing back, an anthropologist might wish to take the very implication of rendering relations external both to the individual organic being and to the conscious person or self *as* an emergent modeling of kinship. The notion of an entity with (external) relations to others echoes some of the ways people of the time were apparently coming to think about kin ties, and this was not confined to England. Eighteenth-century Europe experienced new sentiments of alliance and new patterns of "interlocking networks of kindred" alongside "social and familial endogamy" (Sabean and Teuscher 2007: 16). But while, according to these historians of Europe (see Johnson et al. 2013; Sabean 2007a, 2007b), such patterns displaced structures of inheritance and succession that had led them to talk of patrilines and agnatic lineages, those earlier formations had themselves emerged with new claims for family definitions. The "passage from the

Middle Ages to the early modern period," Sabean and Teuscher (2007: 14–15) write, witnessed "more well-established family strategies," as in the "patrilineal and similarly exclusive conceptions of kin organization [that] acquired an almost constitutional status." What conceptions of individuals were evolving here? Is this identity already in the making? In the language I have been using, do kin alliances as such come to enact a form of external relations between units increasingly imagined as discrete—whether between lineages, families, or conjugal households?

This is worth briefly enlarging upon. Various developments seem to have coalesced in the seventeenth century. These included a shift from what writers refer to as kin connections based on extensive collateral relations, with women as well as men having interests in family property, to the delineation of those lineages emphasizing descent and property accumulation through men. While these changes clearly affected those with property, they were not confined to such considerations. Davis (1978) describes family strategies in sixteenth- and seventeenth-century France that came from a wide social spectrum and involved a consciousness of family history and family futures, meaning the conjugally based household. As significantly for our interests, Davis (1986) observes that, like families, individuals were acquiring a distinct sense of their life histories. But for those of much or little means, the 'individuality' of people and families might sharpen certain identities at the expense of others. "Women," Duhamelle (2007: 133) states, "were gradually excluded from participating in the circulation of wealth between the lineages as their shares in family goods were progressively diminished," culminating in a decision in 1653 to abolish women's inheritance claims in favor of "a new self-representation [i.e., the family] that enhanced male descent." Aspects of this account of German nobility (the Rhenish imperial knighthood) could as well have been written of ordinary folk in England. In 1670, the English Parliament intervened in the administration of probate (settling the inheritance of a deceased's estate), with the effect of undermining ordinary women's entitlement to personal property. Diverse writings on political theory of the time, Erickson (1993: 230) adds, made an "overt identification of 'the individual' [person] with the male individual."

Touching on ideas about relatedness, a momentary turn to procreative idioms of blood, away from those of flesh, enabled 'lines' of blood to be identified.[20] Here one might wonder at the role of reproductive material in rendering external relations distinct and concrete. A naturalist connotation of corporeal entities as belonging to a physical world implied their being identified, and thus fixed, in relation to one another, and this went for procreative elements as well. Thus, it came to be assumed that the contributions and reproductive organs of the sexes had distinct properties with respect to each other. Drawing on materials from Italy, one historian directly addresses the development of a 'naturalist theory' of bodily transmission through inheritance: "[B]lood was identified as the substance that transmitted qualities from one generation to the next" (Delille 2013: 130). It also circulated. In seventeenth-century Europe at large, "each consanguineal link could be a conduit of blood, and each alliance, a sharing of blood ... [So] a group of males, an agnatic line, a house ... could express the marriage of one member with another house as a mingling of blood: [such] an alliance could only be thought of ... through a language of flows, channels, conduits, coursings, and circulations" (Sabean 2013: 145). That heritage was conferred by 'nature', blood being the carrier, is arguably what was new (Delille 2013: 127, 130).[21] Blood was not alone—semen and milk had similar properties. The specific interest in blood is that it "replaced the medieval notion that generation was the result of contact between flesh" (ibid.: 135).[22] If external relations between (individual) familial units were visualized in terms of flowing blood, such units in turn acquired specific identities: "Families or lineages were natural beings whose social personality rested on a foundation which today we would term biological" (ibid.: 132).

What then was to gather momentum in the eighteenth century was a stress on alliances between families through marriage, alongside the (social) class-consciousness of desirable investment in same-status matches. This contributed to a fresh focus on conjugality, for "marriage-as-alliance ... expressly put the interest of the new [conjugal] unit above the interests of either of the spouses' natal families" (Perry 2004: 231).[23] One may wonder in fact whether the pleasures and perils of close marriage typical of the (upper) middle-class England of the nineteenth century were not a hypertrophied outcome of the value placed on seeking 'good connections'. This was a time when marriages between cousins or brothers- and sisters-in-law were as common among doctors, lawyers, and clergymen as they were in business, not to mention the intellectual and scientific bourgeois (Kuper 2009: 135). Often the unions were explicitly between families, such as among elite Quakers prominent in banking. Crucially, marriage repeated between families merged into a sense of marriage "within the family" (ibid.: 27), an ideal arrangement of the Victorian novel, for example, being adoption "into the family [of] someone who is almost a member of the family already" (Valerie Sanders, cited in ibid.: 17).

We might detect a naturalist cosmology in the naturalization of substances. Anticipated in the period of biology before biology, so to speak, we might also detect that there is nothing innocent in the naturalization of relations either.

Language Effects and Concealments

Carsten's (2004: 107) rethinking of personhood and kinship led her to call for an appreciation of Western people's "everyday sense of relationality." The question, then, as she makes clear, is how the world ever made such an appeal to an appreciation of relations necessary. What is being emphasized and what gets overlooked? Her point is that discussions of the person that emphasize "the notion of an abstract and legally defined entity, the bounded individual with rights over property ... [has] obscured the most obvious contexts in which relationality as an aspect of personhood is expressed" (ibid.), namely, kinship. In other words, it is the relationality of kins*persons* (the linguistic relationality of kin designations never being in doubt) that is obscured. Carsten refers to these (interpersonal) relations as intrinsic to the person. Was it descriptions and enactments of relations—including kin relations—as external to the person that obscured them?

For users and speakers of English, there is particular significance to the local expositions mentioned here. The foray into European kinship was intended to localize or parochialize the English examples. Clearly, events were happening elsewhere of which developments in England were but one version, and its spokesmen (to put it like that) but players on a wider stage. Israel's (2001: 515) reference to the Anglomania that swept Europe in the 1730s and 1740s, when Locke—along with Bacon and Newton—were "almost everywhere eulogized and lionized," is in the context of a reflection on the radical potentials of European intellectual life at large. Locke, intellectually 'safe' in his view, contributed little and late to the European Enlightenment. But ideas flow with language regardless of their credibility. The entwining of kinship ties and relations may have been an incidental division of subject matter in Locke's account. However, and peculiar to linguistic idioms in English, the entwining was concretized in the idiomatic adoption of relations as a substantive for kinsfolk: relations, relatives, meaning kin. Its wide usage dates from the seventeenth century. One wonders what English users anywhere would have made of relations as an abstract object of knowledge when so much weight seems to have been put on their externalizing effects. And for non-English speakers, the kin usage might have seemed puzzling.

Recall the language of symbiosis and those findings of zoological science that "animals [among other organisms] are composites of many species living, developing, and evolving together," presented as a matter of "inter-active relationships among species" (Gilbert et al. 2012: 326). In English, this last phrase is likely to evoke external relations. In the seventeenth century, which is when ideas about kinship were being reconfigured by the abstract term 'relation' for kinsfolk, it was arguably becoming possible to conceive of an individual person plus his or her relations or of the (conjugal) family plus its relations. Here would have been an enactment of external relations indeed—both in the way the individual entity is at once separated from such relations (i.e., [other] kinsfolk) and related to them *and* in the substantive 'relation' itself as an object of reflection.

Narrativizing the concepts of 'identity' and 'relation' may have thickened an appreciation of the naturalist insistence on external relations 'between' self-contained terms. Self-containment, held in place when one distinct thing is defined by its relation to another distinct thing, gives us entities with properties but without internal relations. Philosophers debate the extent to which all relations might be internal, that is, whether any relation can leave unaffected its terms or bearers (Johansson 2014). Yet common conceptions were and are otherwise. In asking how this form of conceptualizing external relations becomes habitual, overlooking any perception of intrinsic kin ties, might we imagine that certain possibilities for reflection on new apprehensions of knowledge were long ago hidden within the naturalist concept of identity? Relations of an external kind were its correlate. That external relations (which kept nature and culture distinct) could often be reformulated as internal ones (each being implicated in the other) was the kind of uncovering of the 'obvious' that could become a fertile source of critical debate.[24] When describing relations in the abstract, Locke himself anticipated the move in talking of concealment. Seemingly absolute terms contain relations, Locke ([1690] 1975: chap. 25:3, 320) argued, for there are "relative terms" that "under the form and appearance of signifying something absolute in the subject, do conceal a tacit, though less observable, relation," an example being the word 'stores' (as a ship lays in stores) in its having a relation to future use.

When thought of as external, relations were to give endless and highly productive trouble to an anthropology concerned with non-Euro-American forms of kinship and aspects of Euro-American forms too. Sahlins's (2013) recent synthesis may be read as uncovering the creativity of internal relations. His formulation of "mutuality of being" as implying "people who are intrinsic to one another's existence" (ibid.: 2) perhaps holds a message for the symbioticists. Whatever new vocabulary those who look to symbiogenesis may find for what English speakers currently cast as relations, internal or external, it might be helpful to be reminded of this concept's early modern molding. It is not nature versus culture, the body-mind split, the separation of the substantial being from consciousness of the self that is only of interest. The silent absence of kinship from learned discussion about the identity of either human beings or persons arguably has had consequences for biology and anthropology alike.

Acknowledgments

My warm thanks to Casper Bruun Jensen and Atsuro Morita for the opportunity to revisit nature-culture and for the particular stamp they have put on the enterprise. I am grateful to Louise Braddock, Natalie Zemon Davies, Jeanette Edwards, and Aparecida Vilaça for conversations on many aspects of these issues and, most enduringly, to Donna Haraway.

Marilyn Strathern had the good fortune to receive initial—and indelible—training in Papua New Guinea, which led to work among other things on kinship and gender relations. In the United Kingdom, she subsequently became involved with anthropological approaches to the new reproductive technologies, intellectual property, audit cultures, and interdisciplinarity. Now retired from the Cambridge Department of Social Anthropology, she is (honorary) Life President of the Association of Social Anthropologists of the UK and Commonwealth (ASA). Strathern is currently working on issues in the conceptualization of relations, some of which are sketched out in her book *Kinship, Law and the Unexpected: Relatives Are Always a Surprise* (2005).

Notes

1. I do not wish to imply familiarity with the journal; the piece was sent to me by Donna Haraway, who has long been concerned with the inherent relationality of the living world. The present chapter is a tangential response to a question of hers, namely, whether contemporary realizations about species symbiosis might be equal in their import to the historical moment at which Euro-American ideas about generation became ideas about production and reproduction. If one transformation happened, could another?

2. For instance, by Bowker (2010) and in actor-network theory, insofar as it "dispenses with any *a priori* delimitation of what can count as a relation" (Jensen and Winthereik 2013: 29). A simple superfluity of interactions in communication networks does the job too. Jensen and Winthereik also comment on Deleuze's view that "the individual, so dear to liberal philosophy and politics, is washing away in a sea of data" (ibid.: 160).

3. Viveiros de Castro (2004) himself goes on to make an argument about internal and external relations in order to engage a debate with representational thinking and its 'relativism', which is to one side of my intentions here. In quite different contexts, the concepts of internal and external relations may be used recursively, as, for example, when they correspond to or evoke a notion of the inside and outside of things. This is done by Morita (2014) in an elucidation of Mumford's machine that, in working, becomes a part of the connections surrounding it, embodying the connections in the design of its parts. Jensen's (2012: 49) distinction is close to that pursued here: "If relations are extrinsic it means that they connect terms, persons or whatever, that remain unchanged regardless of the connection. If they are intrinsic it means that relations come first, shaping the terms that are purportedly connected."

4. As discussed by Jensen and Winthereik (2015), following Latour.

5. Reflecting semi-autobiographically on how to make an anthropology of the 'Moderns' possible, Latour (2013a) refers to frenzied users of nature-culture schema as 'Naturalists'. The way ahead, as he sees it, is in discarding the smokescreen thrown up by notions of nature and an exterior material world. In practice, he adds, the frenzied users of this schema do something else entirely. However, Descola (2013) is more interested in 'naturalism' as itself a permutation of other possibilities, so it is appropriate for his argument to keep certain established characterizations of nature-culture intact.

6. Such marriages were confined very largely to that century. In Britain, cousin marriages were legally permissible, but morally often the source of soul-searching.

7. Specifically, and notoriously peculiar to England, the permissibility of a man's marriage with a deceased wife's sister (see Kuper 2009).

8. The idea that each species acts according to its own nature has a long history in European thought. However, by contrast with the 'chain of being' that "from the early seventeenth century onward … gradually lost its analogical dimension and soon was employed only as a familiar metaphor in the service of naturalist ontology" (Descola 2013: 205), nature in the sense of a quality intrinsic to something seems to have been reinforced by the new concept of identity.

9. What to naturalists is uncertainty, or inadequate knowledge, can be held at bay in an analogic cosmology by rearranging the elements in question (e.g., through omen and revelation). Naturalists cannot 'control' the natural world in this way. They can uncover it, exploit it, change it, and in that sense master it with human inventions. But they cannot reorder it, insofar as each epistemic reordering is attributable to

filling a gap in human knowledge and thus appears as a human intervention (reordering understood as an act of human interpretation).

10. Not just "the modern western conception of the human" (Vaisman 2013: 106), but a specific concept of the 'individual' appears at the same time as the separation of nature and culture. In bringing together these two confluences, Vilaça (2013: 364) adds that it is hardly "a novel correlation" (citing Dumont).

11. Witness the definitive volume of Ingold and Palsson (2013), which takes up what has long been a dominant theme in Ingold's *oeuvre*, the mutual interpenetration of biological and social understandings in a larger understanding of life.

12. 'New' in the sense of reconceived or reformulated, not originary.

13. Although there was a precursor in French and late Latin, as far as English is concerned, the 1979 *Oxford English Dictionary* (p. 1368) remarks of this period: "Various suggestions have been offered as to the formation. Need was evidently felt of a noun … to express the notion of 'sameness', side by side with those of 'likeness' and 'oneness.'" 'Individual' also came into its own at this time. Originally a term for an indivisible entity, it became used in the seventeenth century for separate entities and (as an adjective) for some thing distinguished from others by attributes of its own, or (as a noun) for an object determined by properties peculiar to itself, as well as for a single member of a natural class or group.

14. I talk of Locke in part for the popularity his writing came to acquire, in part because there are interesting pointers to kinship usage in his *Essay Concerning Human Understanding* ([1690] 1975)—a (re)source for discussion, with no imputation as to any originating role it may have played.

15. As in the case of one of Locke's pupils, Shaftesbury, ruminating on the circumstances under which "'I [may] indeed be said to be lost, or have lost My Self'" (Porter 2000: 166).

16. Substance as a mass of matter has its own type of identity. Here Locke is talking of the identity of an individual organism that has a typical and distinct form, and an individual life, or what we may gloss in the case of man as referring to "human individuals" (Balibar 2013: 57). Attending to its textual location and context in arguments of the time, we may add that Balibar credits Locke with inventing the concept of consciousness.

17. "This also shows wherein the identity of the same man [as the human individual organism] consists; viz. in nothing but a participation of the same continued life, by constantly fleeting particles of matter, in succession vitally united to the same organized body" (Locke [1690] 1975: chap. 27:6, 332). Where modern readers might look forward to a nature-culture dichotomy, over Locke's shoulder were contemporary debates on the resurrection. The being accountable for his or her actions could not be the bodily enfolded and corruptible 'man' but the moral 'person' or self with its enduring identity (Sandford 2013: xxx–xxxi).

18. No mention is made of kinship although the chapter on identity and diversity is sandwiched between extensive discussions on different kinds of relations. It is the place of kin relations in Locke's account that concerns me. This is separate from the question as to whether his notion of personal identity can be parsed as a relational one (see Fausto 2012: 36, following Balibar 2013).

19. When Locke brings these concepts together, it is seemingly for purposes other than an inquiry into identity. In the introductory section on relation, a person (Caius) is taken as a "positive being" who can be described either through attributes, such as his being a man or white, or through a relative term, such as "husband," which links him to some other person, or the comparative "whiter," which links him to some other thing (Locke [1690] 1975: chap. 25:1, 319). Thought is led beyond the

initial subject, says Locke, and in this sense any idea may be the foundation of a relation. This is an instance of (affinal) kinship being used to exemplify a logical relation—that of comparison. Here the fact that the example is of a person does bring kinship to mind, if only one among other possibilities: Caius is later imagined as compared to several persons, someone "being capable of as many relations as there can be occasions of comparing him to other things" (ibid.: chap. 25:7, 322).

20. I am very grateful to Jeanette Edwards for pointing me to Johnson et al.'s (2013) collection and for her specific comments (Edwards 2014). Carsten's (2013) work on blood is highly germane. See also both Weston and Bildhauer in Carsten (ibid.).

21. Blood flowed between parents and children and, in a restricted sense, specifically between father and child. Thus, sons might be conceived as "part of the bodies of fathers who pass on their glory to their sons," as opposed to an idea of nobility being "in the human soul" (Delille 2013: 127). In some formulations, maternal blood was externalized by its circulating properties. The time span that Delille discusses ranges from the latter half of the fifteenth to the seventeenth century, by which time these ideas were consolidated. He also describes opposition to these theories from both church and state.

22. Flesh, like blood, had it own genealogy, one that we cannot pursue here. When it was 'flesh' that depicted the (carnal) union of spouses and their procreative intent, some of the virtues of 'blood' were instead bound up with the blood of sacrifice and its analogy with baptismal water in Christian thought.

23. Following the arguments of Trumbauch, Perry (2004) is comparing eighteenth-century aristocratic and middle-class marriages in England.

24. This is exactly the move made by Wagner (1977) in the famous opening to "Analogic Kinship." Against prevailing assumptions about the innateness of kin differentiation, he asks us to imagine that "all human relationships [including all kin relations] are analogous to one another" (ibid.: 623).

References

Balibar, Étienne. 2013. *Identity and Difference: John Locke and the Invention of Consciousness*. Ed. Stella Sandford; trans. Warren Montag. London: Verso. First published in 1998 as *Identité et différence: L'invention de la conscience*.

Bowker, Geoffrey C. 2010. "A Plea for Pleats." In *Deleuzian Intersections: Science, Technology, Anthropology*, ed. Casper Bruun Jensen and Kjetil Rödje, 123–138. New York: Berghahn Books.

Carsten, Janet. 2004. *After Kinship*. Cambridge: Cambridge University Press.

Carsten, Janet, ed. 2013. *Blood Will Out: Essays on Liquid Transfers and Flows*. Malden, MA: Wiley-Blackwell.

Davidoff, Leonore. 2012. *Thicker Than Water: Siblings and Their Relations, 1780–1920*. Oxford: Oxford University Press.

Davis, Natalie Z. 1978. "Ghosts, Kin, and Progeny: Some Features of Family Life in Early Modern France." In *The Family*, ed. Alice S. Rossi, Jerome Kagan, and Tamara K. Hareven, 87–114. New York: W. W. Norton.

Davis, Natalie Z. 1986. "Boundaries and the Sense of Self in Sixteenth-Century France." In *Reconstructing Individualism: Autonomy, Individuality, and the Self in Western Thought*, ed. Thomas C. Heller, Morton Sosna, and David E. Wellbery, 53–63. Stanford, CA: Stanford University Press.

Delille, Gérard. 2013. "The Shed Blood of Christ: From Blood as Metaphor to Blood as Bearer of Identity." In Johnson et al. 2013, 125–143.

Descola, Philippe. 2013. *Beyond Nature and Culture*. Trans. Janet Lloyd. Chicago: University of Chicago Press. Originally published in 2005 as *Par-delà nature et culture*.

Duhamelle, Christophe. 2007. "The Making of Stability: Kinship, Church, and Power among the Rhenish Imperial Knighthood, Seventeenth and Eighteenth Centuries." In Sabean et al. 2007, 125–144.

Edwards, Jeanette. 2014. "Tugging on a Thread (of Thought): A Comment on Marilyn Strathern's 'Anthropological Reasoning.'" *HAU: Journal of Ethnographic Theory* 4 (3): 39–44.

Erickson, Amy L. 1993. *Women and Property in Early Modern England*. London: Routledge.

Fausto, Carlos. 2012. "Too Many Owners: Mastery and Ownership in Amazonia." In *Animism in Rainforest and Tundra: Personhood, Animals, Plants and Things in Contemporary Amazonia and Siberia*, ed. Marc Brightman, Vanessa E. Grotti, and Olga Ulturgasheva, 29–48. New York: Berghahn Books.

Gilbert, Scott F., Jan Sapp, and Alfred I. Tauber. 2012. "A Symbiotic View of Life: We Have Never Been Individuals." *Quarterly Review of Biology* 87 (4): 325–341.

Ingold, Tim, and Gisli Palsson, eds. 2013. *Biosocial Becomings: Integrating Social and Biological Anthropology*. Cambridge: Cambridge University Press.

Israel, Jonathan I. 2001. *Radical Enlightenment: Philosophy and the Making of Modernity, 1650–1750*. Oxford: Oxford University Press.

Jensen, Casper Bruun. 2012. "Proposing the Motion: The Task of Anthropology Is to Invent Relations." *Critique of Anthropology* 32 (1): 47–53.

Jensen, Casper Bruun, and Brit Ross Winthereik. 2013. *Monitoring Movements in Development Aid: Recursive Partnerships and Infrastructures*. Cambridge, MA: MIT Press.

Jensen, Casper Bruun, and Brit Ross Winthereik. 2015. "Test Sites: Attachments and Detachments in Community-Based Ecotourism." In *Detachment: Essays on the Limits of Relational Thinking*, ed. Matei Candea, Joanna Cook, Catherine Trundle, and Thomas Yarrow, 197–218. Manchester: Manchester University Press.

Johansson, Ingvar. 2014. "All Relations Are Internal: The New Version." In *Mind, Values, and Metaphysics*, ed. Anne Reboul, 225–240. New York: Springer.

Johnson, Christopher H., Bernhard Jussen, David W. Sabean, and Simon Teuscher, eds. 2013. *Blood and Kinship: Matter for Metaphor from Ancient Rome to the Present*. New York: Berghahn Books.

Kuper, Adam. 2009. *Incest and Influence: The Private Life of Bourgeois England*. Cambridge, MA: Harvard University Press.

Latour, Bruno. 2013a. "Biography of an Inquiry: On a Book about Modes of Existence." *Social Studies of Science* 43 (2): 287–301.

Latour, Bruno. 2013b. *An Inquiry into Modes of Existence: An Anthropology of the Moderns*. Trans. Catherine Porter. Cambridge, MA: Harvard University Press.

Law, John. 1994. *Organizing Modernity*. Oxford: Blackwell.

Locke, John. (1690) 1975. *An Essay Concerning Human Understanding*. Ed. Peter H. Nidditch. Oxford: Clarendon Press.

Morita, Atsuro. 2014. "The Ethnographic Machine: Experimenting with Context and Comparison in Strathernian Ethnography." *Science, Technology & Human Values* 39 (2): 214–235.

Perry, Ruth. 2004. *Novel Relations: The Transformation of Kinship in English Literature and Culture, 1748–1818*. Cambridge: Cambridge University Press.

Porter, Roy. 2000. *Enlightenment: Britain and the Creation of the Modern World*. London: Allen Lane.

Sabean, David W. 2007a. "Transition 1: From Medieval to Early Modern Kinship Patterns. Outline and Summaries." In Sabean et al. 2007, 51–56.

Sabean, David W. 2007b. "Transition 2: From Early Modern to Nineteenth-Century Kinship Patterns. Outline and Summaries." In Sabean et al. 2007, 187–193.

Sabean, David W. 2013. "Descent and Alliance: Cultural Meanings of Blood in the Baroque." In Johnson et al. 2013, 144–174.

Sabean, David W., and Simon Teuscher. 2007. "Kinship in Europe: A New Approach to Long-Term Development." In Sabean et al. 2007, 1–32.

Sabean, David W., Simon Teuscher, and Jon Mathieu, eds. 2007. *Kinship in Europe: Approaches to Long-Term Developments (1300–1900)*. New York: Berghahn Books.

Sahlins, Marshall. 2013. *What Kinship Is—and Is Not*. Chicago: University of Chicago Press.

Sandford, Stella. 2013. "Introduction. The Incomplete Locke: Balibar, Locke and the Philosophy of the Subject." In Balibar 2013, xi–xlvi.

Taylor, Charles. 1989. *Sources of the Self: The Making of the Modern Identity*. Cambridge: Cambridge University Press.

Vaisman, Noa. 2013. "Shedding Our Selves: Perspectivism, the Bounded Subject and the Nature-Culture Divide." In Ingold and Palsson 2013, 106–122.

Vilaça, Aparecida. 2013. "Reconfiguring Humanity in Amazonia: Christianity and Change." In *A Companion to the Anthropology of Religion*, ed. Janice Boddy and Michael Lambek, 363–386. Malden, MA: Wiley-Blackwell.

Viveiros de Castro, Eduardo. 2004. "Exchanging Perspectives: The Transformation of Objects into Subjects in Amerindian Ontologies." *Common Knowledge* 10 (3): 463–484.

Wagner, Roy. 1977. "Analogic Kinship: A Daribi Example." *American Ethnologist* 4 (4): 623–642.

Chapter 2

BETWEEN TWO TRUTHS
Time in Physics and Fiji

Naoki Kasuga

This chapter conducts an anthropological analysis of time, beginning with an examination of the Fijian movement Viti Kabani (Fiji Company). The examination is based on an ontological consideration. Although there are exceptions (e.g., Gell 1992), anthropological theory has basically presupposed time as a given. Since the 'ontological turn', this tendency has begun to change, but the situation formerly indicated by Nancy Munn (1992: 93), according to whom "the topic of time frequently fragments into all the other dimensions and topics," remains much the same. In most cases, time appears as little more than a component of other themes, such as 'prisons' (Reed 2003), 'knowledge' (Riles 2004), 'alternative currencies' (Maurer 2005), 'collection' (Moutu 2007), 'arbitrage' (Miyazaki 2013), and so on.

It was the difficulty of understanding the power of the leader of Viti Kabani over his followers and their truth claims that compelled me to undertake this ontological investigation (Kasuga 2008). The worshippers continued to put into practice his orders to actualize his 'Time = Era' (*Na Gauna*), even though those

Notes for this chapter begin on page 44.

orders, delivered in secret from his place of exile, caused physical, economic, and political hardship. Why were the worshippers so attached to his predictions, delivered one after another, although none of them came true? This question led me to ontological questions regarding time: What kind of passage of time enabled Fijians to accept their leader's orders? What characterized their time and what, indeed, could be 'His Time'? I decided to approach this problem by conducting a series of 'thought experiments'. Their starting point is in Fijian ethnography, but they proceed by way of a comparison with the truth claims of modern physics.

My reason for making a comparison with physics is that this science continues to reign as the king of the natural sciences: it has brought about the 'conversion to physics' of various fields; it provides knowledge and practice that have made possible much of our technological environment; and its truth claims offer the most robust basis for various realities. Indeed, as Peter Galison (2003) has made clear, since relativity arrived in the early twentieth century in response to global socio-technological demands, our present existence would be impossible without the time of physics. Ironically, this is the case although as relativity established a closer relationship with quantum mechanics in the 1970s—incidentally, a field born in the same period as relativity and disliked by Einstein—it also had to learn to tolerate a certain temporal vagueness.

The present chapter thus compares time as conceived by the Viti Kabani with modern physics, which has explicitly tried to deal with the ontological problems of time. The comparison proceeds via reference to criticisms of physics made by the analytical philosopher Huw Price and the works of the quantum theorist Satoshi Watanabe. Gradually, the analysis expands our understanding of the Viti Kabani movement, while also raising questions about our own understanding of time and of the relation between time and the technological environment in which we live. Combining the notions of the heretical physicist Julian Barbour with Alfred Gell's later work, this chapter then presents an alternative ontology for the activities of Viti Kabani—one in which the absolute separation between qualia and quanta has been ruptured. Developing this theme also allows me to offer some responses to various criticisms of the 'ontological turn'.[1]

The Hidden Company

Judging from oral surveys of elders, taken in Fiji's main island of Viti Levu, and from records of civil servants, missionaries, and colonists, it seems that the Viti Kabani movement, Oceania's largest native movement, inspired people by means of the following argument: why are white people rich and Fijians poor? Apolosi Nawai, the movement's leader, had the following response: "Because Westerners hide good and proper things from us and try to show us nothing but bad things."[2] The hidden thing was Viti Kabani, the 'company' that Fijians had founded in order to take the agricultural trade into their own hands. By early 1914, the colonial government became aware of this movement and Apolosi, its central figure who came from Nadi in western Viti Levu. Making full use of his eloquence, Apolosi, traveled all over Fiji, collecting funds for the foundation of the 'company'. The movement gathered strength and soon spread across the whole territory, helped by a growing sense of fear among the Fijians that changes in government land policy would lead to the loss of their lands.

Apolosi was said to be accompanied, and protected, by the twin gods, *Na Thiri*, known throughout Fiji. These gods were otherwise believed to have left Fiji for Europe long ago with all their wealth. Wherever Apolosi visited, people were eager to sense, or witness, *Na Thiri*. The twin gods had given Apolosi *mana* that enabled him to "know the things," "speak it to materialize it," and to "save" Fiji. The movement was also called *Lotu ni na Gauna vou*, (Christianity of the New Time or Era), or more commonly *Na Gauna*—the Time that foretold an age in which Apolosi would rule the world in place of Jesus Christ.[3] Many believed that Christianity and the wealth that the whites had brought to Fiji originally belonged to the Fijians, and that the strong Fiji of former days would now be restored by Apolosi, who had laid bare the white men's secrets and would multiply the original wealth through the 'company'.

Apolosi exploited the conflation of the church and chiefly systems established by the government. The church system and the chiefs, who embodied and were mediums for gods and spirits, supported one another. Christianized Fijians maintained friendly relations with the ancestral spirits and gods of the land by regarding Jesus and Jehovah as strong 'chiefs' (*turaga*), or even by identifying them as *Na Thiri*. Apolosi, who was under the protection of *Na Thiri*, brought these gods and spirits into the church system and made the church itself an affiliate of the Viti Kabani. To raise funds, he appropriated the style of the 'church collections' (*soli ni lotu*), which Western missionaries had labored to establish. A man chosen from the people of the village kept accounts of the names, amounts, and dates of donations. In principle, each house would share the burden equally.

Apolosi also exploited relationships between lands and chiefs. In Fijian, everything from kin and ritual group to chiefdom and the level of confederation is referred to as 'land' (*vanua*). While the chiefs 'attend to each other' (*veiguaravi*) in relation to each of these lands, a 'chief-vassal hierarchy' (*guaravi turaga*) also developed. Apolosi set up locally born activists as mediators and toured the various regions, impressing on the chiefs that he was 'strong' (*kaukauwa*) and 'true' (*dina*)—both of which are synonyms for having *mana*. Eloquent, surrounded by followers, and demonstrating in both word and deed his fearlessness of great chiefs and the government, Apolosi blessed the lands that welcomed him. His blessing acted as a predication. The chiefs and those in his group supported Apolosi by believing in the special links between their land and his/him. These links were confirmed by what Apolosi did with the lands. Past relations, related events, and anecdotes worked toward such confirmation. Whatever the case might be, Apolosi actualized the superior power of local gods and captured the imagination of how ancestors had lived with the gods in the old days. Although the various lands maintained their conflicts and sense of rivalry, they were united through their connections with Apolosi.

The meetings of the Viti Kabani recorded in detail the vast number of 'gifts of the land' (*soli vaka vanua*) that were offered to Apolosi, since he was received as a guest in the manner of the paramount chief. People gave him enormous sums of money in the hope that, in his hands, the money would show incredible 'growth/multiplication' (*tubu ni lavo*) or, as we might say, would earn interest. Yet even while tax payments to the government slowed and the church began to lament its financial difficulties, the 'company' office set up in Fiji's capital city Suva hardly engaged in any business activities. Instead, the vast quantities of agricultural products and cash that had been collected became the basis for Apolosi's luxurious living and generous behavior.

Needless to say, the government was under pressure to take severe counter-measures. It established native ordinances to block the movement, punished a stream of activists, and deported Apolosi to a distant Fijian dependency, Rotuma Island. In fact, between 1917 and 1924, 1930 and 1940, and 1940 and 1946, the year of his death, Apolosi spent most of his time following the 'company' in exile. Thorough suppression led to the severing of Viti Kabani's vertical command structure and its horizontal solidarity. Lacking these, it was confined to remote areas and fell into decline. Even then, dozens of copies of Apolosi's letters would somehow evade strict censorship and make their way to his supporters.

Containing a mixture of religious and secular elements, these messages were referred to as 'orders' (*ota*). They included orders not only for making purification rites to call forth ancestral spirits and the gods of the land, but also for the re-establishment of the 'company', the participation in some new business, the shareholding of all the large companies,[4] and the creation of schools to learn business from Indo-Fijians. While the orders were full of biblical quotations and metaphors, they were always directed to people or districts that would have to raise a certain amount of money. As before, records of the donors' names and the amounts given were entered in account books, and the money was taken to Viti Kabani's treasurer in Lautoka and from there conveyed in secret to Apolosi.

How people understood Apolosi's orders is not easily comprehended. Here is an example: "J.C. will come in the year 1944, see Revelation 14:14–18, Matthew 13:38–39 and 25:31. It is there revealed the second coming of Christ … We shall meet in the sky and then proceed together to the New Jerusalem which is prepared for the just. The wicked people will be destroyed … the period of the 'New Time' will commence."[5] This otherwise fanatic expression suddenly turns practical toward the end, telling people about the participation status of the 'New Time' that commenced in 1937, and asking for a subscription of one shilling and six pence for all able-bodied men, and as much as could be afforded for elders, women, and children. These funds were meant to prepare to "meet in the sky and then proceed together to the New Jerusalem." Thus, dreamlike stories and biblical quotations were interwoven with Apolosi's concrete business plans. Even if based on the Scriptures, the movement can thus be regarded as secular in its plans. Only when it was driven into a corner did it retreat into mysticism.

But given this secular penchant, how can the movement survive beyond Apolosi's death up to the present day? Moreover, what accounts for the fact that many people still continue to 'miss' him?

What 'His Time' Could Be

From the early twentieth century, people received Apolosi's orders and donated money and food. As 'slaves of His Time', they went as manual laborers to Suva and the trading post Levuka, or they withstood the harsh labor conditions of the sugar plantations, all the while making 'donations' from their meager wages. The return of Apolosi was never realized, and the 'company' never even began to function. For decades, the only recurrent happening was repeated orders to work for the 'company'. Moreover, even in the face of certain punishment from the government, and despite hearing about Apolosi's extravagant living, his supporters held on to the belief that he is immortal and will return, and they continued to make small-scale donations—even after his death. Why did they do it?

The simplest explanation—because of their belief—does not provide an answer but rather transports us into a thicket of questions. Corroboration for belief, which would come from Apolosi's *mana*, should have easily failed, because his 'true' words consistently failed to materialize. Thus, for example, predictions about hurricanes that would arrive on a specific date to smite those who failed to obey Apolosi's orders repeatedly missed their marks.

Another explanation might be fear. For example, one of the inhabitants of Yasawa was menaced by Apolosi, thinking that he would sell people's land if they disobeyed his orders: "It seemed as if the minds of the people were frightened by his threatening words and so they fell in with him, although some of them unwillingly, as would have been done by our forefathers in olden times."[6] Although no one raised doubts about Apolosi's *mana*, there may have been some surreptitious criticism that he 'misused' (*yaga tani*) it. However, it would be inappropriate to portray these donations, which had been made without realizing any return, as a form of blackmail, for while people repeatedly made donations in fear of Apolosi, they simultaneously hoped for the coming of a different reality. And so Apolosi's messages continued to emphasize that 'the New Time' would arrive, "this time, for sure":

> Fiji lives. All nonsense and deception will be ceased. The progress of Fiji will not be halted.[7] (February 1925)

> It is my desire that you repent immediately and take the right path to follow. I will then forgive the sin of the Society and will be able to cleanse it so that we may reach the 'New Time'.[8] (June 1938)

> Keep your spirit up, boys, or the jar may break in the doorway, as the place from which it is brought is too far.[9] (September 1941)

Even cognitive dissonance appears insufficient to explain the persistent beliefs of Apolosi's followers, who did not solve discrepancies between promise and reality "by transposing the theodicy either to another world or to another reality somehow hidden within this one" (Berger 1967: 70). As exemplified above, the world to be actualized was religious *as well as* secular, with no detachment between this world and another.

The questions that the oral material and the vast quantities of written records put to me ultimately remain unresolved. Why did Apolosi's worshippers continue to follow orders to actualize 'His Time' even though doing so caused hardship? Why were they so attached to his predictions despite the fact that none of them came true? Why did they continue to wait for his return? The more unsolvable these questions seem, the more condensed the nature of their unintelligibility becomes. Eventually, it is compressed into a question of time: what kind of passage of time enabled them to accept Apolosi's orders? By asking what their time is, or what 'His Time' could be, rather than how they perceive time, this question becomes ontological.

Measuring Time in Physics

When considering time in the Viti Kabani movement from an ontological point of view, physics offers an appropriate frame for comparison. This discipline has shown the reality of black holes, Higgs particles, and dark matter. It provides the foundation for technologies that support our daily lives. And it possesses the most radical realism about time. Yet only a small number of physicists think that the question 'what is time?' has actually been answered by relativity theory. Most maintain a cautious attitude or avoid the problem. The reason lies in Einstein's 10 equations, which presuppose universal laws that are unrelated to the direction of time. However, during the 1920s, it became clear that their solutions necessarily change with time.

When the observation of cosmic background radiation established the Big Bang in the 1960s, quantum theory was adopted to determine the period in which the universe came into existence. When the principles of quantum theory were added to the time-space of relativity, it became clear that the deterministic assumptions held up that point were no longer tenable. Because it was impossible to explain various curious motions of quanta by means of pre-existing theories, physicists had by then abandoned any claim to be able to state definitively when things actually happened. Instead, they had created special principles to determine the attributes of quanta at the point in time at which observations were concluded.

The typical example of quantum vagueness is the case of recording time variations of the universe in terms of the motion of elementary particles. Because the motion of these particles is also a measure of time, as in the case of caesium clocks, the curious character of elementary particles must be 'bound up' with time. In consequence, generally defined time disappears.[10] As Galison (2003) shows, Einstein constructed a physics that suited the clock-coordinating procedure in the electro-technical world of his own time. However, he probably did not foresee that this would develop to a point where clocks would come to embed the quantum vagueness that he strove to avoid. Nevertheless, research linking relativity and quantum theory has by now developed into a fundamental branch of physics. In a dimension cut off from the ontology of time, physicists produce theories grounded in abstract mathematics and high-level observation technologies, considering the matter of quantum vagueness to be an issue of 'interpretation'.

The Past as Inaccessible

The philosopher Huw Price (1996) was among the first to search for a solution to this curious situation. His arguments are valuable in that they put forward 'interpretation' as a new ontology for time and thereby encourage a reconfiguration of physics. Price argues that the curious motions of quanta, which make it impossible to understand when something has occurred, should be understood in terms of phenomena in which causal relationships operate not from the past to the present, but rather the opposite—from the present into the past. With the introduction of such backward causality, the laws of physics ensure symmetry with time and acquire consistency and universality.

In order to carry this idea into the core of modern physics, Price educes the conditions for evading the 'bilking argument' put forth by Max Black (1956), which specifically denies backward causality. The bilking argument works by inserting a third event C between an earlier event A and a later event B and by establishing a positive correlation between A and C, as well as a negative correlation between C and B. The implication is that causation from B to A is necessarily blocked. To evade this consequence and bring backward causality into effect, Price exploited a form of logic introduced by Michael Dummett (1978), who cited the example of imaginary rites related to African initiation ceremonies. Price (1996: 175) states that "it is possible to avoid the bilking argument so long as one confines oneself to the claim that one can affect bits of the past which are epistemologically inaccessible at the time that one acts." Advocating the possibility of a new co-existence between quantum mechanics and relativity, Price thus uses 'inaccessible' in the sense of 'unobservable' and 'immeasurable'.[11]

From the fact that Price is almost completely ignored by the important figures whom he criticizes (for details, see Price 1996: 87), it is easy to conclude that his arguments appear irrelevant to physicists. This is indeed an unavoidable situation, because all the theorems, arguments, and paradoxes that Price uses are out of date. Meanwhile, he makes no reference to space, mass, or gravity, all of which are indispensable to the theory of time of modern physics.

Nevertheless, the time lived by the Viti Kabani activists becomes more understandable when considered from the point of view of Huw's concept of the inaccessible past. In particular, one must pay close attention to the fact that the space in which this past manifests itself is presented as "the gap between the past and the accessible past" (Price 1996: 180). If the first past is the vague history of Fiji before the present, including myths and oral tradition, the second (accessible) past consists of the combined set of records, using written words, maps, and numbers, observed and stored during the process of Christianization and colonization. The Viti Kabani movement spread across Fiji at a time when the colonial government dispatched officials of the Native Land Commission to different parts of the country, where they began measuring land, specifying the groups to which it belonged, and establishing orders of precedence inside and outside those groups. This ushered in a series of stark dissociations: in place of vague agreements reached by mutual consent came numerous orders that were both clear and difficult to accept. Even more, the familiar story of the strong Fijians was replaced by daily proofs of their powerlessness. A situation was thus produced in which, to quote Price (1996: 178), "two conventions give different answers and we have to make a choice."

At this time, Apolosi attempted to topple authority relationships, laying bare the secret that the wealth that had previously existed in Fiji had been taken across the seas by the twin gods of mythology, and that currently white people were increasing it by means of the 'company'. As far as Fijians were concerned, Apolosi himself was certainly another god who had gained the protection of the twin gods—the true form of Jehovah and Jesus. Here we recognize that the inaccessible past has been created in the gap between the general past and the accessible past. This gap can be called the 'mythical past'. Wherever Apolosi went, he manifested this past by invoking the twin gods and the gods of the lands through his behavior and words, summoning images that were both clear and specific.

Unlike the backward causality promoted by Price, the inaccessible past accomplished by Apolosi moved neither from the future into the present nor from the present into the past. Rather, it demonstrated the possibility of reconstructing both present and future. Thus, Apolosi's predictions can be said to originate in his retrodictive ability, as declarations of a link with the past that he alone could access and with a future that he knew would be actualized. But this, in turn, raises a new question for the truth claims that physics makes about time. Although predictability plays a crucial role for the evaluation of reasonable theories and models, what would physics make of the kind of retrodictive ability that made the Viti Kabani movement possible? The physicist Satoshi Watanabe offers a daring answer to this question.[12]

Compression of the Past-Present-Future

Watanabe begins with the question of how humans, as living creatures, have constructed physics. Living in irreversible time, humans have derived conclusive and temporally symmetrical logic and laws, placing them on a foundation of probabilistic causal relationships of the form 'If A, then probably B'. However, using Bayes's theorem, Watanabe makes clear that while the laws of physics are appropriate for prediction, they are not suitable for retrodiction.

$$p(I_i/F_j) = \frac{p(F_j/I_i)\ p(I_i)}{p(F_j)}$$

$\{I_i\}$: a set of initial states at t_I
$\{F_j\}$: a set of final states at t_F

This classic theorem—derived from the empirical fact that the ratio between retrodictive and predictive probability must be equal to the ratio between the prior event and the subsequent event probability—plays a vital role in information processing today. If we put retrodictive probability $p(I_i/F_j)$ on the left side of the equation, the right side must be predictive probability $p(F_j/I_i)$ times prior event probability $p(I_i)$ divided by subsequent event probability $p(F_j)$. For predictive probability, it is possible to apply the laws of physics, to make experiments based on these laws, and to determine probabilities by repeating the experiments.

However, retrodictive probability is predetermined not by physical laws, but rather by information and speculation concerning what happened at an initial time. Moreover, 'pre-existence credibility' is brought into play in the form of artificial manipulations. Thus, a kind of logic from outside the realm of the laws of physics comes into operation.[13] Although the laws of physics work in both directions of time, the people who make use of them live in irreversible biological time, and this makes prediction and retrodiction asymmetric.

Watanabe revealed the conditions necessary to solve the Schrödinger equation, which represents the motion of quanta, by a route opposite to that taken by conventional physics. He indicated the kinds of limits that would need to be assigned to make it physically possible to determine the probability of retrodiction. These can be broadly classified as either (1) uncontrollable cases, in which it is impossible to select the probability of either prior facts or subsequent facts, or (2) cases in which there is a one-to-one relationship between prior facts and subsequent facts. Because both kinds of cases are exceptional, it becomes clear that deterministic probability should be sought in prediction. In fact, after creating conditions that exclude condition (1) above, macroscopic experiments in physics are designed to convert observation results to data as prior facts and thus to derive predictive probability.[14] Watanabe's original treatise, published in the 1950s, is an unusual thought experiment by today's standards; however, advanced modern physicists cannot ignore the points he makes (see Watanabe 1955a, 1955b). This is because no matter how often various researchers may try to sever the ontology of time, the ontological handling of time is still embedded within the practice of experimentation.

From the perspective of this chapter, what matters most is that Watanabe's arguments can play an important role in understanding Viti Kabani. After all, is there not some similarity between the anthropologist—harboring the question 'Why?' regarding the Viti Kabani movement—and the physicists who derive predictive probabilities by analyzing observed data? Thinking that the worshippers of Apolosi could have foreseen that his words would not become reality by comparing them with the to-them accessible—that it to say, observable—past, I cannot understand why they did not do so. Here, as with physicists, the procedure of making predictions based on prior facts has been introduced as an obvious premise. However, since Apolosi so splendidly revealed his retrodictions, in which the laws of physics do not hold true, his worshippers have continued to accept his predictions, captivated by the inaccessible past, which includes his existence.

Precisely this logic can be elucidated by Watanabe's argument. For if one accepts retrodictive probability $p(I_i/F_j)$ and the probability of phenomena that should have occurred in the past $p(I_i)$ as absolutes—that is to say, both as '1'—on the right-hand side of the equation, only the predictive probability $p(F_j/I_i)$ remains, and the left-hand side becomes 1, so that the predictive probability $p(F_j/I_i)$ must also become 1. In other words, the prediction must become reality. Hence, the unintelligibility of Viti Kabani time has its origins in the time of physics, which seeks predictive probability based on observations, and in a place that excludes both the inaccessible past and the realm opened up by retrodiction.

But what are the circumstances in which it is possible to specify prior events, retrodiction, subsequent events, and prediction with absolute certainty? The development of the Viti Kabani movement can be portrayed as a great broadening of the inaccessible past in the very midst of the present. At the same time, it elicits a situation in which the expected future is continuously revealed. Wherever and whenever Apolosi went, he was in the company of the twin gods. Protected by the gods, he pronounced curses and blessings and made predictions concerning Fiji and the world. Even if direct observation of occurrences in the past, present, and future is impossible for Viti Kabani followers, the implication is that these people continue to share with Apolosi the ongoing creation of space-time from which they are able to command a bird's-eye view of the past-present-future. It is this very compression of the past-present-future that enables the absolute confirmation of all retrodiction, prediction, prior events, and subsequent events.

Reconsidering Unobservability

Some may argue that the situation of the Viti Kabani is made possible by an inaccessible past taking the form of what we might call the 'supernatural'. This would render the comparison with physics irrelevant. It is true that in physics unobservable phenomena have been dealt with by the development of detectors, by progress in methods of observation, and by the creation of models that can be linked to measurable physical quantities. Nevertheless, at the very core of modern physics there is an inaccessible phenomenon whose acceptance has been unavoidable, even though these methods do not work with it. This phenomenon, the so-called collapse of the wave packet, typifies the aforementioned quantum vagueness.

The problem, which arose when quantum theory was in its infancy, can be summarized as follows. The wave functions that record quanta depict the superposition of multiple eigenvectors, so it is to be expected that wave packets are produced in which different waves move as one. However, when one collides electrons in an experiment and observes the particles, only a single point shines, for which reason one must think that the wave packet has collapsed. As no one has observed it, the collapse must have occurred faster than light, which is impossible. Nevertheless, a majority of physicists accept this inaccessible phenomenon as a premise so that they can develop arguments making full use of wave functions. Accordingly, the question redirected from the Viti Kabani to physics concerns the extent to which this discipline has adopted a procedure that relies upon, or even justifies, unobservability.

In fact, Price and Watanabe both developed their arguments with this question in mind. As noted, these arguments have had no influence since they stray from the path of problems acceptable to modern physics. As one might expect, physicists indeed influence physics. One explanation offered by the physicist Hugh Everett (1956), in a paper titled "The Theory of the Universal Wave Function," is now known as the many-worlds interpretation.[15] The significance of Everett's explanation lies in seeing the wave function not as a depiction of the state of particles but as the fundamental entity, thereby redefining the problem of observation by means of a deterministic linear wave equation. Accordingly, it becomes possible to depict the particle observation process as the 'state function' of the composite system of the observer and his or her object-system, which must satisfy the wave equation. This makes it possible to present the collapse of the wave packet as the effect of the wave's continual diffusion. In line with the equation, the superposition of eigenstates is absolutely constant, while the composite system forks with every observation.[16]

Everett's theory is extremely difficult to prove, yet seemingly logically consistent. Presumably, it is a nuisance to physicists, who have had to accept an unobservable phenomenon at the core of their discipline. Martin Gardner's (2002) position that Everett's argument can be defended as mathematical truth, although it is not truth in physics, suggests that this question, about which physics has reservations, has been resolved mathematically. Stephen Hawking describes the situation as unproblematic and self-evident, entailing nothing more than a calculation of "conditional probabilities" (cited in Ferris 1997: 345). This expedient obviates the whole problem posed by the fact that the probability derived from the wave function retains its role by excluding the interpretation problem.

Thus, modern physics has exploited observability by means of experiments that have maintained a primordial, unaffected unobservability at their core. In contrast, Apolosi's predictions can be authenticated by their unobservability. It is thus possible to say that while Viti Kabani, which obtained a grounding in unobservability, has been able to continue without generating any substantial results, modern physics has continued to produce remarkable results precisely by keeping its foundation uncertain.

Conclusion, or an Other Reality of Time

After having considered the truth claims of physics from the point of view of the ontology of time, the nature of time that has supported the truth claims of the Viti Kabani is no longer totally incomprehensible. As a result of a comparative study of the ontologies undergirding the truth claims of both Fijians and physicists, the way in which time is handled in the Viti Kabani has been thrown into relief. On the one hand, this thought experiment based on ethnography converts the unknowable into the knowable, while on the other it transforms the known into the unknown.

If it is true that the results of physics, which have internalized ungroundedness, continue to construct our technological environment, what does this say about the reality in which we are living? In the same manner as physicists, do we not construct our lives on the assumption of the possibility of observation, while the unobservable lurks underneath? For example, the very problem of history may have been established on a basis that makes final 'resolution' impossible, no matter how much effort is made to verify the accessible past.

The ontological contrast of the two truth claims shows that the levels of qualia and quanta are connected in a way that strengthens criticisms of the nature-culture dichotomy that have gained ground in recent years. While grappling with the difficulties of the qualia of other people, anthropologists are also able to develop arguments that re-examine physics as the pursuit of universal quanta and the reality made possible by this pursuit. Indeed, such studies can take as their subject the qualia of physicists as practitioners of the supreme knowledge of quanta.

Meanwhile, this re-examined physics hints at the possibility of reimagining the (non-physicist) people studied by anthropologists through the question of quantum vagueness. In this way, there is no need to classify the inflection of the 'ontological turn' carried out in this chapter as instantiating any kind of 'cultural relativism' (see Carrithers et al. 2010; Paleček and Risjord 2012). Moreover, this turn does not in any way posit a pure Other or an attempt to access that Other by means of 'meta-ontology' (see Heywood 2012; Laidlaw 2012). In neither the case of the Viti Kabani nor that of modern physics can such a pure Other be located. Nor, as we have seen, is it necessary to resort to meta-ontology to access either of them.

I would like to end by engaging in a final thought experiment concerning time in a space where the absolute border between qualia and quantum has collapsed. As I have emphasized, anthropologists doing ethnography rely very much on accessibility—on engaging with observable states. But it is worth questioning what it is that guarantees observability. In the case of historical perception, there are concrete forms, such as documents, pictures, and numbers, as well as testimonies and memories. These are confirmed by the perceptions that we bring to bear on them, and they hold good as long as we trust these perceptions. One could thus say that the past is merely acknowledged as a product of trust in one's current perception, that is, 'the Now'. If this is the case, however, we need to contemplate how the Now is interwoven with the past and the future. We also need to consider the link between this Now and the following Nows—both forward and backward. Unfortunately, according to Carnap (1963: 37), this issue is beyond the scope of physics: "Once Einstein said that the problem of the Now worried him seriously. He explained that the experience of the Now means something special for man, something essentially different from the past and the future, but that this important difference does not and cannot occur within physics."

This does not mean that no physicists are dealing with the issue of the Now. Julian Barbour (1999), for example, posits a timeless theory of quantum gravity on a universal scale, which makes infinite Nows describable. Although his argument remains in the minority, once again with no prospect of being linked to measurable physical quantities, I take inspiration from it in order to present the time of Viti Kabani activists in an ontological space where neither qualia nor quanta can stand on its own. Physicists often express a four-dimensional state that includes time by means of three-dimensional special icons. In contrast, Barbour expresses the notion that the history of the universe is composed timelessly.[17] In opposition to conventional physics, which has represented the fourth dimension using three dimensions, he argues that what we sense as four-dimensional history is a component of the three dimensions.

Interestingly, if we increase the number of dimensions by one, this is equivalent to the contrast between Western art and the art of the Marquesas Islands proposed by Alfred Gell (1998). Gell argues that Western art is a representation of three dimensions by two dimensions, while the Marquesas Islanders compose two dimensions by three dimensions. In modern physics, this is analogous to the contrast between orthodox kinetics, in which three dimensions represent four dimensions, and radical theories that deny motion itself, thus recomposing three dimensions four-dimensionally. This structural transformation can be used to make a final remark on the Viti Kabani.

Originally, gift-giving rituals gave concrete shape to Apolosi's movement. To borrow from Strathern (1988), gifts were artifacts exchanged and evaluated aesthetically. Rather than viewing Apolosi's worshippers as representing and consuming an immense amount of time using thinly sliced time-spaces—gift-giving rituals—we might think of them as composing those rituals by means of a four-dimension-like relationship of past-present-future. Their time is thus one of (continuing to give) gifts. This is not to pose another truth claim but, subjunctively, to open up other alternatives for thinking about anthropology and time.

Acknowledgments

I am grateful to the original panel participants for their useful comments. I especially thank Marilyn Strathern for her insightful response. I also wish to thank Yoichi Kazama, a quantum physicist, for his critical and instructive comments. As usual, this research owes much to the encouragement of Hirokazu Miyazaki and Annelise Riles. Last but not least, I thank Casper Bruun Jensen and Atsuro Morita for their invitation to the panel.

Naoki Kasuga is a Professor of Anthropology at Hitotsubashi University. He has written on a wide range of topics from mathematics to crime novels. Among his many publications are *Rasputin in the Pacific: The Historical Anthropology of the Viti Kambani Movement* (2001, Kyoto: *Sekai Shisosha*, in Japanese) and "Total Social Fact: Structuring, Partially Connecting, and Reassembling" (*Revue du MAUSS*, 2010).

Notes

1. For a general view of responses to such criticisms, see Holbraad (2012), Holbraad et al. (2014), Pedersen (2012), and Viveiros de Castro (2011). The comparison I develop here owes much to the pioneering work of Strathern (1988, 1991) and to anthropological studies influenced by her research. For a good example, see Jensen (2011).
2. Apolosi Nawai to Governor E. B. Sweet-Escott, 27 November 1917: "E ra dau vunia e matai keimami na ka vinaka ka savasava ka ra sa dau vakaraitaka ga vei keimami na vei ka ca" (in Fijian).
3. The definite article 'Na' added to 'Gauna' (time) implies 'His Time'.
4. The companies included the Colonial Sugar Refining Company (CSR), Barnes & Phillips (BP), and Morris Hedstrom (MH).
5. Apolosi Nawai to the heads of the Gaunavou Society of Fiji, 28 June 1938.
6. A letter from a villager to the acting inspector general, March 1926.
7. Napitalacagi Japeuni to Uaia Nakobua, 4 March 1925.
8. From Apolosi Nawai to all the Heads of the Gaounavou Society of Fiji, 28 June 1938.
9. From Apolosi Nawai to the leaders of the New Age, Rt. Semesa N., Aisea N. and everyone in Fiji, 4 September 1941.
10. For more on this history, see *About Time: Einstein's Unfinished Revolution* by Paul Davies (1996).
11. What quantum physics describes as the 'entanglement' of particles contradicts relative theory in breaking the global/local distinction. Although Einstein's criticism attracted the physicists of his day (see Einstein et al. 1935), John Bell (1964) and contemporary physicists have proved its lack of validity. Price's point is that by considering backward causality in relation to quantum mechanics observations, new links between relativity theory and quantum dynamics can be explored.
12. Among a number of arguments against time asymmetry in physics, the most prominent of which is by Ilya Prigogine, I have chosen to discuss only two: one by Huw Price and the other by Satoshi Watanabe. The first introduces the distinction between the 'inaccessible past' and 'accessible past', while the second outlines the contrast between 'prediction' and 'retrodiction'.
13. As long as we accept the presumption that no manipulation has taken place, retrodiction holds true.
14. The two previous paragraphs are based on Watanabe (1969, 1978).
15. "The Theory of the Universal Wave Function" was originally Everett's (1956) PhD thesis. DeWitt and Graham (1973) described his theory as a 'many-worlds interpretation'.

16. There are different versions of many-worlds interpretation. Everett saw the wave function as universal, not simply as a description but as the non-linear reality of the universe itself.
17. Physicists like Rovelli (2006) and Zeh (2008) have also discussed timeless histories of the universe.

References

Barbour, Julian. 1999. *The End of Time: The Next Revolution in Our Understanding of the Universe.* Oxford: Oxford University Press.
Bell, John. 1964. "On the Einstein Podolsky Rosen Paradox." *Physics* 1 (3): 195–200.
Berger, Peter. 1967. *The Sacred Canopy: Elements of a Sociological Theory of Religion.* New York: Doubleday.
Black, Max. 1956. "Why Cannot an Effect Precede Its Cause?" *Analysis* 16 (3): 49–58.
Carnap, Rudolf. 1963. "Autobiography." In *The Philosophy of Rudolf Carnap*, ed. Paul Arthur Schilpp, 37–200. La Salle, IL: Open Court Publishing.
Carrithers, Michael, Matei Candea, Karen Sykes, Martin Holbraad, and Soumhya Venkatesan. 2010. "Ontology Is Just Another Word for Culture." *Critique of Anthropology* 30 (2): 152–200.
Davies, Paul. 1996. *About Time: Einstein's Unfinished Revolution.* New York: Simon & Schuster.
DeWitt, Bryce S., and Neill Graham, eds. 1973. *The Many-Worlds Interpretation of Quantum Mechanics.* Princeton, NJ: Princeton University Press.
Dummett, Michael. 1978. *Truth and Other Enigmas.* London: Gerald Duckworth.
Einstein, Albert, Boris Podolsky, and Nathan Rosen. 1935. "Can Quantum-Mechanical Description of Physical Reality Be Considered Complete?" *Physical Review* 47: 777–780.
Everett, Hugh. 1956. "The Theory of the Universal Wave Function." PhD diss., Princeton University.
Ferris, Timothy. 1997. *The Whole Shebang: A State-of-the-Universe(s) Report.* New York: Simon & Schuster.
Galison, Peter. 2003. *Einstein's Clocks, Poincaré's Maps: Empires of Time.* New York: W. W. Norton.
Gardner, Martin. 2002. "Many Worlds? A Response to Bryce DeWitt's 'Comment.'" *Skeptical Inquirer* 26 (3): 61.
Gell, Alfred. 1992. *The Anthropology of Time: Cultural Constructions of Temporal Maps and Images.* Oxford: Berg.
Gell, Alfred. 1998. *Art and Agency: An Anthropological Theory.* Oxford: Clarendon.
Heywood, Paolo. 2012. "Anthropology and What There Is: Reflections on 'Ontology.'" *Cambridge Anthropology* 30 (1): 143–151.
Holbraad, Martin. 2012. *Truth in Motion: The Recursive Anthropology of Cuban Divination.* Chicago: University of Chicago Press.
Holbraad, Martin, Morten Axel Pedersen, and Eduardo Viveiros de Castro. 2014. "The Politics of Ontology: Anthropological Positions." *Cultural Anthropology*, 13 January. http://culanth.org/fieldsights/462-the-politics-of-ontology-anthropological-positions (accessed 6 March 2017).
Jensen, Casper Bruun. 2011. "Introduction: Contexts for a Comparative Relativism." *Common Knowledge* 17 (1): 1–12. Special issue titled "Comparative Relativism."

Kasuga, Naoki. 2008. "Gift and Commodities in Repetition: The Viti Kambani Movement in Fiji." Paper presented at the "Permeation of Monetary Resources in Gift-Exchange Economies Conference," Taj Goa, 18 December 2005. http://www.soc. hit-u.ac.jp/∼kasuga/kasuga04.pdf (accessed 17 February 2017).

Laidlaw, James. 2012 "Ontologically Challenged." *Anthropology of This Century* 4. http://aotcpress.com/articles/ontologically-challenged/.

Maurer, Bill. 2005. *Mutual Life, Limited: Islamic Banking, Alternative Currencies, Lateral Reason*. Princeton, NJ: Princeton University Press.

Miyazaki, Hirokazu. 2013. *Arbitraging Japan: Dreams of Capitalism at the End of Finance*. Berkeley: University of California Press.

Moutu, Andrew. 2007. "Collection as a Way of Being." In *Thinking Through Things: Theorising Artefacts Ethnographically*, ed. Amiria Henare, Martin Holbraad, and Sari Wastell, 93–112. London: Routledge.

Munn, Nancy D. 1992. "The Cultural Anthropology of Time: A Critical Essay." *Annual Review of Anthropology* 21: 93–123.

Paleček, Martin, and Mark Risjord. 2012. " Relativism and the Ontological Turn within Anthropology." *Philosophy of the Social Sciences* 43 (1): 3–23.

Pedersen, Morten Axel. 2012 "Common Nonsense: A Review of Certain Recent Reviews of the 'Ontological Turn.'" *Anthropology of This Century* 5. http://aotcpress.com/articles/common_nonsense/.

Price, Huw. 1996. *Time's Arrow and Archimedes' Point: New Directions for the Physics of Time*. Oxford: Oxford University Press.

Reed, Adam. 2003. *Papua New Guinea's Last Place: Experiences of Constraint in a Postcolonial Prison*. New York: Berghahn Books.

Riles, Annelise. 2004. "Real Time: Unwinding Technocratic and Anthropological Knowledge." *American Ethnologist* 31 (3): 392–405.

Rovelli, Carlo. 2006. *What Is Time? What Is Space?* Trans. J. C. van den Berg. Rome: Di Renzo Editore.

Strathern, Marilyn. 1988. *The Gender of the Gift*. Berkeley: University of California Press.

Strathern, Marilyn. 1991. *Partial Connections*. Lanham, MD: Rowman & Littlefield.

Viveiros de Castro, Eduardo. 2011. "Zeno and the Art of Anthropology: Of Lies, Beliefs, Paradoxes, and Other Truths." *Common Knowledge* 17 (1): 128–145.

Watanabe, Satoshi. 1955a. "Symmetry of Physical Laws. Part II: Q-Number Theory of Space-Time Inversions and Charge Conjugation." *Reviews of Modern Physics* 27 (1): 40–76.

Watanabe, Satoshi. 1955b. "Symmetry of Physical Laws. Part III: Prediction and Retrodiction." *Reviews of Modern Physics* 27 (2): 179–186.

Watanabe, Satoshi. 1969. *Knowing and Guessing: A Quantitative Study of Inference and Information*. Chichester: John Wiley.

Watanabe, Satoshi. 1979. *Jikan to Ningen*. [In Japanese.] Tokyo: Chuokoron.

Zeh, H. Dieter. 2008. *The Physical Basis of the Direction of Time*. Berlin: Springer.

Chapter 3

NATURES OF NATURALISM
Reaching Bedrock in Climate Science

Martin Skrydstrup

How are nature(s) connected with and/or separated from culture(s)? What are the analytical implications and political stakes involved in holding them apart or combining them? And what remains of the great nature-culture divide in the Anthropocene? Reflecting on Western notions of nature and culture and their interrelations, Marshall Sahlins (2008) quotes Nietzsche, who says that deep issues are like cold baths: one should get quickly in and out again. Along the way, Sahlins argues that we are still very much entrenched in the nature-culture divide: "As enchanted as our universe may still be, it is also still ordered by a distinction of culture and nature that is evident to virtually no one else but ourselves" (ibid.: 88). In light of this proposition, it makes sense to explore this distinction by probing what Casper Bruun Jensen and Atsuro Morita refer to in the introduction to this book as a conjunction between "the possible existence of multiple nature-cultures" and "the definite existence of diverse anthropological

Notes for this chapter begin on page 63.

traditions." However, such an exploration seems troubled by a conceptual predicament, which Jensen and Morita diagnose as follows: "The present moment testifies to a relativization, if not a collapse, of both nature and culture. It is no longer clear that there is 'one' of either. Indeed, it is no longer certain that nature and culture constitute encompassing domains at all." It might then seem that any interrogation of the nature-culture divide should indeed be limited to a short bath, or we might run the risk of never getting out again.

Here I argue that we might gain some perspective on this 'collapse and relativization' scenario by way of recalling three Parisian attempts to conceptualize nature-culture as a continuity rather than a contrast. Half a century ago, Claude Lévi-Strauss ([1949] 1969: 4) asked: "Where does nature end and culture begin?" Taking the incest taboo as his *vexata quaestio*, he maintained that it is easy to perceive universality in nature and norms in culture as aspects of "two mutually exclusive orders," presenting anthropology with "conflicting features" (ibid.: 8). When Lévi-Strauss spoke of nature, he was referring neither to the physical environment nor to what the field of science and technology studies (STS) typically subsumes under the rubric of 'non-humans'. What he had in mind was the biological and existential realities of bodies. In the Lévi-Straussian analytic, 'nature out there' is constituted by particular and shifting environments of flora and fauna, which at once provide the building blocks for human perception and cognition and for a universal theory in which "culture is not merely juxtaposed to life nor superimposed upon it, but in one way serves as a substitute for life, and in the other, uses and transforms it, to bring about the synthesis of a new order" (ibid.: 4). Thus, Lévi-Strauss assumed a conceptual continuum between nature (particular environments with plants and animals) and culture (a reservoir of myths, norms, and institutions). This is why, as Philippe Descola (2013: 24–25) concludes, one looks in vain for a culture-nature binary in Lévi-Strauss's oeuvre. Instead, one finds a matrix of multiple natures providing food for thought for a single culture. The Lévi-Straussian formula of structural anthropology therefore offers a radically different alternative to the notion of multiple nature-cultures to which Jensen and Morita (this volume) call attention.

Perhaps the most articulate, ambitious, and bold attempt to think of the world without distinguishing culture from nature can be found in Descola's (2005) *Par-delà nature et culture*. In it, Descola argues that the contemporary nature-culture views assume an epistemological continuum, which shapes how relations between societies and their environments are perceived (ibid.: 119–120). According to Descola, rethinking the relational continuities and discontinuities between humans and their environments entails engaging in an 'anthropology of nature', which identifies four experiential orders: totemism, analogism, animism, and naturalism. Particularly interesting for my purposes is Descola's notion of naturalism, described as an inversion of the "cultural construction of nature," an experiential mode in which people extend material continuities between non-humans separate from and before cultural aptitudes (ibid.: 279). Overall, *Par-delà nature et culture* reads as a reflexive treatise on epistemological categories—an ambitious attempt to rethink the conditions of possibility for doing anthropology. Yet while Descola doubts the autonomy of nature, he is not dubious about naturalism, which he sees as an experimental, non-reductive, and autonomous order (ibid: 107).

In a short, insightful article titled "Perspectivism," Bruno Latour (2009) contrasts Descola's four ontological modes of ordering with Eduardo Viveiros de Castro's 'Amerindian perspectivism'. Latour argues that the two are incommensurable: "If there is one approach that is totally anti-perspectivist, it is the very notion of a type within a category, an idea that can only occur to those Viveiros calls 'republican anthropologists'" (ibid.: 2).

Leaving open for now the question of whether Descola's and Viveiros de Castro's approaches are indeed incommensurable, I continue with an ethnographic exploration of a domain located firmly within what Descola designates as naturalism. This domain is climate science conducted on the empirical terrain of Greenland's ice. But let me first introduce another Parisian alternative to the nature-culture binary.

In *We Have Never Been Modern*, Latour (1993) convincingly argued that starting with the mechanical revolution in the seventeenth century, science and technology have not ceased to create hybrids of nature and culture. The paradox of modernity is that this process is rendered invisible by the persistence with which moderns purify these hybrids and locate them in two separate ontological domains—nature and culture, science and politics. Accordingly, access to nature through scientific laboratories is a primary distinguishing feature between moderns and non-moderns. In his more recent *An Inquiry into Modes of Existence* (2013), Latour reasserts this position. He sees geologists' use of the term Anthropocene as indicative that "we have no hope whatsoever—no more hope in the future than we had in the past—of seeing a definitive distinction between Science and Politics" (ibid.: 9). For Latour, contemporary phenomena of the Anthropocene, such as climate change, have put us in an entirely new situation where the 'modernization front' is collapsing.

We have moved from a concept of multiple natures encompassed by a single culture (Lévi-Strauss) to an idea of the autonomy of an ontological/experiential order of naturalism (Descola), and on to the idea of ever more hybridized and entangled nature-cultures, which are believed by the moderns to be separable (Latour). But what then to make of naturalist cosmologies that are thoroughly modernist in the Latourian sense, yet also harbor reflective understandings of multiple natures? As I discuss below, the climatologists I studied were familiar with critiques of scientific realism and worked within a framework of multiple natures, but they nevertheless also maintained the boundary between epistemic (climate) and material (ice) objects. The anthropological challenge in what follows is to remain faithful to the ways in which scientists draw seemingly modern boundaries and at the same time offer analytical alternatives to those boundaries.

I tackle this challenge by offering an analysis that brings together fieldwork, during which I followed the dramas of deep ice core drilling in Greenland, and a later presentation of this work to the scientists after their return to Copenhagen, where they questioned and challenged my ethnographic account. My ethnography portrays a transnational team of climatologists drilling through the ice sheet of Greenland with the goal of obtaining a record of so-called Eemian ice. I develop the argument through four parables, each of which displaces the perspective on multiple nature-cultures. The first parable doubles as a presentation of the architecture of ice core research and the multiple cultures of camp life. The second offers an ethnographic study of how bedrock was reached and how nature was defined as a form of consent and public ritual. In the third parable, the media-saturated account of reaching bedrock is challenged by the scientists, who replace it with what they call 'versions of nature', carefully distinguishing the epistemic object from the material scientific object. Finally, the fourth parable traces the representational and objectifying techniques of what the scientists refer to as the 'reconstruction' of the Eemian from what later turned out to be 'disturbed' ice. The key argument is that although the scientists in one sense operated squarely within a naturalist cosmology, they also enacted a reflective repertoire of multiple natures, whereby they distinguished 'versions' from 'layers' of nature.

Camp Cultures and the Non-Greenlandic Nature of NEEM

At the time of my fieldwork, the research station known as the NEEM (North Greenland Eemian Ice Drilling) camp was situated on the northwestern part of the Greenland ice sheet. Located at 77°27'N 51°3.6'W, this particular site was chosen based on systematic airborne recognizance across the entire Greenlandic ice sheet, which measured the thickness, density, and layers of the ice sheet from planes equipped with sophisticated radars. The NEEM site offered the most promising prospects for obtaining Eemian ice. Previously layers of snow, now compressed as ice, Eemian ice contains information about earlier climatic periods. In the current era, ice from the Eemian period, which began about 130,000 years ago and ended about 115,000 years ago, has garnered much interest because it is estimated to have been 5 degrees Celsius warmer than it is now and thus offers an analogue for global warming. Finding Eemian ice and deciphering its messages thus implies gauging future scenarios of climate change.

The infrastructures, logistics, and fiscal expenditure of drilling an ice core almost three kilometers deep through the ice sheet of Greenland and distributing it, in bits and pieces, across laboratories from Copenhagen to Tokyo make NEEM exemplary of what Latour (1987, 1999) has called 'late modern technoscience'. Yet the project doubles as a kind of science fiction time machine with which to reconstruct the past to foretell the future.

Organized as a scientific collaboration between 14 nations, the NEEM project was managed by the Center for Ice and Climate (CIC) at the University of Copenhagen's prestigious Niels Bohr Institute (NBI) in Denmark. It encompassed nine different research consortia working with different fragments of the ice cores. Their focus of their analyses ranged from the physical properties of the ice to the atmospheric gases trapped inside the core.

The NEEM base was operational between 2007 and 2012. It was inhabited between mid-May and mid-August by the 'NEEM community', which included climate scientists (from principal investigators to graduate students) and field technicians (from drilling engineers to cooks) and numbered anywhere from 3 to 34 persons at a time. Accessible by air, entry to the NEEM camp was by invitation only. Spending anywhere from one to twelve weeks in camp, scientists and technicians were flown in with United States Air Force ski-equipped Hercules planes.

The camp architecture centered on the Main Dome (fig. 1), often dubbed 'the mother ship' by the scientists. The mother ship housed the kitchen, the dining room (featuring a monitor displaying the action in the subsurface drilling trench), leisure activities, and a flight deck from which incoming planes were directed. Around the Main Dome, tents were spread out, and behind it lay the entrance to the subsurface drilling trench and science trench, the adjacency of which blurred the distinction between field science and lab science (Kohler 2002; Latour and Woolgar 1986). In the drilling trench, a team of engineers and scientists drilled around the clock, producing anywhere from 0 to 20 meters of ice cores per day. These cores were logged and carried to the science trench, where measurements were conducted along an elaborated assembly line according to complex distribution schemes between different scientific consortia. These measurements gave the scientists an initial reading of messages from 'the abyss'

FIGURE 3.1 The Main Dome of NEEM

Photograph © Martin Skrydstrup

(Helmreich 2009), providing almost real-time analysis of the climatic period in which they were drilling. The more sophisticated work to produce an accurate climatic profile of the Eemian that would with 'match points' to other ice cores in Greenland and Antarctica was saved for the metropolitan labs.

In June 2010, I arrived at the NEEM base with 14 other passengers and a lot of cargo. I had been enlisted as an assistant cook, but during my five weeks of ethnographic fieldwork, I also performed as an ice core logger in the drilling trench and contributed photographs to the NEEM field diary. The diary, which was the official account of what happened in camp, was uploaded to the CIC hosting site directly from camp. The CIC head who had set up the roster had deliberately placed me in the kitchen, since he thought this was the "hub of camp life" where "all the vibe is, and you can observe the group dynamics and interactions between the scientists when they are at ease and off duty."[1]

Thinking that I had this republic of science—populated with 14 different nations and nine scientific consortia—all to myself, I was surprised to learn on my very first day that another social scientist was already there. He was employed by the US military to conduct a field survey on group dynamics in isolated settings, a topic he was unable to divulge further details about since it was classified. During the few hours he spent in camp, he invited me to a 'focus group session' with three camp scientists. I recorded the following exchange between the four interlocutors:

> American social scientist: Could you please summarize your field experience in this extreme environment?
>
> French climatologist: I would say that one month on the ice is one month of vacation in one big family ... I just feel being part of one global family!
>
> Australian climatologist: Yes, very true. It feels like being on a holiday with family and with friends. I am just having a nice time, you know. We are working together, cooking together, and riding skidoos [snowmobiles] together.
>
> American climatologist: Ahh, this must be your first field season. For me it's just hard work.
>
> American social scientist: Are there lessons to be taken away from NEEM for other polar camps? I mean, what have you done here to have a better functioning group?
>
> French climatologist: The lesson to take away from NEEM is that you have built a family spirit here.
>
> American social scientist: Do you take over a new culture when you're here, or do you retain your background culture while you are here?
>
> American climatologist: I don't know. I am American, and they say Americans don't have any culture.

Apparently satisfied with this double entendre response of humor and ethnographic refusal, the surveyor thanked the scientists for their time and made his way to the Hercules. When I caught up to him as he boarded the aircraft, he confided that, two years earlier, when conducting fieldwork on the mental states of researchers overwintering at the McMurdo station in Antarctica, he had identified "seven different cultures ... the Italian one, German, Swedish, American, Swiss, French, and ... ah, I can't remember the last one."

I do not invoke this piece of meta-anthropology ironically. The point is that the situation attests to the sense in which the modern notion of multiple cultures enacted on the stable background of a single nature is shared between the climatologists and the social scientist. Significantly, this stable canvas of nature is never referred to as Greenlandic. Instead, the landscape is seen as a vast nothingness where the forces of nature reign.

In the Latourian sense, then, the NEEM collective appeared thoroughly modern. Its members subscribed to an ontology of multiple cultures on the backdrop of a generic nature. At the level of camp cuisine and Saturday night entertainment, these multiple cultures were celebrated and orchestrated. In the drilling and science trenches, cultures might converge, diverge, or enter into conflict. But cultures never entered the borehole. This layering also explains why, from the perspective of the scientists, the proper place for an anthropologist was in the kitchen. They expected that I would study the multiple cultures of camp life as it unfolded at the surface level. Genuinely surprised that I was interested in the experiential realities of the drilling trench and science trench, they could not fathom why an anthropologist would delve into the manufacture of facts and knowledge in the subsurface trenches.

Hybrid Natures

Remote sensing had established that Eemian ice could be found in the layers approximately 2,400 to 2,500 meters below the snow surface. They further estimated the depth of the ice sheet to be approximately 2,545 meters. Thus, the Eemian ice—and with it the entire scientific rationale of the project—was sitting just some 50 meters above bedrock. When I arrived at the camp in June, the driller's depth stood at 2,270 meters. During the first two weeks of July, we raced toward bedrock, with up to 25 meters of ice core being produced in a day. Bedrock seemed within reach during the 2010 field season, and excitement and anticipation ran high. Then the weather changed, and a storm hit the camp so badly that it qualified as a 'whiteout'. This is an odd phenomenon, because even though there is plenty of light, you cannot see your own hand stretched out in front of you. Emergency procedures and way ropes were put in place, and drilling slowed down to five meters per day. Continuing at this pace, we were unlikely to reach bedrock within the field season. After the storm, the drillers therefore mounted new asymmetrical shoes and steep cutters on the drill. On the evening of 17 July, I ran into the deputy field leader, toothbrush in hand. Before going to bed, he wanted to check the latest results on the real-time monitor in the Main Dome. On entering, we saw that about half of the camp population had gathered in anticipation. When the result of a core measuring 3.4 meters was displayed, we all rejoiced. Bedrock was once again within reach.

On 22 July, the drillers began to recover ice cores containing cloudy, 'silty' bands of basal material, which were revealed to consist of mud. The crystals in the ice also got bigger. This was a tangible sign of approaching bedrock, and anticipation in the camp heightened further. Over the next two days, drilling was cumbersome, with many broken core cutters and several 'zero runs'. However, on 24 July, an ice core came up from the abyss: a 5-centimeter-long stone that looked like granite and was embedded in a 10-centimeter silty band very close to the outer diameter of the core. Almost every camp member came to inspect this ice core, and speculation flourished. Did the drill go through the stone? How close are we? For the scientific consortium studying basalt material close to bedrock, this was a spectacular yield, since what the scientists referred to as the 'impurities' in the ice core could potentially tell the story of what life had looked liked in a Greenland with no ice. Yet afterward drilling got increasingly difficult. At this point, the field leader deployed a new grinder drilling head, even though it would compromise the integrity of the scientific material. Called 'Arnold', the new drilling head was named after a Californian governor of Austrian origins with a reputation for causing considerable collateral damage during his missions.

On 26 July, everybody in camp followed the lowering of Arnold into the borehole. After more than three hours, the drill came up with a 10-centimeter-long crystal clear ice core. Since crystal clear ice without any impurities seemed to indicate that we were far from bedrock, the drillers were puzzled, not to say bewildered. What had been expected was an ice core with even more impurities than the earlier one, perhaps even bigger stones and more basalt material. Among old-timers, I heard recollections of when bedrock was reached in the North Greenland Ice Core Project (NGRIP) camp in 2003: the last ice core that came up from the abyss was a pinkish, alien-like core dubbed 'the Thing'. The next day yielded nothing but zero runs and damaged cutters. The field leader had a long conversation with the drillers. It seemed that any attempt to penetrate further, even with Arnold's assistance, would be in vain.

Yet something was in the air, and preparations for a big celebration were in the making. As the drilling activities came to a halt, the activities in the Main Dome began to center on where the champagne glasses had been hidden and how they could be brought to the drilling trench. Later that day, bedrock was officially proclaimed at 2,537.46 meters, and champagne was poured in the drilling trench. Each nation gave a speech, and the field leader was photographed holding the penultimate ice core from 24 July as a trophy (see NEEM 2010). The entry in the official NEEM field diary for 27 July, entitled "Bedrock!!!" reads: "After a few runs with no penetration and totally grinded down cutters we made the decision to terminate the deep ice core drilling. We celebrated this with a glass of champagne in the drill trench and every nation present gave a small speech. Later we all went by skidoo to the shallow drill site 3 km from the NEEM camp to enjoy an afternoon of scones with whipped cream and strawberry jam. We all dressed for a party and had a wonderful evening with big smiles everywhere. To imagine—it is done!!" (ibid.).

At the gala dinner that evening, I asked the drillers if they thought we had reached bedrock. They replied that there were still several meters of ice under

FIGURE 3.2 NEEM scientists celebrate in the drilling trench having reached bedrock

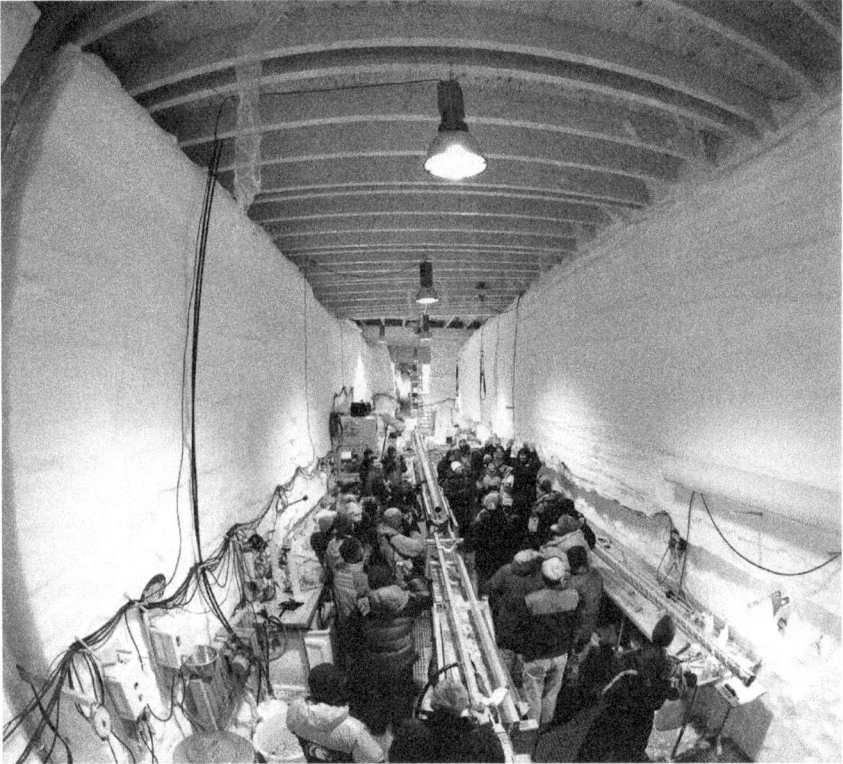

Photograph © Martin Skrydstrup

the drill head, but as one driller put it, with apparent relief: "Maintenant, c'est les vacances!" (Now, it's time for vacation). Further discussion of the circumstances and timing of reaching bedrock made clear that there were as many interpretations around the table as persons seated. One driller argued that bedrock had been reached because the drill could not penetrate any further. Another asserted that we had reached bedrock because we had. A third took the view that bedrock had been reached today because all the drillers had to leave camp tomorrow. Another person said that bedrock had been reached because another field season would be too expensive. On the next day, 28 July, the Hercules plane arrived. On the third attempt, it took off with three pallets of ice cores and 23 people from NEEM, including the three drillers who had reached bedrock.

In another piece (Skrydstrup 2012), I have argued that bedrock/nature was defined by the NEEM collective as a product of the social order (the departure dates of its members) and the goal-oriented agency and reading of the plot by the field leader. Although this argument and my ethnographic account are illustrative of how the social order and material practices of scientists mutually construct nature, I remain uncomfortable with the term 'social construction'. With Ian Hacking (1999), I would now be inclined to ask, the social construction of what?

Bedrock, yes, if something can be both real and constructed. However, my account has also foregrounded a fair amount of contingency in scientific practices. Nature resists. Apparatus is modified, and ultimately Arnold-the-drill is mounted. But the larger point is that examining the conditions of possibility for the emergence of bedrock based on a notion of science as material engagement (i.e., what happens in the drilling trench) is but only one mode of analysis. In the third parable, I discuss how my account of the experiential reality of the drilling trench in Greenland fared back in the scientific headquarters in Copenhagen.

Versions of Nature

In December 2010, about the time of the UN's Climate Change Conference, or COP 15, held in Copenhagen ('Hopenhagen', as the meeting was called in great anticipation), and the so-called Climategate event (see Skrydstrup 2013), a lot seemed at stake in doing ethnographies of climate science. Thus, when I was asked by CIC to present my work in their Friday seminar series, a peculiar timidity took hold of me. Preparing my talk, I tried to figure out whether and how the potential gaps and tensions between my ethnographic account and the scientists' official field diary might be bridged. Particularly troublesome was my knowledge that the photograph of the field leader holding up the 98-centimeter bedrock with the 10-centimeter stone inside that had been featured in the press release was actually the penultimate ice core, which had come to the surface several days before bedrock had officially been reached. Was I taking the Latourian imperative to follow scientists to where they were most vulnerable—to the very frontier of their own uncertainty about nature—a step too far? Or would the scientists welcome my ethnographic rendition of reaching bedrock as a realist account in the spirit of demystifying their practices?

I structured my presentation in two parts. The first was a walk through my black-and-white images of the camp,[2] which triggered stronger reactions than I had anticipated. "Why not digital color?" asked one. "Why did you choose to curb the horizon and distort the proportions of camp?" ventured a climatologist. It was obvious that their aesthetic sensibilities preferred realism in color to distortions in black and white. I explained that I intended to convey the planetary dimensions of the project, which was why I used extreme wide-angle perspectives that made it look like they were on top of planet Earth. Moreover, I had used black-and-white film as an aesthetic strategy to convey a different reality of camp than that rendered by snapshots in digital color (Skrydstrup 2014).

In the second part, I juxtaposed my image of reaching bedrock with the official one. Both images depict the field leader holding up the penultimate core in triumph; however, my wide-angle image shows the conspicuous presence of the media, which is absent in the official image. In my presentation,

I continued to depict NEEM as a public experiment, and I accounted for the presence of the media in the drilling trench when bedrock was reached as an explanatory idiom, which made the staging of the penultimate ice core understandable. In hindsight, this probably came from a certain connivance with my subjects. After all, I wanted to describe their practices in order to understand them, not to reveal them as manipulative or disingenuous. But to my surprise, the scientists contended that I exaggerated the role of the media. More significantly, they also took issue with my account of reaching bedrock by distinguishing material practice from the epistemic object of science. In the words of a young Dutch researcher: "What we find from the ice cores in terms of climate change, that is what we consider scientific facts. Bedrock just means the moment we decide to terminate the drilling. I was reading the online field diaries because I was not in the field, and what you conveyed today was exactly what came across in the diaries—that is, we didn't get anywhere with the drilling, so let's call it bedrock."

Another climatologist concurred, but doing so he turned bedrock into one version of nature and climate change into a co-construction:

So, could you imagine the field leader holding up the small piece of ice [refer-ring to the ultimate 10-centimeter crystal clear ice core] saying, "This is where the climate record ends"? Nobody claimed that the ice core the field leader is holding is bedrock. It's just a freaking good picture. It's a kind of versionizing. You have to target different audiences in different ways. To us, bedrock is the end of the core. It's not a definite definition. It limits how much ice we have, but that's it. Climate change is something, where fact meets society. Climate change is constructed between nature, scientists, and society in a much more dynamic way than the length of an ice core.

Yet another climatologist defended the use of the penultimate ice core as evidence of bedrock, while also characterizing it as a construction:

What gets sold to the media is a cover image of a rock in an ice core. That's what makes the front page. The significance of bedrock is a construct because, from a climate point of view, the story got messy a hundred meters before that, when we saw the first wiggles. You know that only four scientists were puzzled with calculating where bedrock was, mainly from an operational risk perspec-tive. However, for the community, our interest was to understand those wiggles in the climate record.

I return to those 'wiggles', the presumptively real concern of the climatologist, in the final parable. Here, I highlight that there does not seem to be such a big difference between what science does (in the drilling trench) and what it says (in an official field diary). Contrary to Latour (1987), this means that science does not always attempt to cover its own tracks and separate all-too-human affairs from non-human facts. Indeed, the climatologists seemed quite comfort-able with a constructivist notion of bedrock as one version of nature, insofar as they could also draw a boundary between this construction and the epistemic object of climate science. Bedrock was not a scientific fact; rather, it was an internal ritual marking the end of the drilling season and a specific version of nature sold to the media.

The juxtaposition of my ethnographic account and black-and-white images with the official field diary and press release photograph of the same event accentuates the somewhat troubled relationship between science and science studies. Recently, Latour (2013: 12) has argued that "the very words 'network' and 'fabrication' are sometimes enough to shock our interlocutors, which only shows how badly we have gone about it." For Latour, ethnographies should make room for multiple ontologies, should stay loyal to the values that scientists hold dear, should be conducted in a diplomatic way, and should make it possible to regain trust in science at last. Yet this is a tall order, and Latour himself seems to have doubts (ibid.: 17). Significantly, however, despite their critique, the scientists offered to include the 'distorted' black-and-white images on the NEEM website. What this suggests is that both scientists' and modified ethnographic descriptions of the adventure of science can become constructively entangled.

Layers of Nature

When the driller's log depth passed 2,300 meters during the first week of July, the Icelandic master driller proudly proclaimed: "We're in the Eemian now!" Significantly, this statement was not based on the interpretive work of a sophisticated instrument, but on physical evidence from the freshly drilled core. Gradually, the core became completely transparent—an indication of the transgression from the glacial (cold) to the interglacial (warmer Eemian) period. Moreover, the size of the crystals grew larger, often up to several centimeters. This suggested that the snow deposited and stored in the core had fallen during a warmer climate.

However, if the physical properties visible in the ice cores were clear, the messages from the science trench were more ambiguous. When I talked with the young German scientist operating the DEP machine (which measures the dielectric properties of the ice core) and the ECM machine (which performs electric conductivity measurements), he said that the measurements largely confirmed that we were drilling Eemian ice. Yet the measurement of the isotopic composition of the ice (delta-O-18), which scientists consider the most robust proxy for climate, did not correspond to the DEP and ECM measurements. Moreover, the match points with the NGRIP ice core drilled only about 300 kilometers away also did not correspond. On 4 July, the official field diary (NEEM 2010) phrased the conundrum in this way:

> Right now, we simply don't know the reason for the dissimilarities of the two ice core records. It may be that they are 'true' differences caused by the different drill site locations, local changes in the height of the ice sheet during the Eemian, changes in the position of ice divides, changes in past accumulation

patterns etc. There is of course also the possibility that the layering is somehow disturbed in this deep part of the NEEM core like it was the case for the GRIP and GRIP2 ice cores. At this point, we can say nothing for certain.

These were the 'wiggles' that caused confusion about the climate story. During the first two weeks of July, the NEEM collective was consumed by this enigma. For some it was a concern, while for others it was exciting. Could the Eemian have regional variations? Were we getting a real climate signal from the core, or were the measurements 'corrupted'? Was the ice perhaps 'disturbed' or 'folded'? All options were entertained in discussions that culminated during Science Night, which was held in the early evening of 8 July in the Main Dome. The field leader introduced the rationale for choosing this exact NEEM drilling location by explaining that it is "*the* site on the Greenland ice sheet where the ice did not move very much." She admitted that the "wiggles looked strange," but insisted that the larger question was whether "the ice had been folded."

After a theoretical presentation by a French climatologist, the young German climatologist presented "the view from the science trench." He confirmed that the time-scale was right and that we were indeed in the Eemian, but he noted the "big shock for everyone that the delta-O-18 measurements did not fit at all. They showed a strong peak in a totally wrong position compared with the GRIP ice core." The field leader responded that she hoped the CFA (continuous flow analysis) lab could get to the bottom of this. The German climatologist responded that it was unlikely that either the DEP or ECM measurements were incorrect. More probably, the NEEM core was disturbed. It was clearly difficult for the field leader to accept that the ice might be folded, for it would mean that the entire rationale for drilling at just this site had vanished, and with it many years of work and resources. The field leader thus ended by emphasizing that at this stage nothing definite could be concluded.

Here I cannot do justice to the long, complex route between these 2010 'wiggles' of uncertainty and the eventual 2013 publication in *Nature* of "Eemian Interglacial Reconstructed from a Greenland Folded Ice Core" by the NEEM community (see Dahl-Jensen et al. 2013). Instead, by way of contrast with the previous constructivist parable, I tease out the concept of nature that the 'reconstruction' of the Eemain from a folded ice core depended upon.

As we have seen, from the perspective of the NEEM collective, the 'versionized' nature of bedrock is at once social and material. The particular circumstances that composed the bedrock in question were not at issue for the scientists, since multiple versions of bedrock can exist as events in time. Some versions of nature are performed, orchestrated, and enacted in practice, for example, when reaching bedrock is turned into a ritual to close the field season or a play enacted for the media. As noted, however, the climatologists were still keen to separate bedrock constructed as a socio-material fact from their epistemic object, which was constituted by the 'wiggles' in the ice core.

In July 2010, these 'wiggles' were presented as specific scientific facts because it was still too early to draw any general conclusions from them. As scientists saw it, these were laboratory facts, not social or cultural ones. Yet once we shift to an STS perspective, laboratory facts are seen as being produced by 'inscription devices' (Latour 1987) in the specific socio-material settings of the lab. This is where the tension between science and science studies tends to erupt, although we might perhaps circumvent this tension by a double analytical move. On the one hand, we can hold on to the separation of socio-materialities from epistemic objects (too quickly collapsed by social constructivism). On the other hand, we can pay closer attention to how scientists distinguish different notions of nature.

If the climatologists understood bedrock as a 'construction' or 'versioning' of nature, then the Eemian was understood as a 'reconstruction', based on layers of nature. In the latter case, one kind of nature had disturbed another by folding the layers of ice, thus producing stratigraphic discontinuities. More specifically, the natural movements of the ice sheet had folded, thereby 'disturbing' the layers of nature that make up the climatic record/absolute stratigraphy of fallen snowflakes. Yet using "globally homogeneous parameters known from dated Greenland and Antarctic ice-core records ... the disturbed record of the deep ice in the NEEM ice core can be unambiguously reconstructed" (Dahl-Jensen et al. 2013: 489, 492). While from the perspective of 'versions of nature' we find a rigid separation of the materiality (physical ice cores) from the general epistemic object (climate), from the perspective of layers of nature, multiple natures can co-exist, interact, and cause mutual disturbances. Only in the former version do circumstantial facts and socio-material orders define nature. However, both bear witness to a distribution of nature ontologies having the modernist idea of multiple nature-cultures as a backdrop.

There is perhaps nothing surprising in the fact that the NEEM collective takes for granted that it can distinguish between matters of nature and matters of society. What is more significant is that multiple natures are organized as versions or layers within this naturalist cosmology. In fact, Descola's (2005) definition of naturalism as material continuities from which cultural aptitudes are separated seems largely congruent with the perspective of the NEEM collective. It is as if, starting from the gravity of naturalism, multiple nature-cultures bifurcate outward along the coordinates of layers and versions, but without ever breaking the overall form. Descola's ontological architecture, however, ceases to offer assistance when it comes to accounting for the reflexive play of these multiple natures within a naturalist cosmology.

Reaching Bedrock in a Post-foundational Era

In these times of anthropogenic climate change, the question of where nature ends and culture begins seems not only wide open but also subject to collapse. Even if 99 percent of the world's scientists agree that global warming is happening (IPCC 2013), there is still controversy about whether the cause is to be found in the magnetic activities of the sun, natural cycles, or other naturally occurring phenomena (nature), or in the rise of atmospheric CO_2 emissions in consequence of human activities (culture). Within the endless iterations of these debates, the tenacity of the distinction between natural causes and human activities is indicative of just how strongly the Cartesian dualism between nature and culture is entrenched.

Each of the four parables presented here has sought to crack open this entrenched dualism. Inverting the perspective of the American social scientist who identified seven different cultures on a research station in Antarctica, I have explored the many 'natures' that I observed at NEEM. Indeed, searching for a multiplicity of natures within naturalism has been the leitmotif of this chapter. Thus, I have highlighted both the co-existence of multiple natures and their complex layering and versioning. The NEEM collective bears witness to a naturalist cosmology of naturalism, which is at once thoroughly modern in the Latourian sense but also harbors reflective understandings of multiple natures.

Here I can return to the question of whether, as suggested by Latour (2009), Viveiros de Castro's perspectivism is indeed incommensurable with Descola's fourfold ontological scheme. For Viveiros de Castro (1998: 470), 'multinaturalism' is a key contrast between Amerindian perspectivist cosmologies and Western 'multiculturalist' cosmologies. Amerindian thought thus offers an inversion of Western cosmology in which a single nature serves as a background to multiple cultures. In Amerindian thought, it is culture that is universal while nature is particular. What strikes me as particularly illuminating about Viveiros de Castro's rendering of 'perspectivism' is the assertion that "if Western multiculturalism is relativism as public policy, then Amerindian perspectivist shamanism is multinaturalism as cosmic politics" (ibid.: 472). In this sense, the NEEM scientists would share a project with Amerindian perspectivist shamanism, namely, aligning the scales between multiple natures (air bubbles trapped in ice cores and atmospheric fluctuations) so that they can end up as a cosmic politics. In the end, I venture, Viveiros de Castro's radical perspectivism is more adequate to the ethnographic material presented here than Descola's notion of naturalism, since it captures the cosmopolitical dimension of the NEEM scientists' work. Their production of proof (ice cores) aims to give the atmosphere a memory that can serve as a 'new nature' for the global politics of the Anthropocene.

The second leitmotif of this chapter has been the relation between contemporary anthropological and STS calls to study science as material engagement with the world and the distinctions climatologists maintain between their epistemic object (climate) and their material practices (ice core drilling). While science studies puts the socio-material processes of science in action at the center of study, to an extent the socio-material process of ice core drilling is merely theater—a ritual at NEEM and a showcase for the public and the funders. In contrast, the puzzle that climatologists hold dear is how to profile the Eemian. The epistemic object does not coincide with the material object of science. I have therefore argued for the importance of simultaneously following this distinction, which belongs to a naturalist cosmology, while staying attuned to the multiple natures of this cosmology. Ultimately, the attempt to think of the world as the scientists do, rather than reconfiguring our conceptual repertoire to better capture their objectifying techniques and realist strategies, might perhaps produce new relationships between those who study scientists and those who are scientists.

Anna Tsing (2013, 2014) has recently explored the possibilities and limits of different descriptive techniques and knowledge strategies that speak to—rather than against—each other. By inviting an anthropologist to conduct fieldwork at NEEM and by accommodating a gallery of what the scientists perceived as distorted images on their own website, the first steps toward such an entangled experimentation was taken by the scientists. The next move seems to be mine. An addendum to this chapter in the form of a fifth parable, which responds to Tsing's call by aiming to be faithful to the distinctions maintained by the scientists, might contribute an answer to Latour's (2013: 17) recent question: "Can we finally offer a realistic description of the modern adventure, one that will allow us to give comparative anthropology a more credible basis for comparison?"

Acknowledgments

I want to thank all the scientists at NEEM and CIC who patiently answered my questions and contributed their valuable time toward my project, especially Sune for acting as my 'ground truth'. I also wish to thank Finn Aaserud at the Niels Bohr Archive for generously sharing his material and views on ice core research. The European Research Council supported this research from 2009 to 2011 (ERC Advanced Grant No. #229459). I extend thanks to Kirsten Hastrup for her encouragements when I first pitched this project on the deck of a small fishing boat in Ameralik Fjord on a freezing day in February 2007 and to my former colleagues at Waterworlds, Department of Anthropology, University of Copenhagen, for our many conversations. This chapter was prompted and nurtured by Casper Bruun Jensen's generous readings and substantive critiques of my drafts. Finally, I thank my family for bearing with my absence during a critical transition period between Kenya and Denmark, when this chapter was written.

Martin Skrydstrup is an Associate Professor at the Copenhagen Business School. He earned his MPhil and PhD in Cultural Anthropology at Columbia University and holds an MA in Social Anthropology from the University of Copenhagen. He has also studied Philosophy and History at Eberhard Karls Universität in Tübingen and has held visiting appointments at SciencePo and Université Paris V René Descartes. His current research interests sit at the intersection of expertise, governance, and the constitution of natural resources. He is the editor with Kirsten Hastrup of *The Social Life of Climate Change Models: Anticipating Nature* (2012). His postgraduate research has been supported by a number of excellence grants, such as the Wenner-Gren Foundation, the National Science Foundation, the European Research Council, and the Sapere Aude elite grant awarded by the Danish Council for Independent Research.

Notes

1. All the research participants are quoted with reference to their titles in cases when anonymity is not requested and under pseudonyms when anonymity is preferred.
2. These images are available at http://www.iceandclimate.nbi.ku.dk/anthropology.

References

Dahl-Jensen, Dorthe, Mary R. Alpert, Alda Aldahan, et al. 2013. "Eemian Interglacial Reconstructed from a Greenland Folded Ice Core." *Nature* 493: 489–494.

Descola, Philippe. 2005. *Par-delà nature et culture*. Paris: Gallimard. Published in 2013 as *Beyond Nature and Culture*, trans. Janet Lloyd. Chicago: University of Chicago Press.

Descola, Philippe. 2013. *The Ecology of Others*. Trans. Geneviève Godbout and Benjamin P. Luley. Chicago: Prickly Paradigm Press.

Hacking, Ian. 1999. *The Social Construction of What?* Cambridge, MA: Harvard University Press.

Helmreich, Stefan. 2009. *Alien Ocean: Anthropological Voyages in Microbial Seas*. Berkeley: University of California Press.

IPCC (Intergovernmental Panel on Climate Change). 2013. *Fifth Assessment Synthesis Report AR5*. http://www.ipcc.ch/report/ar5/.

Kohler, Robert E. 2002. *Landscapes and Labscapes: Exploring the Lab-Field Border in Biology*. Chicago: University of Chicago Press.

Latour, Bruno. 1987. *Science in Action: How to Follow Scientists and Engineers through Society*. Cambridge, MA: Harvard University Press.

Latour, Bruno. 1993. *We Have Never Been Modern*. Trans. Catherine Porter. Cambridge, MA: Harvard University Press.

Latour, Bruno. 1999. *Pandora's Hope: Essays on the Reality of Science Studies*. Cambridge, MA: Harvard University Press.

Latour, Bruno. 2009. "Perspectivism: 'Type' or 'Bomb'?" *Anthropology Today* 25 (2): 1–2.

Latour, Bruno. 2013. *An Inquiry into Modes of Existence: An Anthropology of the Moderns*. Trans. Catherine Porter. Cambridge, MA: Harvard University Press.

Latour, Bruno, and Steve Woolgar. 1986. *Laboratory Life: The Construction of Scientific Facts*. 2nd ed. Princeton, NJ: Princeton University Press.

Lévi-Strauss, Claude. (1949) 1969. *The Elementary Structures of Kinship*. Trans. James H. Bell, John R. von Sturmer, and Rodney Nedham. Boston: Beacon Press.

NEEM (North Greenland Eemian Ice Drilling). 2010. "Field Diaries." http://neem.dk/field_diaries (accessed 6 March 2017).

Sahlins, Marshall. 2008. *The Western Illusion of Human Nature*. Chicago: Prickly Paradigm Press.

Skrydstrup, Martin. 2012. "Modelling Ice: A Field Diary of Anticipation on the Greenland Ice Sheet." In *The Social Life of Climate Change Models: Anticipating Nature*, ed. Kirsten Hastrup and Martin Skrydstrup, 163–182. New York: Routledge.

Skrydstrup, Martin. 2013. "Tricked or Troubled Natures: How to Make Sense of 'Climategate.'" *Environmental Science & Policy* 28: 92–99.

Skrydstrup, Martin. 2014. "Planetary Perspectives: A Note on the Optical Sub-Consciousness in Ethnographic Fieldwork." *Anthropology News*, 16 April. http://www.anthropology-news.org/index.php/2014/04/16/planetary-perspectives (accessed 25 July 2014).

Tsing, Anna. 2013. "More-Than-Human Sociality: A Call for Critical Description." In *Anthropology and Nature*, ed. Kirsten Hastrup, 27–42. London: Routledge.

Tsing, Anna. 2014. "Strathern beyond the Human: Testimony of a Spore." *Theory, Culture & Society* 31 (2–3): 221–241.

Viveiros de Castro, Eduardo. 1998. "Cosmological Deixis and Amerindian Perspectivism." *Journal of the Royal Anthropological Institute* 4 (3): 469–488.

··:::::··

Chapter 4

RAW DATA
Making Relations Matter

Antonia Walford

Drawing on an ethnographic study of the everyday scientific practices per-
taining to the production of observational environmental data in the Brazilian
Amazon, this chapter demonstrates some of the different sorts of relationality
that are constitutive of scientific data.[1] The chapter will concentrate on a form
that observational scientific data takes known as 'raw data' (in Portuguese,
dados brutos), which is data that has come straight from the instrument without
having passed through any sort of quality control process. It is data with noise,
gaps, and errors in it. It contains 'impossible' measurements and does not display
the relations between variables that it must in order to be considered 'certified
data' (*dados certificados*), ready for use by other researchers. By concentrating
on uncertain, unstable, and ambiguous raw data rather than certain and stable
certified data, the chapter seeks to interrogate the relationship between stability
and relationality from an empirical perspective. This also provides a vantage
point from which to rethink the way that facts and relations might themselves
relate to ideas of nature and culture.

Notes for this chapter begin on page 77.

I will start by reiterating an observation that has been made several times (including in the introduction to this volume): how the relationship of nature to culture seems to kaleidoscopically shift, forming a "matrix of contrasts" (Strathern 1980: 177) that does not hold steady across space or time. As also noted in the introduction, from a relational perspective the fact that there might be more than one way to relate nature to culture means not only that there is more than one 'culture' in the world; it also means that there is more than one 'nature'—an insight that has galvanized a great deal of contemporary work in anthropology and science and technology studies (STS) (Haraway 1991; Latour 1993, 1999; Viveiros de Castro 1998, 2004).

But this observation has other related and equally kaleidoscopic effects, one of which I will concentrate on in this chapter: namely, while (scientific) 'facts' can be opposed to (social) 'relations' (in the same way that nature can be opposed to culture, such that Western scientific knowledge production about 'nature' can be seen to be reductively 'cutting out' culture), 'facts' can also be seen to be themselves constituted by 'relations' (in the same way that 'culture' has always been 'in' nature, in different ways) (see, e.g., Hayden 2012; Law 2002; Strathern 1992; Wagner 1977). The tension arises from the imbricated co-existence of a relation of opposition and a relation of implication. As Geoffrey Bowker (2013: 168) puts it in another form: "The social, then, is other than the natural and should/must be modeled on it; and yet the natural is always already social."

An example of this tension plays itself out within STS and related disciplines. One of the most powerful of STS's (often feminist-inspired) interventions into our understanding of the scientific production of nature is its emphasis on all the unseen or eclipsed relations that go into the production of scientific knowledge and that permit the enactment and existence of certain sorts of 'facts' or 'objects'. But if certain social critiques then highlight the way in which Western science removes all traces of these socio-cultural relations in its quest for objectivity (thus defining these two categories as being against each other), STS approaches such as actor-network theory (ANT) further demonstrate how these social relations were in fact *there all along*. On the one hand, then, whereas scientific objectivity has been accused of 'reductionism', on the other, ANT offers the opposite: the accumulation and endless multiplying of connections and relations. From this view, facts, objects, and certainty—in short, reality as we know it—are a result of these relations, rather than opposed to them.

Based on an ethnographic study of raw data, the chapter will take this argument in a slightly different direction by exploring how observational scientific data is not only composed of, or constituted by, particular relations—as if it were the sum result of them—but is also itself a relation of sorts. Given the theme of this book (see also Coopmans et al. 2014; Lynch and Woolgar 1990), we might say that data is already a form of relating nature to culture (although its relational capacity is not restricted to this particular dichotomy). As I shall argue in this chapter, and in terms more familiar to my informants, observational scientific data is itself a relation between what is data (i.e., what is fact) and what is error (i.e., what is artifice). Indeed, data can be seen as a particularly interesting case for examining 'multiple nature-cultures' in this sense because it slips between these categories. For example, certified observational data is not considered the same as a 'natural' object, sample, or phenomenon, nor is it considered an abstract scientific law. As such, this chapter suggests that we see the relational work that goes into the stabilization of data (and other scientific informational entities) not as the establishment of the existence of this or that fact, but rather as the establishment of specific kinds of relations. By focusing on the raw data, I demonstrate that not only are natures and cultures, or data and errors, enacted through the quotidian practices of scientific endeavor. In fact, it is the relation that constitutes the dualism of these forms that is being forged. That is to say, the relation is also an end and not simply a means.

Raw Data as an Oxymoron

In 2010, I spent a year conducting fieldwork with researchers and technicians involved in a Brazil-led scientific project, the Large-Scale Biosphere-Atmosphere Experiment in Amazonia (LBA). Initiated in 1998, the LBA is responsible for managing, collecting, and making available data from a long-term data collection project that has spanned 10 years, with the intention of ascertaining the role of the Amazon forest in the global carbon cycle. It thus brings together hundreds of researchers in different scientific disciplines. With help from collaborative partnerships with the National Aeronautics and Space Administration (NASA) of the United States and various other Brazilian, European, and North American institutions, the LBA built meteorological towers that stretch more than 20 meters above the top of the forest canopy, up to almost 70 meters in places. These towers have a profile of equipment on them that measures different sorts of meteorological variables, including wind speed and direction, rainfall, air temperature, and air humidity. Some towers also have specific equipment that measures carbon flux—the rate and volume of carbon moving vertically up and down, being exchanged between the biosphere and the atmosphere.

The data that these instruments produce is either collected weekly by a technician or sent in real time via telemetry to the LBA head office, which is in the city of Manaus, Amazonas. During my fieldwork, I spent a great deal of time with the LBA micrometeorology team that is responsible for this tower data. This involves work both 'in the field' (*no campo*)—that is, in the forest with the towers and the instruments—and back at the LBA head office on the computer, processing or 'cleaning' (*limpando*) the data that arrives from the forest. This clean data is then stored in several databases and made available to the wider LBA community and beyond.

The data that the LBA micrometeorology team collects and processes evolves and changes as it is transformed from raw to certified. The members of the micrometeorology team discuss 'the data' (*os dados*) all the time without necessarily having to refer to any specific stage, because the context makes this clear: the question "did you collect the data?" implies one sort of data, while "did you send the data to [so-and-so]?" implies another. Raw data was almost always explained to me as something still unfinished—"data that has not been cleaned yet" or, as one researcher put it, that still has to be "lapidated" (*lapidar*). Raw data, I was told, should not be passed on for use by other researchers until it is cleaned.

A recent edited volume makes a case for the provocative argument that raw data is an oxymoron (Gitelman 2013; cf. Bowker 2005). The thrust is that the imagery of rawness eclipses the fact that raw data is the result of an enormous amount of intervention, manipulation, and hard work. Indeed, the sheer amount of effort necessary to produce raw data is very apparent in the case of the LBA: funds have to be obtained from foreign institutions or from the Brazilian government; collaborative links need to be established between institutions and governments; visas need to be negotiated; data policies have to be established. After a series of expeditions to different possible sites in the forest, which can involve trekking in intensely hot and difficult conditions, a research site must be chosen—often as far from urban settlements and roads as possible. Once a site is selected, it must be ascertained that a tower can indeed be built there, which means a team of engineers must be hired to 'probe' the area (*fazer sondagem*). If the tower is to be built near indigenous territory, as was the case with one tower, the LBA needs to send someone to ensure that the indigenous people know and accept what they are doing.

Once the research site has been settled upon, the materials for the tower's construction must then travel up the Amazon to Manaus and be transported to the research site. The difficulty of this journey depends a great deal on the time of year, as the river can sometimes be too swollen from rains for a safe passage or too low for any boats to pass at all. International and domestic transportation laws must also be negotiated here, and the tower materials can be held for several weeks at customs. Once they have arrived at the research site, the tower must be built. This involves recruiting a team of people to work shifts in the forest over an extended period. Holes must be bored deep enough for the cement foundation of the tower to be laid, which in turn involves the back-breaking work of carrying all the building materials from the river to the research site. The tower is then assembled, level by level, often between massive rainstorms that make it too dangerous to construct the upper levels for fear of lightning strikes. A lodging house or camp must also be established near the site for those who are involved in constructing the tower, or subsequently, in maintaining the instruments or collecting data.[2]

Clearly, a myriad of relations is forged between people, objects, instruments, and institutions in order to produce raw data from the forest—relations that are unlikely to make it into the published papers, reports, or other artifacts of knowledge that come out of the data. Yet the initial establishment of the research site and tower is only the first step. What follows is an ongoing effort involved in then continuously collecting the raw data. And just as building the tower is particularly arduous exactly because the desirability of the research site is based on its inaccessibility, collecting the data that the instruments on the towers produce is difficult for the same reason and requires just as much effort. For example, raw data from a tower near the city of São Gabriel da Cachoeira, in the north of the Amazon, arrived by airplane. The tower there was very isolated, several kilometers along a dirt road that frequently floods and then about two kilometers or so along a particularly precarious trail that has been cut through the forest. A single technician collected data from this tower and maintained the instruments in good working condition. He went to the tower whenever he could, downloaded the data onto an interface, and uploaded it to a CD before putting it on the next flight to Manaus. This was easy for him as he also worked at São Gabriel's tiny airport.[3]

As such stories make clear, an enormous amount of effort is expended in order to establish a research site, build a tower, and collect the raw data from the forest. This effort is necessary because the research sites are so isolated; as a result, the raw data is highly prized by the scientific community, of which the LBA is a part. On several occasions, I heard researchers remark that "this has never been done before" or that "this would be the first time [this variable] was measured in the Amazon." On one occasion, a German researcher told me that it was probable that the data produced in the Amazon would be published even if it were of lower "quality" than data from elsewhere, simply because there was no other data like it. This is why researchers will go to such lengths to obtain it. The possibility of obtaining raw data on something that has never been measured before means that many different researchers from all over the world are drawn to the Amazon forest and to the LBA.

Mark is one such researcher. Based at Harvard University in the United States, Mark, a specialist in laser engineering, instrumentation, and trace gas measurements, came to Manaus to install a new piece of equipment on one of the LBA towers. His instrument could measure not only carbon dioxide (CO_2) and water (H_2O), but also carbon monoxide (CO). When he arrived at the LBA headquarters in Manaus, the leader of the micrometeorology team suggested that they install his instrument on one of the towers. Mark was very excited because, as he explained, this would be the first time this sort of data had been obtained in 'real time'—immediately available and even, Mark hoped, directly transmitted to his desk at Harvard. Furthermore, adding the measurements of CO to those of methane (CH_4) and CO_2 already being taken by the instruments on the tower would provide a unique picture of the chemical relations in the air. As Mark explained to me, the relation of these gases to each other is very important in global atmospheric chemistry directed at understanding climate change. CO produces ozone (O_3) and CO_2, so the global CO_2 estimate in part depends upon the presence of CO in the atmosphere. This in turn depends on knowing how CO behaves in tropical biomes—of which the Amazon forest is the largest in the world. However, just measuring isolated concentrations, Mark told me, "isn't chemistry." You need simultaneous measurements of all of the gases to be able to see the way in which they are interacting. This sort of chemical measurement had never to his knowledge been done in the Amazon before—which is why he was so excited.

Mark was therefore willing to overcome all sorts of obstacles in order to collect this data. Alongside trying to ensure that a clean energy supply reached his highly sensitive instrument, Mark also had to work out a way to protect the instrument from the heat and from the bees, which like to make hives in any inviting cubbyhole they can find. After spending some time toying with ways to outsmart the bees, Mark eventually decided that he would just have to sit and watch over the instrument up on the tower in the blazing heat while it was running. When packed in a protective box, the instrument weighed 60 to 70 kilograms, and it took two people to hoist it up the tower, using a rope and pulley system, and another two people to guide it so that it did not bang into the tower on its way up. Once it was there, Mark managed to get the instrument working to his satisfaction, but given the unpredictable weather conditions, he was worried. In fact, he was so worried about the instrument overheating that he left it running a total of only about five hours, during which time he sat with the instrument in the tower by himself. Yet he seemed unfazed by the ordeal. "That'll be some good data," he told me, looking pleased.

It required an enormous amount of work to install Mark's instrument in the middle of the Amazon forest. Clearly, he would not have been able to collect any data had it not been for the actions of others, as Mark himself impressed upon me several times. Those difficulties are one reason why Mark's data is one of a kind. In one sense, the raw data is thus unique simply because it is from an isolated research site. Looking more closely at what is involved in its production, however, we might say that it is unique also because of the particular relational demands that the isolated research site makes. The raw data does not just emerge from the isolated patch of forest. Without the ongoing relational work that ranges from international data policies between countries to collectively working out how to think like a bee, this particular Amazonian data would not exist. Its uniqueness is due not to its isolation, as such, but to the very particular relational configuration from which it emerges.

Raw Data's Ambiguity

However, this highly sought-after Amazonian raw data is not only unique. What in fact makes it 'raw' for the researchers and technicians I spent time with is that it is uncertain and not yet 'trustworthy'.[4] Whereas Mark was conducting a short pilot experiment and therefore could sit in the tower with his instrument, the bulk of the data from the towers is collected over years and stored automatically, which means that the instruments are left out in the forest for long stretches of time. The implication for the researchers and technicians is that the raw data from the towers could potentially be full of errors and gaps and therefore highly uncertain. As I shall now show, this uncertainty is also the result of a certain sort of relationality.

Some uncertainty in the raw data is inevitable, arising from the fact that, as a metrological technician told me, "no sensor is perfect." In other words, no sensor can measure without an element of observational uncertainty. One cause of this is the undesired effect of measuring *in situ*. For example, air temperature sensors heat up exactly by being 'in' the heat, so the heat they measure is partly their own rather than solely that of the air. There is also uncertainty in the measurement system due to the loss of information in the conversion of analog signals into digital, a conversion that takes place automatically in the instruments in order to give the data. No less important is the fact that all instruments function with a larger or smaller uncertainty factor, which is provided by the manufacturers. An uncertainty factor of, for example, 10 percent means that if that instrument measures 25° C, this value actually could be anywhere in between 22.5° C and 27.5° C. This factor, a result of the metrological testing and calibration undertaken by the manufacturers, is unavoidable when making measurements.

Further sources of uncertainty are inherent in more complicated measuring methods. Consider the technique for measuring carbon flux, known as the eddy covariance method. The carbon flux system installed on the LBA towers comprises a sonic anemometer and what is known as an open-path infra-red gas analyzer (IRGA). The sonic anemometer measures wind direction in three axes using sound waves that are pulsed between three triangulated detectors, corresponding to three spatial dimensions: vertical, horizontal, and lateral. These pulses are interrupted by the turbulent vortices and eddies created by the interaction of the wind with the tops of the trees in the forest, and from this interference the sonic anemometer infers wind turbulence direction and speed. The IRGA also measures the concentration of CO_2 and H_2O in the air at very high frequencies. By correlating the concentration of CO_2 with eddy direction and speed, the eddy covariance method can give a measurement of carbon flux—that is, how much carbon is moving per area per unit squared. However, these calculations get rather complicated, partly because of the rapidity with which carbon molecules move about, and partly because a lot of different factors have to be taken into account. In fact, some factors that are known to influence flux, such as mixing ratio and air density, are many times knowingly omitted from calculations, despite the method being state-of-the-art. This omission imparts a certain level of uncertainty that accompanies the eddy covariance method irrespective of where it is applied.[5]

Furthermore, specific uncertainties that in other settings are minimal are magnified considerably when measuring carbon flux in the forest. One of these sources is the 'footprint' of the tower, that is, how far the IRGA and the anemometer can 'see'. The footprint is calculated based on the assumption that the terrain in question is flat, being in pastureland, for example. As several researchers impressed upon me, the towers are therefore conventionally understood to measure vertical carbon flux only, as the horizontal axis can be taken as homogeneous. However, the Amazon forest is far from flat. This means that there is horizontal or lateral carbon and energy flux as well: the CO_2 'rolls' down hills and collects in basins and valleys. As a result, the raw data from the towers also includes the effect of this horizontal carbon flux caused by the topography of the land—something the researchers have only recently become aware of, as one LBA researcher told me. This poses a serious problem: the researchers had assumed the vertical measurement to be total when in fact it captured only part of the carbon that was moving around the forest.

On top of these issues are the problems of installing and maintaining electrical instruments in the forest, which interferes unremittingly. As the tower can move about alarmingly in a rainstorm, the anemometer can often slip very slightly, thus affecting the calculations of the directionality of the wind eddies. At the more remote towers, the technician would sometimes arrive to find the instruments disconnected or turned upside down, as if a curious passer-by, or some animal, had decided to take a look. Bees colonize the boxes that house the data logger and slowly turn it into a hive, coating it in wax. When it rains, the open-pathway IRGAs cannot take measurements because raindrops on their detectors do not evaporate due to the intense humidity. The manual for these instruments, intended for temperate climates, warns users only about the effects of snow. But the most substantial problem is also the simplest: dirt. It piles up on the instruments, coats the IRGAs, and spreads over the radiometers, requiring someone to constantly remove it and thoroughly clean the instruments as frequently as possible. Dirt offers the most vivid illustration that the very presence of the instruments in the world, in the forest, affects the data that is being produced.

Despite the best efforts of the micrometeorology team, raw data is therefore always a measurement *plus something else*. As the head of the team told me, "dirt kills the curve" (*a sujeira mata a curva*). What he meant was that the dirt on the instrument will affect the shape of the graphed line of the data because it is included in the measurement. What is thus interesting about the raw data is not only that it emerges out of all the relational, intentional work that went into its production. More striking is the fact that what emerges from all this effort is not stable at all but inherently uncertain and unstable—'untrustworthy', as the researchers put it. As I have tried to demonstrate, this uncertainty is also constituted by a whole host of relations. Indeed, the raw data is constituted as much by these relations—between bees and wax and the data logger, or between the instruments and rainstorms—as by the network of social, legal, and institutional relations, associations, and negotiations that I described earlier. Even with cutting-edge instruments, meticulously planned logistics, and access to a team of willing people who know the forest and can help you, it is very hard in the first instance to produce Amazonian carbon flux data that is singular in meaning. What is produced instead is very raw data that is inherently semiotically uncertain. Alongside being a measurement of a particular phenomenon, it also contains connections to all sorts of other entities, such as insects, rainstorms, air vortices, meddling passers-by, and so on.

Making Relations Matter

In this section, I want to return to the question of how facts and relations are associated, concentrating on one particular and very influential way in which 'facts' and 'relations' have been understood in STS. Perhaps unsurprisingly, I have in mind the dynamic characterized by ANT, whereby the accumulation of associations in a network successively establishes the reality of a fact (Callon 1999; Latour 2005; Law 2003). The central point is that the establishment of facts, or more radically truth, is a result of collective and contingent processes of connection, enrollment, and relating between entities in a network. These processes might include the persuasion of colleagues, the enrollment of funders, the cajoling of objects, the creation of an audience, and more—all in order to achieve *"well-articulated actors*, associations of humans and non-humans" (Latour 2004: 86; original emphasis; cf. Bowker and Star 2000; Gerson and Star 1986).

In Latour's (1987) now classic *Science in Action*, the methodological emphasis is on 'following' the multiple entities that need to coalesce around a task before scientific knowledge can be made. For this reason, the emphasis in such studies is often on the entanglement between science and entities conventionally deemed to be 'non-scientific' (e.g., Derksen 2000). Latour's (1988; cf. Callon 1999: 81; Latour 1999a: 311) examination of Pasteur, for example, traces the articulation and 'translation' of the interests of not only the most obvious human (Pasteur) and non-humans (the anthrax), but also French farmers, statisticians, public health workers, Pasteur's colleagues, and the French public, as well as a host of sundry non-humans (cf. Latour 1999a: 113–173). More 'focused' laboratory ethnographies (e.g., Amann and Knorr-Cetina 1990; Knorr-Cetina 1981) often center on showing the process through which alternative interpretations of experimental results or "inscriptions" (Latour 1987: 79) are progressively discarded or refused by the scientists in favor of a single interpretation, which comes to be seen as true. This has been variously described as "black boxing" (ibid.: 21), "fixation of evidence" (Amann and Knorr-Cetina 1990: 88), and "controlling interpretative freedom" (Collins 1985: 106). Whatever the designation, and wherever the ethnographic setting, the transformation of ambiguous results into singular meaning through socio-material means, often considered to lie outside of objective scientific practice, is frequently highlighted as the governing dynamic.

An interesting double quality characterizes the reduction in meaning that such descriptions catalogue. Paradoxically, the fact-to-be (or 'matter of concern') assumes a singular meaning (becomes a 'matter of fact') exactly by being increasingly 'articulated' into networks of different sorts of entities. The more connections and articulations it has, the more indisputable and therefore singular it becomes: as more and more humans and non-humans are convinced of and enrolled into its existence, the fact becomes more stable and real. As Latour (2004: 85) writes: "Reality grows precisely to the same extent as the work done to be sensitive to differences. The more instruments proliferate, the more the arrangement is artificial, the more capable we become of registering worlds." Whereas a paucity of connections surrounds a proposition that is ambiguous and plural in meaning, as the number of connections, associations, and actors increases—as the network grows—this ambiguity decreases.[6]

Certainly, the production and collection of raw data that I have described entails all sorts of associations, articulations, connections, and negotiations. Nevertheless, from the perspective of the LBA researchers and technicians, the problem that raw data presents has to do not only with forging stable relations, but also with the fact that the raw data is already connected in more or less unpredictable ways to a host of other entities in the world. The 'problem' itself is that these connections are the 'wrong' sorts of relations. The extraneous relations that the raw data has—with bees and lightning and dirt, or with non-linear effects of the environment, or with curious passers-by—obscure the representational potency presumed to be lurking within it. Whereas ANT might argue that the data's singular meaning emerges as a result of a whole array of relations that are constantly being enacted and tested, the same can be said of its lack of a singular meaning.

Another way of saying this is that 'the network', as it were, does not exhaust the relational repertoire of the raw data.[7] In fact, what makes the raw data 'raw' is precisely the tension between the work of those actors in the network that toil toward eliciting a stabilized set of certified data, on the one hand, and those connections and relations that lie outside this network, anchoring the raw data in the liminal state between meaning and lack of meaning, on the other.

We might therefore observe that certainty and uncertainty are equally relational effects. And thus, rather than being a question of the accumulation of associations in a network, the stability of data is created by the gradual substitution of certain relations for others. The raw data might in this way be thought of as being constituted by a sort of relational friction. It is composed of all sorts of relations to entities that the researchers do *not* want, in combination (they hope) with the relations that they *do* want and have struggled to elicit. Processing or cleaning the raw data, which results in certified data that can be shared among researchers, is a matter of sorting out those relations—keeping some, forging others, and getting rid of still others. At the end of this process, the result is stable certified data that can travel to other institutions and researchers and, indeed, forge yet more relations.

That ambiguous raw data is also composed of relations may seem a somewhat banal conclusion, as everything in ANT is understood to be the result of the network.[8] Yet it helps to clarify how facts and relations come to be co-implicated in the production of data. If the dynamic that emerges is not of relational accumulation that produces facts, but rather of a progressive substitution of relations, then in the same way it follows not only that there are relations always already behind or within the data, but also that there are relations always already behind or within the relations (cf. Strathern 1995). A second implication is that the relations that compose the raw data are relations that are somehow excessive to meaning and therefore excessive to the network. This in turn means that raw data (or uncertainty) is not, in fact, a result of the network in the way that a fact (or certainty) is. In ANT idiom, one might describe raw data as emergent from the overlapping interstices of two networks that are qualitatively different. But it is descriptively and analytically difficult to imagine the bees, the wax, the lightning, the passers-by, the rain, the non-linear effects of heat, and so on as being a 'network' in the ANT sense—that the LBA researchers are 'enrolling' these entities into producing an uncertain object. We might say therefore that raw data sits at the point at which the image of the network no longer has that much traction. In other words, it would be imprecise to say that raw data is ambiguous because it is pulled between two different networks and that, as a result, it is composed of too many relations. Rather, it is ambiguous because it pre-exists the one relation that is necessary for it to be considered a fact—or not.

Not Data, But Not 'Not Data'

Raw data is understood by the researchers and technicians I worked with to be unfinished, awaiting transformation. In paying attention to it, one finds one's attention constantly directed elsewhere—to what it will become, rather than what it is. Thus, the uncertainty around the raw data is not in terms of content, that is, what it means numerically as such; rather, it concerns the question of whether it is even data at all. If it is, then it will *always* have been data. If it is not, then it will *never* have been data. In a certain sense, it becomes what it already is.[9]

All data that is unable to lose its rawness sufficiently is defined by an unfixed relation of data to error, and the LBA researchers and technicians deal with this lack of fixity on a daily basis. One PhD student I spoke to, for example, had found that their data on water vapor flux was "very strange." The balance did not "add up." "In fact, I thought they [the data] were wrong," she explained further. "But then, when one of the reviewers of the committee read [my thesis], he told us that it was something he had noticed about the river himself." According to this committee member, it was not necessarily an error. He had seen the same anomaly in another part of Brazil. "It's a question of the lateral transport of energy," the student continued. "It's like what [another LBA researcher] saw, only he saw it for CO_2, and mine is humidity ... So, it isn't an error, but to prove this, I need more data ... We're not certain because we need a longer series of data."

"Why not just accept it as an error?" I asked.

"The first time you see it, you think it's an error because the difference is really big," she responded. "So, it could be an error associated with, let's say, the calibration of an instrument. But it is actually the same sensor that measures these two. So ... I thought there was a possibility ... that there might be a calibration error ... or it might be the lateral transport of heat. Of vapor in fact, of humidity, right? When the reviewer read my thesis, he was like, 'Ah, I saw the same thing. And I think the problem you have is nothing to do with calibration, it's not an error, it's lateral transport' ... I know it wasn't an error ... you are never certain, though, right? You imagine that it's an error. But now, after the [committee members'] result, I know that it could be ... *could be* [an error]. I am also not certain that it is lateral transport. That's why I need more data." As her supervisor told me, it is a question of 'mistrust' (*desconfiança*) because they "don't know exactly what it is."

A similar uncertainty is captured in Susan Leigh Star and Elihu M. Gerson's (1987) work on anomalies in science. Star and Gerson are dissatisfied with what they see as a tautology in Thomas Kuhn's description of anomalies, which suggests that an anomaly is only an anomaly because it does not fit with the current paradigm—that is, something is an error if it is wrong. They suggest that this can be refined by looking at the history of an anomaly and how it can change status very rapidly, not simply because it becomes logically wrong or right as a paradigm changes, but because of the constantly changing context—or what they call "work organization" (ibid.: 149)—from which both the anomaly and the paradigm emerge. Regarding a certain anomaly in neurophysiological research, they write that " its centrality to the problem structure of brain research became clear; it was defined and redefined to fit the need of an emerging work organization and the victorious school of thought in a debate. The anomaly went from mistake to artifact to discovery—even through accusations of fraud—until it was made tractable enough to be absorbed into an ongoing enterprise" (ibid.: 160). Star and Gerson are interested in a very different set of questions from those that animate the present discussion, but this observation resonates. What their analysis further demonstrates is the extent to which an anomaly, like raw data, is in constant transformation and thus always seen as something other than it is. I would like to draw attention explicitly to the conceptual potential of this characteristic. Raw data is neither phenomenon nor artifact, neither data nor error. Instead, raw data instantiates the moment before any of these positions is even ascertainable.

The technicians and researchers do not know the relation of their raw data to the world when they collect it, or whether it is error or data. Both these positions are contained within it, because what will end up being data will have *always been* data, and what will end up being error will have *always been* error. What ends up as error is in fact simply the relations that the researchers are not interested in. However, until analyzed in this way, the raw data is thus still not exactly data, nor is it 'not data'. From this perspective, all the effort that the LBA puts into collecting raw data in the first instance generates neither data nor error, but rather the endless potential for constantly creating the relation between them.[10]

Conclusion

I will conclude by briefly returning to the question of the co-implication of nature and culture with which I started. In this chapter, I have tried to hint at an unstable analogy between facts and relations and nature and culture. I have suggested a shift in emphasis, from seeing the result of scientific work as the production of facts that are constituted by a myriad of relations to seeing the result of scientific work as the production of the relation that makes the distinction between facts and relations possible. Finding out that raw data is what it has always already been—either one or another of the terms of the relation between data and error—eclipses the fact that it is the potential for this relation itself that is being forged over and over again. Extending the analogy to anthropology and STS, it is likewise possible that if nature is understood to always already include culture within it—to be a 'nature-culture'—we risk eclipsing the potential that both contain to be related very differently in different times and places.

Acknowledgments

This research was funded by the IT University of Copenhagen and a travel grant from the Danish Research School for Information Systems. I would like to thank Casper Bruun Jensen and an anonymous reviewer for their comments. I am extremely grateful to Mark C. Witinski for reading and correcting an earlier draft. I would also like to thank the members of the LBA for being so patient with me.

Antonia Walford is currently a Teaching Fellow in Digital Anthropology at University College London and a Postdoctoral Research Associate at the Centre for Social Data Science (SODAS), University of Copenhagen. Previously, she was a Research Associate at the ESRC Centre for Research on Socio-Cultural Change (CRESC). Her research explores the effects of the exponential growth of digital data on social and cultural imaginaries and practices, focusing particularly on large-scale digitization in the environmental sciences. She has published in several major journals and is preparing a book manuscript.

Notes

1. I will be using a relatively wide notion of relationality that will take advantage of the slippage between 'relations' and 'culture', which I go on to explore below, and the corollary sense in which relations are therefore opposed to facts and often associated with connectivity.
2. At one isolated camp, there was also a satellite dish so that the construction workers who spent several months in the forest at a time could watch serial dramas (*telenovela*). Mysteriously, the dish received the right channel only if a potato was carefully balanced on the connection between it and the television.
3. Unfortunately, the tower at São Gabriel fell down in June 2010, halfway through my fieldwork.
4. In a subsequent telephone conversation, Mark told me that in fact he had not used the data in a publication. Some of it was good, but there had been too many errors, resulting in not enough data "to draw trends."

5. When I asked about this, one researcher told me that the scientific community knows about these issues, of course, but at the present time the eddy covariance method is considered to be the best way available to measure flux, so they keep using it. The uncertainty of the method does not mean that it is redundant.
6. As an aside here, it is worth noting that the entities that Latour (and others) discuss have often been discovered or fabricated in a laboratory. In such a setting, it makes intuitive sense to picture lone researchers at their desks, with suspicions that they might have 'discovered' something of note and their subsequent attempts to convince colleagues that they have indeed done so—what Donna Haraway (1997: 31) refers to as the 'heroic' depiction of science. This plays into an idea of the increasing connectivity and stability (and therefore the 'constructed' nature) of such discoveries in the world. This narrative is arguably more convincing when the setting is a laboratory.
7. See also feminist critique of ANT here, such as Star (1991).
8. For another view on this matter, see Lee and Brown (1994).
9. I am here appropriating an idea from Marcio Goldman's (2009: 121–123) analysis of Afro-Brazilian *candomblé*.
10. The dynamic I am pointing to resonates with Morten Axel Pedersen's (2012) argument regarding 'post-relational' anthropology, particularly the challenge he puts to reductionist understandings of the apparently non-relational (see also Candea 2010). I am not so sure, however, that the relational 'reinvention' of scientific practice that I am here engaged in contributes to exhausting the conceptual capacity of the relation, as Pedersen would have it. See also Casper Bruun Jensen and Brit Ross Winthereik's (2015) argument regarding the necessary interplay between different sorts of relationality (cf. Candea et al. 2015b).

References

Amann, Klaus, and Karin Knorr-Cetina. 1990. "The Fixation of (Visual) Evidence." In Lynch and Woolgar 1990, 85–122.
Bowker, Geoffrey C. 2005. *Memory Practices in the Sciences.* Cambridge, MA: MIT Press.
Bowker, Geoffrey C. 2013. "Data Flakes: An Afterword to *'Raw Data' Is an Oxymoron.'*" In Gitelman 2013, 167–172.
Bowker, Geoffrey C., and Susan Leigh Star. 2000. *Sorting Things Out: Classification and Its Consequences.* Cambridge, MA: MIT Press.
Callon, Michel. 1999. "Some Elements of a Sociology of Translation: Domestication of the Scallops and the Fisherman of St Brieuc Bay." Abridged version. In *The Science Studies Reader*, ed. Mario Biagioli, 67–83. London: Routledge.
Candea, Matei. 2010. "'I Fell in Love with Carlos the Meerkat': Engagement and Detachment in Human-Animal Relations." *American Ethnologist* 37 (2): 241–258.
Candea, Matei, Joanna Cook, Catherine Trundle, and Thomas Yarrow, eds. 2015a. *Detachment: Essays on the Limits of Relational Thinking.* Manchester: Manchester University Press.
Candea, Matei, Joanna Cook, Catherine Trundle, and Thomas Yarrow. 2015b. "Introduction: Reconsidering Detachment." In Candea et al. 2015a, 1–31.
Collins, H. M. 1985. *Changing Order: Replication and Induction in Scientific Practice.* Chicago: University of Chicago Press.
Coopmans, Catelijne, Janet Vertesi, Michael Lynch, and Steve Woolgar, eds. 2014. *Representation in Scientific Practice Revisited.* Cambridge, MA: MIT Press.

Derksen, Linda. 2000. "Towards a Sociology of Measurement: The Meaning of Measurement Error in the Case of DNA Profiling." *Social Studies of Science* 30 (6): 803–845.

Gerson, Elihu M., and Susan Leigh Star. 1986. "Analyzing Due Process in the Workplace." *ACM Transactions on Office Information Systems* 4 (3): 257–270.

Gitelman, Lisa, ed. 2013. *"Raw Data" Is an Oxymoron*. Cambridge, MA: MIT Press.

Goldman, Marcio. 2009. "An Afro-Brazilian Theory of the Creative Process: An Essay in Anthropological Symmetrization." *Social Analysis* 53 (2): 108–129.

Haraway, Donna J. 1991. *Simians, Cyborgs and Women: The Reinvention of Nature*. London: Free Association Books.

Haraway, Donna. J. 1997. *Modest_Witness@Second_Millenium.FemaleMan°_Meets_ OncoMouse™: Feminism and Technoscience*. New York: Routledge.

Hayden, Cori. 2012. "Rethinking Reductionism, or, the Transformative Work of Making the Same." *Anthropological Forum* 22 (3): 271–283.

Jensen, Casper Bruun, and Brit Ross Winthereik. 2015. "Test Sites: Attachments and Detachments in Community-Based Ecotourism." In Candea et al. 2015a, 197–218.

Knorr-Cetina, Karin. 1981. *The Manufacture of Knowledge: An Essay on the Constructivist and Contextual Nature of Science*. Oxford: Pergamon Press.

Latour, Bruno. 1987. *Science in Action: How to Follow Scientists and Engineers through Society*. Cambridge, MA: Harvard University Press.

Latour, Bruno. 1988. *The Pasteurization of France*. Trans. Alan Sheridan and John Law. Cambridge, MA: Harvard University Press.

Latour, Bruno. 1993. *We Have Never Been Modern*. Trans. Catherine Porter. Cambridge, MA: Harvard University Press.

Latour, Bruno. 1999. *Pandora's Hope: Essays on the Reality of Science Studies*. Cambridge, MA: Harvard University Press.

Latour, Bruno. 2004. *Politics of Nature: How to Bring the Sciences into Democracy*. Trans. Catherine Porter. Cambridge, MA: Harvard University Press.

Latour, Bruno. 2005. *Reassembling the Social*. Oxford: Oxford University Press.

Law, John. 2002. "Objects and Spaces." *Theory, Culture & Society* 19 (5–6): 91–105.

Law, John. 2003. "Networks, Relations, Cyborgs: On the Social Study of Technology." Published by the Centre for Science Studies, Lancaster University. http://www.lancaster.ac.uk/fass/resources/sociology-online-papers/papers/law-networks-relations-cyborgs.pdf (accessed 6 March 2017).

Lee, Nick, and Steve Brown. 1994. "Otherness and the Actor Network: The Undiscovered Continent." *American Behavioral Scientist* 37 (6): 772–790.

Lynch, Michael, and Steve Woolgar, eds. 1990. *Representation in Scientific Practice*. Cambridge, MA: MIT Press.

Pedersen, Morten Axel. 2012. "Proposing the Motion: Morten Axel Pedersen." *Critique of Anthropology* 32 (1): 59–65.

Star, Susan Leigh. 1991. "Power, Technology and the Phenomenology of Conventions: On Being Allergic to Onions." In *A Sociology of Monsters: Essays in Power, Technology and Domination*, ed. John Law, 26–56. London: Routledge.

Star, Susan Leigh, and Elihu M. Gerson. 1987. "The Management and Dynamics of Anomalies in Scientific Work." *Sociological Quarterly* 28 (2): 147–169.

Strathern, Marilyn. 1980. "No Nature, No Culture: The Hagen Case." In *Nature, Culture and Gender*, ed. Carol P. MacCormack and Marilyn Strathern, 174–222. Cambridge: Cambridge University Press.

Strathern, Marilyn. 1992. *After Nature: English Kinship in the Late Twentieth Century*. Cambridge: Cambridge University Press.

Strathern, Marilyn. 1995. *The Relation: Issues in Complexity and Scale*. Cambridge: Prickly Pear Press.

Viveiros de Castro, Eduardo. 1998. "Cosmological Deixis and Amerindian Perspectivism." *Journal of the Royal Anthropological Institute* 4 (3): 469–488.

Viveiros de Castro, Eduardo. 2004. "Perspectival Anthropology and the Method of Controlled Equivocation." *Tipití* 2 (1): 3–22.

Wagner, Roy. 1977. "Scientific and Indigenous Papuan Conceptualizations of the Innate: A Semiotic Critique of the Ecological Perspective." In *Subsistence and Survival: Rural Ecology in the Pacific*, ed. Timothy P. Bayless-Smith and Richard G. Feachem, 385–410. London: Academic Press.

Chapter 5

METHODS FOR MULTISPECIES ANTHROPOLOGY
Thinking with Salmon Otoliths and Scales

Heather Anne Swanson

"This is how I know a salmon," George said, handing me a small fleck of white calcified matter (see fig. 1). Sitting in one of the folds in my palm, the object looked like a bit of broken seashell. Instead, it was an otolith, or fish ear bone. George, a long-time fisheries science lab manager at a California university, spends his days working with such bony chips, making them tell stories. He mounts the otoliths on slides and polishes them thin enough so that their tree-like rings can be counted, measured, and analyzed in an effort to learn about salmon life histories. George almost never sees salmon in the flesh. The otoliths that he processes arrive in tiny vials, already separated from piscine bodies. George knows salmon not through fishing or cooking, or even through field-work: he knows them through a microscope and the practices needed to 'read' the patterns on otoliths.

Notes for this chapter begin on page 97.

FIGURE 5.1 A salmon otolith resting in George's palm

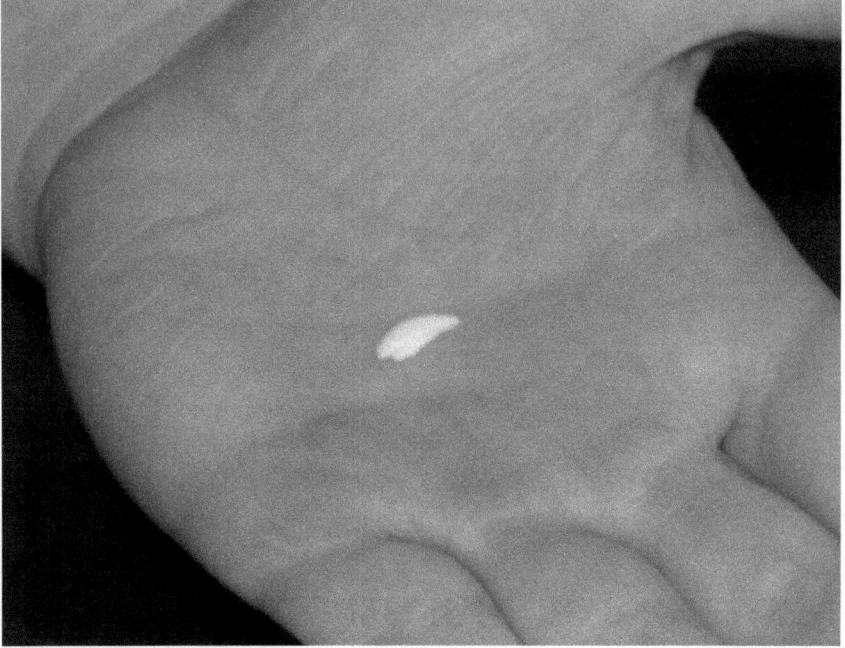

Photograph © Heather Anne Swanson

I begin with this brief description of George because it is part of a familiar genre. The ways that salmon are enacted in laboratory practices are precisely the things that scholars engaged in multispecies anthropology and science and technology studies (STS) have become skilled at studying. Scholars trained in the social sciences and humanities have become adept at asking questions about how different humans know and enact animals, plants, and landscapes.[1] This chapter, however, starts in a different place. It begins not from curiosities about human knowledge practices, but from curiosities about fish, in particular salmon, who also capture George's attention.

In their introduction to this volume, Jensen and Morita draw our attention to what they term "minor anthropologies," that is, anthropologies with "conceptual and descriptive styles that are different from those of the major traditions, without, for that matter, being radically detached from or incommensurable with them." Pointing to Marilyn Strathern and Eduardo Viveros de Castro as examples of scholars who allow their materials to disrupt Western anthropological theory-as-usual, Jensen and Morita suggest that such scholarship pushes us to imagine "forms of anthropology that [take] the practices and cosmologies of people not simply as ethnographic 'information' that could be theoretically processed using the standard anthropological repertoires, but as conceptual starting points for widening, redefining, or challenging them" (this volume). Here I suggest that just as we can explore minor anthropologies through the cosmologies of diverse peoples, it is also possible to imagine new forms of anthropology through the practices of non-humans.[2]

In the following, I aim to allow my curiosities about salmon to generate reflections on the challenges and opportunities that arise within multispecies anthropology. What happens when anthropologists pose new queries—beginning with non-humans or human-nonhuman assemblages—in a field that has a long tradition of starting with people? Undoubtedly, questions of method become central. Anthropology has often defined itself through ethnographic methods. However, the starting point of 'non-humanist' anthropology calls for research practices that rub up against conventional methodological expectations. Accordingly, this chapter centers on some 'minor methods' situated within this friction, asking how they enable us to rethink some of the methodological assumptions of anthropology, including its orientation toward the natural sciences.

Multispecies Anthropology: New Curiosities

Multispecies anthropology is, in many ways, the offspring of poorly disciplined curiosities. Anthropologists who were previously studying properly 'cultural' topics—scientific knowledge-making, political ecology, indigenous peoples' practices of nature management—have started to be more promiscuous, allowing their professional curiosities to be captured not only by human practices, but also by the so-called natural world (Kirksey and Helmreich 2010; Tsing 2014). Scientists-turned-humanists have helped to show the promise of such transdiscipinary desires. Philosopher and physicist Karen Barad (2007) has demonstrated how the double-slit experiment can be an opening to new conceptions of ontology, politics, and ethics. Biologist and STS scholar Donna Haraway (2008) has used her fascination with symbioses, such as that between Hawaiian bobtail squid and *Vibrio* bacteria, to develop concepts of relationality that challenge dominant discourses of individualism. Both of these scholars illustrate that paying attention to the stuff of the world can make a major difference in how one does theory in the social sciences and humanities. Their work gives us permission to search for transformative questions at the edges of existing scholarly formations.

Promiscuous multispecies curiosities, however, come up against the presuppositions of contemporary anthropology and cause disciplinary equivocation (Viveiros de Castro 2004). Over the last century and a half, the space for professional polymaths has shrunk. The ability for one to be equally interested in Iroquois kinship and beaver dam-building practices—as Lewis Henry Morgan was—has fallen victim to specialization. In recent years, the objects of cultural anthropologists' gazes have been greatly shaped by the increasing rigidity of disciplinary boundaries, linked in part to nature-culture divides. Specialized natural scientists got to report on the world; social scientists and humanists were assigned to interpretations of and discourses about it. Yet in this time of expanding environmental crises, some anthropologists have found such approaches insufficient for figuring out how we might co-exist with other beings. Might we need to know more about other beings' life-worlds and how humans participate in them? Multispecies anthropologists have taken a materialist and empiricist approach to this question, asking how humans and non-humans jointly participate in making worlds.

In doing so, multispecies anthropology marks a significant redefinition of the objects of anthropology. Multispecies ethnographers insist that in order to better understand social worlds, we must better attend to the non-human socialities that anthropology, with its narrow definitions of the 'human' and the 'social', has often neglected (Kirksey and Helmreich 2010; Tsing 2014). Anna Tsing (2012: 144) argues that anthropologists have been caught up in pan-disciplinary projects that "imagine human species being, that is, the practices of being a species, as autonomously self-maintaining." Tsing (2014) and others challenge such limited definitions of *anthropos* by insisting that in order to understand 'being human', anthropologists must expand their gazes to include more-than-human relations.[3] Multispecies scholars have therefore urged social scientists to pay attention to non-humans so as not to reproduce the myopias of the human-nonhuman divide that continue to structure much of academia. They ask us to be curious not only about what people like George are doing with and saying about salmon, but also about the lives of such fish.

In doing so, multispecies anthropology becomes a complex disciplinary dance—an articulation of beings such as salmon, typically considered objects of 'biology', within recognizable social science languages. At a certain level, this articulation is well under way, as evidenced by the growing amount of multi-species scholarship. But in terms of method, much remains to be explored. Indeed, while multispecies anthropology has made powerful claims concerning the importance of being curious about non-humans, it has not adequately addressed the methodological dilemmas that such curiosity occasions. Yet how *does* one study non-humans within a discipline whose methods are largely human-oriented? What methodological equivocations might we need?

Methods, Practices, and Instruments

To describe some possible practices for multispecies anthropology, I draw on my own research on Pacific salmon, including the analysis of salmon otoliths and scales. I use the specifics of salmon to argue that the curiosities that multi-species anthropology seeks to cultivate require methods of observation that stretch the boundaries of what we typically think of as 'ethnography'. Salmon socialities (both in relation to and beyond humans) necessitate that anthropologists learn to 'read' salmon bodies. To this end, I propose that we befriend some of the practices and instruments that people like George use to craft knowledge of other species' worlds.

Consider the Pacific salmon species that are the subject of George's research. As they migrate from rivers to the ocean and back, these peripatetic fish know and do landscapes in multiple ways. They follow currents, tracing out complex migration routes and returning to the rivers of their birth. During spawning, they dig nests with their tails that alter river morphology. And when they die, the fishes' rotting bodies release marine-derived phosphorous and nitrogen into freshwater streams, remaking patterns of nutrient cycling across wide swaths of watersheds.

The ways that salmon enact landscapes and waterscapes both entangle with and profoundly transform human lives and histories. Consider how people in indigenous communities have patterned their life-ways according to salmon routes and rhythms. Consider, too, how salmon shape industrial societies. Salmon migration patterns affect both the design of hydro-electric facilities and the amount of power they generate. Furthermore, the fishes' demands for cool, clear streams have led to logging policies that preserve streamside tree cover, ranching regulations that prevent cattle from trampling streambeds, and farming rules that reduce agricultural runoff. Indeed, most land use practices in a salmon watershed find themselves in dialogue with the fish.

But how do anthropologists actually study salmon? Amid the enthusiasm, multispecies ethnography has proved to be challenging, in part because it exposes the vulnerabilities of ethnography itself. It is relatively easy to say that we need to take non-humans more seriously, but it is quite difficult to know what knowledge practices we might use to ask about non-human practices. The classical social science tools that position us well to study the practices through which scientists, fishery workers, and indigenous people know and enact fish tend to come up short for studying non-humans. So, too, do most methods advocated by actor-network theorists and STS scholars. For example, talking with the 'spokespeople' for non-humans—a method advocated by Bruno Latour (2004)—is important, but not always sufficient. What do we do if our curiosities about non-humans are different from those of their biologist or zoologist spokespeople? Similarly, STS approaches that examine how things are 'enacted' or 'done in practices', such as those of Annemarie Mol and John Law, work well for analyzing the liveliness of diseases and technological devices, yet they are insufficient for studying living creatures who are not merely brought into being through human practices, but also participate in world making themselves.[4] At the same time that we ask how George enacts salmon, can we also learn about how salmon enact?

Such a question is fraught with uncertainties and risks—ontological, political, and disciplinary. These are vulnerabilities, however, that I think we must embrace. If we are going to ask how salmon know landscapes, we might have to articulate new modes of knowing with existing social science methods. This move does not, of course, necessitate an abandonment of our own tools of cultural and political analysis; rather, it means embracing responsibility for continuing to build a discipline reflexive about its own methods, histories, and practices, including its legacies of human exceptionalism.

Ethnographic Experiments

Seeking to expand the range of ethnographic practices, multispecies anthropologists have drawn on a number of fields. One of the most common resources has been animal behavior research. Some anthropologists have turned to ethology and animal training (Allen and Bekoff 1997; Hearne 1987; Smuts 2001) to learn how to attune themselves to and interpret non-human actions (Despret 2004; Haraway 2008). When turning to such fields for insight, anthropologists have tended to gravitate toward scholars whose research is loosely epistemologically compatible with their own. For example, some multispecies scholars have entered into fruitful methodological and theoretical collaborations with primatologists, where complex notions of 'culture', 'tradition', and 'personhood' are already on the table.[5]

Yet while multispecies anthropologists' engagements with animal behavior have been incredibly productive, they have also produced some significant lacunae. Animal behavior researchers have overwhelming studied mammals, and multispecies scholars have reproduced this focus. The vast majority of research has featured non-human primates, pets, and farm animals—a rather narrow swath of multispecies life.[6] This topical focus has been largely driven by methods. Existing animal behavior methodologies—which focus on observations of body language and social relations largely visible to the human eye—simply work better for mammals (and birds) than for other forms of life. When brought into dialogue with multispecies anthropology, the approaches of animal behavior set one up well to study relations with dogs but not with, say, bacteria.

Anthropologists working on insects, plants, and fungi have often gleaned insights from natural history and descriptive biology (Raffles 2010). Inspired by the careful noticing and note taking of naturalists and field scientists (Canfield 2011; Herman 1980), as well as its resonances with the descriptions of many classical anthropological texts (e.g., Evans-Pritchard 1940; Malinowski 1935; Rappaport 1968), they are building forms of empirical observation that encompass more-than-human social worlds. One example of this type of work is that of Tsing (2014), who in her work on the forests where matsutake mushrooms grow, has called for anthropologists to engage in practices of transdisciplinary noticing that she calls 'critical description'. Tsing stresses the importance of attention to things as diverse as capitalist practices, forest succession, and forms of fungal growth for understanding the ongoing social histories of landscapes.

However, such natural-history-based approaches also have limitations. While the melding of ethnography and natural history methods has brought human and non-human histories into the same frame, it has retained the focus of both approaches on direct observation by an embodied observer, typically with something close to the naked eye. In many cases, this is an asset in that it brings the situated, embodied nature of knowledge production to the fore (Haraway 1988). But expanding ethnography through natural history observations does not help us methodologically with things we cannot directly and personally see. This is a huge problem for studying a whole range of phenomena, including microbes, ocean currents, long-term evolutionary processes, and, in my case, salmon. Furthermore, by focusing so strongly on fieldwork-based observations, such approaches also skirt some of the epistemological questions of doing 'science' as an anthropologist. Natural history still looks a lot like the 'deep hanging out' that is familiar and comfortable to anthropologists. What happens, however, if we cannot learn something in the field and so turn to chemical analysis in a lab, not as 'participant observation', but as an anthropological practice? Such moves sit more uneasily with some of our disciplinary commitments.[7]

Geographers, whose field has also been shifted by the 'animal turn', have begun to probe the possibilities of mixed methods. Hodgetts and Lorimer (2014) have suggested that animal geographers might make more use of three methods to explore species histories: (1) tracking and data collection devices affixed to difficult-to-follow animals; (2) technologies for investigating animal communicative practices that fall outside the range of human visual and aural practices;[8] and (3) methods of genomic analysis, including phytogeography. Inspired by such work, I explore the possibilities for anthropologists to pursue similar methodological experiments—to stretch ourselves to befriend some of the practices and instruments that people like George use to craft knowledge of other species' worlds.

When Direct Observation Fails: Studying Salmon Lives

Let me turn now to my research on salmon in Japan and the western United States. My focus is on how salmon shape multispecies ways of life in these places—how they participate in the iterative making and remaking of landscapes and waterscapes together with other beings and forces. Such work requires me to know something about how fishing practices, indigenous lifeways, and dam construction practices both respond to and shape salmon lives. But it also requires that I know something about salmon lives as such. Many of the salmon in these regions begin their lives in hatcheries. There, salmon are born in plastic trays, reared in stainless steel tanks, fed a pelleted diet, and regularly weighed and measured. When they are in such facilities, salmon are so visible that traditional modes of direct ethnographic observation work quite well. By carefully noticing and describing the ways that salmon respond to their hatchery environs, one can learn much about their behavior and their relations with their worlds—in this case, largely human-crafted ones. But when juvenile salmon are only a few months old, they are released into the 'wild', migrating to the ocean where they live for several years before returning to the region of their birth.

When salmon swim away from the hatchery, the possibilities for directly observing their social worlds slip away. Ethnography, rooted in direct, embodied observation and participation in salmon lives, seems impossible. In such moments, anthropologists begin to lose their epistemological grip. In these situations, we need new tools to extend our powers of observation.

This kind of challenge is not without parallel in human-centric ethnography. When studying people, we often want to learn about practices and events that we cannot directly observe. This is one reason why we conduct interviews, record life histories, and undertake archival research. There are stories that we know are essential to our work, even if we cannot directly experience them. Indeed, we often use technologies and infrastructures, such as those of libraries and museums, to trace such activities. Without hesitation, we jump into the archives or talk to the elders about the past. In my work in Japan, for example, I often found myself using microfiche readers to wade through old newspaper clippings for information about past fisheries management practices.

Now, I want to engage in a sleight of hand—one that opens up the questions at the core of this chapter. Using the same microfiche device on which I relied in Japan, I want to swap a salmon scale for the old newspaper clipping. This is not merely a hypothetical switch. Microfiche readers are a technology sometimes used for viewing fish scales. With a bit of instruction—far less than that required for me to learn to interpret Japanese-language documents—I can see much about the history of a salmon beyond the periods when I can directly observe it. Salmon scales are like tree rings: as the fish grows, its scales develop additional concentric marks (fig. 2). These marks tell us something about the life histories—the relationalities and temporalities—of fish. The width of these bands tells us about the patterns of fish growth—when the fish were finding abundant food and when they were struggling to find adequate nutrition. Because growth slows in winter, seasonal changes in banding patterns also tell us the age of the fish. Other lines on a scale indicate when the fish transitioned from freshwater to saltwater. From such bands, we can get a sense of how long

FIGURE 5.2 Viewed under magnification, banding patterns in fish scales resemble the growth rings of trees

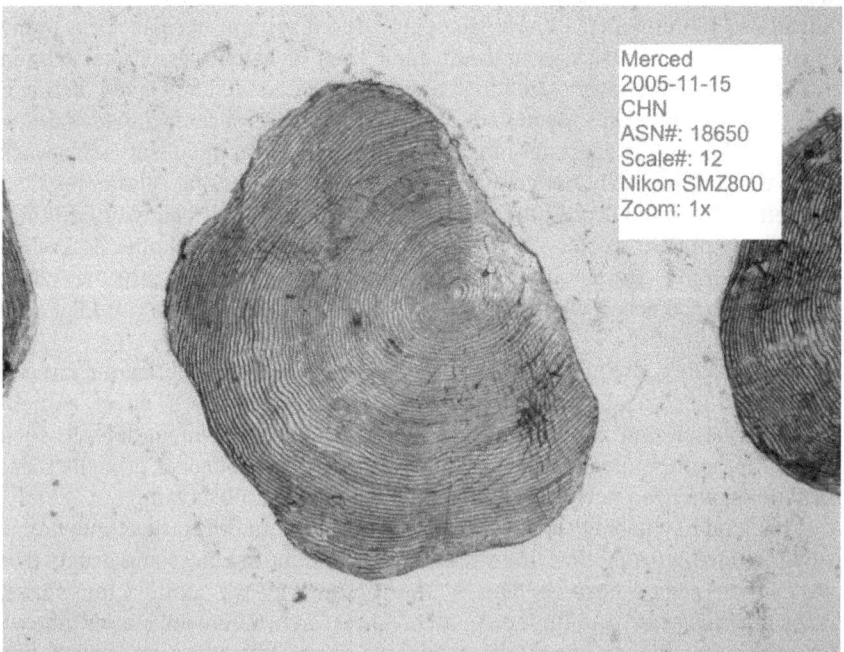

Merced
2005-11-15
CHN
ASN#: 18650
Scale#: 12
Nikon SMZ800
Zoom: 1x

A trained eye can read information about the age of a fish, its growth rates, and its migration patterns from these bands. Photograph © California Department of Fish and Game

a salmon spent in different habitats and how it grew during those periods. Through 'reading' the salmon's 'archive', we are able to learn about salmon modes of knowing and doing landscapes that cannot be easily retrieved through other observational practices.

Tim Ingold (2011: 160) has written that "any thing—caught at a particular place and moment—enfolds within its constitution the history of relations that have brought it there." The phenomenological idea that organisms enfold their history of relations in their bodily constitution is quite literally the case for fish. Although they do not enfold *all* histories of a salmon's encounters, scales carry important piscine history. If life histories, long a key anthropological object of study, are embodied in salmon flesh, we need to learn how to *see* that flesh— how to attend to its markings, articulations, and layered complexities—so as to detect social relations that ethnography cannot. To ask us to do so is not a far-fetched proposal. If anthropologists can use the methods of historiography and the technologies of archival research, should not they be able to use the methods of ecological forensics to know salmon bodies and their archives?

Nearly every anthropologist I know ends up doing archival research despite the fact that very few of us have extensive formal training in historical methods. We depend on our ability to learn the methods of another discipline, in this case history, and to integrate them with our own. Epistemologically, we also cope with the issues that archives present, such as the fact that historical materials are never neutral and that their presences and absences are shot through with relations of power. Sometimes we foreground these issues. At other times, however, we are willing to accept certain pieces of information as 'good enough' to use without extensive explanation about the multiple layers of knowledge production through which they were made. We practice a mix of skepticism, curiosity, responsibility, and openness, destabilizing some points while accepting others in order to tell a given story. I argue that we should approach our engagements with salmon bodily histories in the same way.

Of Otoliths and Collaborations

I turn now to another salmon observation technique: looking closely at the same tiny calcifications that we previously saw in George's hand. Otoliths are small stones in the inner ear of a fish. Composed of calcium carbonate and trace minerals deposited into a protein matrix, otoliths are a different density than the rest of a fish's body. Thus, as the fish moves and experiences vibrations, its otoliths bump up against hair cells inside its cochlea. This process allows fish to sense accelerations and decelerations and to tell up from down (Popper et al. 2005). But otoliths are not only sense organs; they are also, like fish scales, a temporally sequenced record of some parts of a fish's life. However, they enfold different time-space relationalities. While scale bands form irregularly on a semi-weekly basis and primarily document seasonal changes, otolith bands are tightly linked to daily rhythms. Otoliths typically accrete throughout the life of a fish at the rate of one band per day.

Otolith bands—produced through a fish's interactions with food sources, temperature, salinity, photoperiod, other fish, and even the minerals of nearby rock formations—can tell us much about salmon sociality. Wide otolith bands indicate an abundance of food, moderate temperatures, and a lack of competition from more aggressive fish. Narrow bands indicate days when life was more difficult. A dark line on the otolith, called a 'stress check', represents a difficult life transition—a significant metabolic and hormonal stress response that literally makes a mark on the fish. For example, juvenile fish reared in a hatchery and then released into the wild typically lay down a distinctive stress check on the day they are 'freed'. Otolith chemistry can tell us even more. The round holes in the otolith seen in figure 3 are the traces of samples taken for microchemical analysis. Isotopic traces in otoliths can tell us about the mineral composition of the water in which a salmon was swimming at a given point in time, allowing us to piece together a salmon's life history trajectory. The presence of certain elements can also tell us when a fish was eating marine-derived protein and when it was eating freshwater macroinvertebrates. For example, the chemical composition of the bands in an otolith from George's lab shows how one fish initially dined on pelleted hatchery feed made from ground-up marine fish, then stayed in the river and ate freshwater organisms for a few days after its hatchery release before quickly migrating to the ocean, where it resumed a marine-based diet.

These examples highlight only a fraction of the stories in otolith archives. By coupling otolith band patterns with chemical analysis, we can construct partial portraits of a given fish's multiplicity of relations as it navigates the rhythms and fluxes of its aquatic environments. Such techniques are invaluable ways to learn how a fish moves and interacts with others—engaging in aquatic world making—during moments when we cannot directly observe it.

FIGURE 5.3 An otolith cross-section that has been placed under 100x magnification

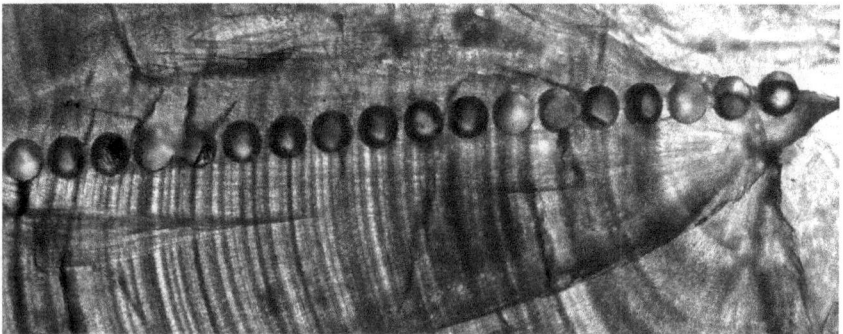

The holes indicate where samples for isotope analysis have been extracted with a mass spectrometer. Each hole is 40 microns wide (1/25th of a millimeter).
Photograph © Rachel Johnson, NOAA Fisheries

Forms of Knowledge-Making in Multispecies Encounters

What new picture of salmon emerges here, and how does it matter for anthropology and STS? Without otolith analysis, anthropologists tend to see salmon primarily in dyadic encounters with humans. We focus on the brief moments when humans directly interact with fish, most often within hatchery cultivation efforts, when they pass through dams, or when they become entangled with a net, trap, or lure. While these are certainly important ways of knowing and doing salmon, they reduce fish worlds to moments of intimate encounter with people. Practices like otolith analysis help us to get the size of humans right. When we look at the stories that emerge from otoliths, we can observe some of the ways that people matter—in a physical sense—to salmon. We can notice how hatchery releases and travels through dams stress fish and create metabolic changes that leave traces in their bones. But we can also see that salmon worlds far exceed these encounters. Otoliths have the potential to show us how salmon bodies are also made up of their engagements with the minerals that leach out of bedrock, the prey they struggle to catch, the predators they work to avoid, the migratory paths they travel, the flux of the seasons, and much more. When brought into dialogue with existing anthropological forms, the stories in salmon ear bones open up possibilities for telling richer histories, situating human-nonhuman encounters within larger webs of multispecies relations.

When George (or an anthropologist) does otolith analysis, we are certainly enacting particular kinds of salmon through our knowledge practices. However, we are also learning something about *salmon* enactments—practices that include, but also far exceed, relations with humans. Otolith analysis is one tool for glimpsing salmon worlds that, while entangled with human ones, are also different. Here I take it as a stand-in for a whole range of science practices that might be able to help us better engage other species in anthropological work. In a moment of climate change, pollution, and mass extinction, it is both practically and politically urgent that we understand how being human happens in worlds of diverse multispecies encounters—and we must have a better sense of what those worlds need in order to survive.

Because otoliths contain information about fish growth rates, they can teach us something about which webs of relations allow fish to thrive—and which do not. When fish are unable to grow, their lives and communities are imperiled. Similarly, the mineral content of otoliths can tell us where fish are traveling and how stressed they are when doing so. By helping to reconstruct fish movements, otoliths can also tell us about the places where salmon can live well, as well as those where they cannot.[9] In these ways, otoliths can provide hints about which kinds of disturbances are bearable for salmon and which push them to their limits, threatening the survival of their aquatic worlds. Looking beyond human-salmon dyads is essential for simultaneously recognizing the profound ways that certain human actions disrupt salmon worlds and remembering that even in the so-called Anthropocene humans are not the only actors who matter.

Sometimes one need not actually perform otolith analysis or a similar observational practice in order to use natural science methods to enrich social science work on non-humans. One can often do so merely by reading scientific papers across the grain, torquing them into a different kind of epistemological practice. But other times, as is the case with otoliths, there is a compelling need to directly inhabit scientific methods as an anthropologist. This is because our questions about non-human socialities are often different enough from those of natural scientists that they have not yet studied what we want to know. In such cases, we can answer our questions only by picking up natural science tools and using them in new ways. For me, otolith analysis is a bit of both. I have learned a lot about salmon life histories from reading published articles, but I also run up against the limits of previous research. For example, I want to know what the otolith rings of spawning salmon might tell us about their relations to their worlds; however, I have found very little data on the outer bands of otoliths—those laid down during the last weeks of a salmon's life—because most of the questions that currently intrigue salmon scientists focus on juvenile fish development. In addition, I am interested in vivid portraits of the lives of individual fish from birth to death, but I have found virtually no research that has examined salmon in that way, even though it is technically possible to do so. For scientists, who have been most interested in statistically analyzing the survival rate of salmon that have different juvenile life patterns, constructing detailed lifespan-long depictions of individual fish has held little allure. The different questions that anthropological training encourages one to ask—and the different knowledges those questions can generate—indicate that there is a real reason for social scientists to engage in practices like otolith analysis.

Concerns about Science

Social scientists tend to be wary of such natural science methods and collaborations despite their utility for learning about non-humans. Are they 'proper' anthropology? Even with caveats, practices like otolith analysis quickly become suspect in anthropology. I realize, therefore, that what I am proposing here is risky business.

I want to be clear that I do not think that science and its tools are the only way to learn about salmon and their worlds. For example, I have learned much about salmon from people who fish, and I do not consider such knowledge secondary. Nets and fishing lines are, like otolith analysis, powerful tools for learning about salmon when they are under water and out of sight. If I emphasize scientific methods here, it is because they are a form of knowledge-making from which anthropologists have systematically shied away—to the detriment of multispecies scholarship. We would not hesitate to pick up a fishing line and try to learn something about salmon while sitting next to a wizened fisherman, yet we are reluctant to engage scientists and scientific methods in a similar kind of collaboration. While the number of anthropologists engaging with scientific methods is growing (see Caple 2017; Hartigan 2017; Mathews 2018), such experimentation remains relatively marginal within the discipline as a whole.

This marginalization has happened for historically important reasons: anthropologists have sought to provincialize the narratives of Western modernity and Enlightenment humanism with which science has been deeply intertwined. While I would not claim that the approaches I advocate in this chapter pose zero risk to the important epistemological work of unsettling the ability of science to tell the master story of the world, I argue that, amid profound environmental crises, the risks of policing the practices that we are allowed to use to know multispecies worlds are far greater. Indeed, science methods are so useful for querying non-humans that it seems irresponsible to refuse to engage with them. Using scientific papers to provide 'background' information—a common practice in anthropology—is not enough; multispecies anthropology requires more intimate negotiations with science.

The tensions among multispecies anthropology, science, and method are almost omnipresent, even if rarely made explicit. Many are linked to the anthropological tendency to contrast animism/non-modern/indigeneity with science/modernity/the West. While animism is seen as enlivening the world—revealing ontological multiplicity and opening up political possibilities—science is often assumed to deaden the world by creating a singular positivist view that shores up already dominant 'modern' ontologies. The sentiments that this binary fosters make it hard to cultivate scientists and scientific practices as allies for querying non-humans. Such reifying tendencies seem more likely to rekindle the 'science wars'[10] than to help us build novel forms of collaboration in their wake—collaborations that contain the potential for doing science otherwise. If we are going to learn about the ontological practices of salmon, indigenous methods of querying salmon should not be discounted. Yet neither should those of the natural sciences. Science does not necessarily have to stand in counterpoint to animism as a practice that produces a 'dead' world with impoverished politics.[11] Science can itself be 'non-modern'—and can be a part of making other worlds. Animistic science is not an impossible neologism.

In rejecting the animism-science binary, I am not proposing that there is an ontologically singular world or that science is the 'master category' against which all other knowledge practices are judged. Instead, I am arguing for a willingness to play the role of the trickster—to move back and forth between worlds, to be oneself multiple, to blur boundaries (Haraway 1988). In order to take up the methods that a serious study of non-humans requires, multispecies anthropology needs to bring back the 'both-and' rather than intensify the 'either-or'.

All methods are contaminated; imperfect tools are the only ones we have. If we police knowledge practices too vigorously, declaring some too contaminated to use, we end up putting on blinders and limiting the ways we can know. Collaborating with natural scientists does not necessarily mean abandoning one's critical stance toward certain kinds of knowledge practices. Referencing Barbara Smith, Jensen and Morita highlight in the introduction to this volume that "scholars are able to produce 'sophisticated conjunctions' of knowledge if they remain scrupulously attuned to, and reflexive about, their different conceptual orientations and assumptions."

Engaging Epistemological and Political Challenges

Feminist science studies provides some clues for how we might engage epistemological and political challenges. Through its attention to the ways that race, class, and gender shape the production of knowledge, feminist science studies firmly critiques many scientific epistemologies and practices, including fundamental ideas of scientific objectivity (Harding 1986; Keller 1982; Longino 1990). Yet feminist science studies scholars are firmly not anti-science; rather, they engage deeply with science and are often scientists themselves. Instead of rejecting science, they simply do it otherwise. Committed to the possibilities of knowing more about the material world at the end of day than at the beginning, they have torqued existing practices in fields such as primatology (Strum and Fedigan 2000), physical anthropology (Tanner and Zihlman 1976), physics (Barad 2007), and biology (Fausto-Sterling 1992). Rather than abandoning commitments to empiricism and objectivity, they have emphasized the political necessity of making reality claims. Finding both classical objectivism and social constructivism untenable, they have stressed that while facts are 'made', they are not 'made up'. Crafting new forms of scientific vision, they have asserted that scientific knowledges are 'situated' and emerge from 'partial perspectives' (Haraway 1988; Harding 1986). While reminding us of the non-innocence of all knowledge practices, feminist scientists and science studies scholars have simultaneously demonstrated that the use of scientific tools and techniques does not automatically lead one into uncritical membership in the culture of no culture.

I suggest that we transfer this kind of orientation toward science to the work at hand. One *can* study salmon social worlds with otolith analysis while keeping critiques of scientific knowledge claims in the frame; indeed, I think it is imperative that we do so. What is particularly exciting about using otolith analysis and similar practices as an anthropologist is not that I am becoming a natural scientist, per se, but rather that, by engaging salmon bodily archives, my practices of seeing social history in material form develop new range and power.

After *Writing Culture* (Clifford and Marcus 1986), anthropologists are certainly alert to questions about the possibilities and limits of what one can know. While some of that alertness has exacerbated anthropologists' fears of objectivity and scientism and has occasionally led to overly reflexive, even solipsistic prose, anthropologists have generally been able to cope with questions of how we know and depict others' lives. Still, the less embodied and less actively collaborative knowledge-making appears to be, the more discomfort we tend to experience. We prefer the image of the anthropologist-cum-naturalist in the field to the anthropologist-cum-high-tech-researcher in the lab. Yet we should not allow such preferences to stop us from engaging in methodological experiments central to multispecies work. After all, while using lenses and technologies—or refusing to do so—certainly shapes one's practices of observation, it does not do so in predictable ways.

Techniques such as otolith analysis do not necessarily lead one toward the sin that Donna Haraway (1988) has called the 'god trick', that is, the adoption of a 'view from nowhere'. Accessing otoliths—getting them to the point where their bands can be seen—takes a lot of work. Otoliths cannot be retrieved from live salmon, so one must begin either by killing fish or by collecting the rotting bodies of the recently deceased. One must then cut open their heads and fish around for the small otolith stones with fingers and tweezers. Retrieved otoliths are then sent to a lab, where they are mounted on slides and polished into thin sections. Otolith analysis, then, is not a disembodied practice that produces 'pure' truth about salmon life histories. Indeed, I compare otolith and scale analysis to archival research in part to emphasize both the embodied work of making inferences from them and the gaps in otolith records themselves. As is the case with traditional archival research, both otoliths and their analysis are partial. Just as colonial archives are skewed toward the bureaucratic, salmon otoliths disproportionately record the metabolic, which although important, does not capture the entire relationality of a fish. Furthermore, research funding, available technologies, disciplinary conventions, and embodied skill shape the inference practices of the humans who read otolith archives. Otolith analysis thus produces patchy and partial reconstructions of fish life histories and salmon social rhythms. The salmon otolith both speaks and is made to speak—and yet much goes unsaid.

If—as part of a commitment to a robust multispecies anthropology—we want to learn about how salmon know landscapes, we cannot take any tools off the table. Practices like otolith observation can certainly be enacted in ways that bolster Western and scientific knowledge practices' false claims to universalism. But they can also be done differently. Diving into otolith analysis, I do not find facts about a singular salmon world. Instead, when I look at the incredible variation in otolith patterns, I notice vast salmon multiplicity. However, it is not the same multiplicity that I saw before, when I relied on interviews and standard modes of participant observation to look at human enactments of salmon. Instead of a multiplicity rooted in human ways of doing salmon, I see a multiplicity rooted in complex multispecies relations, in which human practices play a role, but not necessarily an always dominant one. Seen through their otoliths, salmon are not only *done* in practices but also *do* practices. They have their own multiple ways of knowing and enacting aquatic landscapes, including rivers, riparian areas, estuaries, and oceans. These practices are often intertwined with humans, but are not encapsulated by them.

If we are going to better inhabit human-damaged worlds, we need to begin by noticing and describing the multispecies relations that are happening within them. This kind of storytelling requires that anthropologists know more about other species. Our discipline has spent decades honing its approaches to studying human social relations. Now, our ongoing political-ethical-environmental situation demands that we tell those stories not in isolation, but in relation to non-human socialities. To do the work of crafting multispecies stories, we need George and other scientists, not as objects of study, but as collaborators in learning about non-human worlds.

Reworking anthropology's orientation to the world in this way requires reworking its methodological practices. It demands that we confront the ways in which our current methodological toolbox forces us into human-centric research practices and constrains our abilities to learn about non-human lives and histories. As social scientists, our practices and commitments are tied up with disciplinary histories that make it challenging, but certainly not impossible, to address the questions and challenges that landscape-oriented research entails. What we need is not a rejection of our existing social science methods, which are critical to understanding human practices, but an amplification of the range of our attention so that we can better understand the non-humans who are also on the scene. In light of such needs, observational practices like fish scale and otolith analysis, which draw us into the skills of seeing social histories in bodily form, are important to consider. This chapter, then, marks a call for a further expansion of our methods—a 'becoming-with' new practices including those typically thought of as the tools and techniques of the natural sciences.

Acknowledgments

Drafts of this chapter were presented at the 2012 annual meeting of the American Anthropological Association, at the 2013 annual conference of the University of Manchester/Open University's Centre for Research on Socio-Cultural Change (CRESC), and at the 2014 "Collaborative Moments" workshop of the NOW Project: Living Resources and Human Societies around the North Water in the Thule Area, NW Greenland. It has benefited from comments by Zac Caple, Pierre Du Plessis, Elaine Gan, Casper Bruun Jensen, Marianne Lien, Carol Stack, and Anna Tsing. I also want to thank Rachel Johnson and George Whitman for their material and intellectual contributions. This work was supported by the STEPS Institute for Innovation in Environmental Research at the University of California, Santa Cruz, and by the University of California Pacific Rim Research Program's Advanced Graduate Fellowship. The chapter was revised during a writing retreat funded by the Aarhus University Contemporary Ethnography program.

Heather Anne Swanson is an Associate Professor of Anthropology at Aarhus University. Her interests include environmental anthropology, cultural geography, environmental history, animal studies, and science and technology studies. She is a co-editor of *Domestication Gone Wild: Politics and Practices of Multispecies Relations* (2018, with Marianne Lien and Gro Ween) and *Arts of Living on a Damaged Planet: Ghosts and Monsters of the Anthropocene* (2017, with Anna Tsing, Elaine Gan, and Nils Bubandt. Much of Swanson's research has examined how relations of political economy and histories of nation making shape the bodies of fish.

Notes

1. This literature is diverse, ranging from work on indigenous knowledges (Cruik-shank 2005) to political ecology (Goldman et al. 2010) to animal studies (Grasseni 2004). In relation to salmon, Lien and Law, have shown how social science methods, such as participant observation, allow us to understand how different salmon are enacted in relation to different human practices. See Law and Lien (2013) and Lien and Law (2011).
2. Although this piece focuses on a particular strand of multispecies scholarship, it resonates with other anthropological conversations, particularly those of scholars focused on 'thinking through things' (Henare et al. 2007) and new materialisms (Bennett 2010). This chapter has interesting synergies with that of Holbraad (2011), who has called for modes of inquiry that go beyond "the ethnography of (people's engagement with) things" (ibid.: 16) and instead explore how things 'speak' through their "material characteristics" (ibid.: 10; see also Holbraad 2013).
3. In resonance with actor-network theory (Callon 1986; Latour 2005), multispecies anthropologists have stressed that 'agency' is not a property exclusive to humanity.
4. Multispecies approaches that use STS arguments about multiplicity as a point of departure (see, e.g., Mol 2002) often inadvertently miss the lively practices of non-humans themselves.
5. Primatology has had exceptionally strong non-Western (i.e., Kyoto school), feminist, and interdisciplinary (i.e., ethno-primatology) strands, and thus many of its scholars are already participating in political and epistemological debates. This has made it a relatively easy site for interdisciplinary multispecies experiments (Fuentes 2012).
6. Consider how terms such as 'the animal turn' and 'human-animal relations' are often seen as loose synonyms for multispecies scholarship.
7. Multispecies scholars have also engaged in collaborations with bio-artists as part of their methodological experiments (Hodgetts and Lorimer 2014: 5; Johnston and Kirksey 2014). I suspect that the popularity of bio-art in multispecies scholarship is linked to the awkward relations between anthropology and the natural sciences. The mediation of art seems to help open up spaces between the two disciplines.
8. An example that Hodgetts and Lorimer (2014) offer is olfactory communication among members of the weasel family.
9. The literature on salmon is vast and stretches back to the 1980s. For examples of what it can show about salmon life histories, see Barnett-Johnson et al. (2008), Kennedy et al. (2002), Lind-Null et al. (2008), and Weber et al. (2002).
10. 'Science wars' is a term used to refer to conflicts in the 1990s, mostly in the United States, between social scientists and humanists, who stressed the 'constructed' nature of all knowledge, and scientists, who—incensed by such claims—asserted their ability to produce objective knowledge about the world.
11. Candea (2010) takes a similar approach when he refuses to condemn scientific 'detachment'.

References

Allen, Collin, and Marc Bekoff. 1997. *Species of Mind: The Philosophy and Biology of Cognitive Ethology.* Cambridge, MA: MIT Press.
Barad, Karen. 2007. *Meeting the Universe Halfway: Quantum Physics and the Entanglement of Matter and Meaning.* Durham, NC: Duke University Press.

Barnett-Johnson, Rachel, Thomas E. Pearson, Frank C. Ramos, Churchill B. Grimes, and R. Bruce MacFarlane. 2008. "Tracking Natal Origins of Salmon Using Isotopes, Otoliths, and Landscape Geology." *Limnology and Oceanography* 53 (4): 1633–1642.

Bennett, Jane. 2010. *Vibrant Matter: A Political Ecology of Things*. Durham, NC: Duke University Press.

Callon, Michel. 1986. "Some Elements of a Sociology of Translation: Domestication of the Scallops and the Fishermen of St. Brieuc Bay." In *Power, Action and Belief: A New Sociology of Knowledge?* ed. John Law, 196–223. London: Routledge.

Candea, Matei. 2010. "'I Fell in Love with Carlos the Meerkat': Engagement and Detachment in Human-Animal Relations." *American Ethnologist* 37 (2): 241–258.

Canfield, Michael R., ed. 2011. *Field Notes on Science and Nature*. Cambridge, MA: Harvard University Press.

Caple, Zachary. 2017. "Holocene in Fragments: A Critical Landscape Ecology of Phosphorus in Florida." PhD diss., University of California, Santa Cruz.

Clifford, James, and George E. Marcus, eds. 1986. *Writing Culture: The Poetics and Politics of Ethnography*. Berkeley: University of California Press.

Cruikshank, Julie. 2005. *Do Glaciers Listen? Local Knowledge, Colonial Encounters, and Social Imagination*. Seattle: University of Washington Press.

Despret, Vinciane. 2004. "The Body We Care For: Figures of Anthropo-zoo-genesis." *Body & Society* 10 (2–3): 111–134.

Evans-Pritchard, E. E. 1940. *The Nuer: A Description of the Modes of Livelihood and Political Institutions of a Nilotic People*. Oxford: Clarendon Press.

Fausto-Sterling, Anne. 1992. *Myths of Gender: Biological Theories about Women and Men*. 2nd ed. New York: BasicBooks.

Fuentes, Agustin. 2012. "Ethnoprimatology and the Anthropology of the Human-Primate Interface." *Annual Review of Anthropology* 41: 101–117.

Goldman, Mara J., Paul Nadasdy, and Matthew D. Turner, eds. 2010. *Knowing Nature: Conversations at the Intersection of Political Ecology and Science Studies*. Chicago: University of Chicago Press.

Grasseni, Cristina. 2004. "Skilled Vision: An Apprenticeship in Breeding Aesthetics." *Social Anthropology* 12 (1): 41–55.

Haraway, Donna. 1988. "Situated Knowledges: The Science Question in Feminism and the Privilege of Partial Perspective." *Feminist Studies* 14 (3): 575–599.

Haraway, Donna. 2008. *When Species Meet*. Minneapolis: University of Minnesota Press.

Harding, Sandra. 1986. *The Science Question in Feminism*. Ithaca, NY: Cornell University Press.

Hartigan, John, Jr. 2017. *Care of the Species: Races of Corn and the Science of Plant Biodiversity*. Minneapolis: University of Minnesota Press.

Hearne, Vicki. 1987. *Adam's Task: Calling Animals by Name*. New York: Alfred A. Knopf.

Henare, Amiria, Martin Holbraad, and Sari Wastell, eds. 2007. *Thinking Through Things: Theorising Artefacts Ethnographically*. London: Routledge.

Herman, Steven. 1980. *The Naturalist's Field Journal: A Manual of Instruction Based on a System Established by Joseph Grinnell*. Vermillion, SD: Buteo Books.

Hodgetts, Timothy, and Jamie Lorimer. 2014. "Methodologies for Animals' Geographies: Cultures, Communication and Genomics." *Cultural Geographies* 22 (2): 285–295.

Holbraad, Martin. 2011. "Can the Thing Speak?" Open Anthropology Cooperative Press, Working Papers Series No. 7. http://openanthcoop.net/press/http:/openanthcoop.net/press/wp-content/uploads/2011/01/Holbraad-Can-the-Thing-Speak2.pdf (accessed 6 March 2017)

Holbraad, Martin. 2013. "Things as Concepts: Anthropology and Pragmatology." In *Savage Objects*, ed. Godofredo Pereira, 17–30. Lisbon: Imprensa Nacional Casa da Moeda.

Ingold, Tim. 2011. *Being Alive: Essays on Movement, Knowledge and Description*. London: Routledge.

Johnston, Marnia, and S. Eben Kirksey. 2014. "Multispecies Salon." http://www. multispecies-salon.org (accessed 6 March 2017).

Keller, Evelyn F. 1982. "Feminism and Science." *Signs* 7 (3): 589–595.

Kennedy, Brian P., Andrea Klaue, Joel D., Blum, Carol L. Folt, and Keith H. Nislow. 2002. "Reconstructing the Lives of Fish Using Sr Isotopes in Otoliths." *Canadian Journal of Fisheries and Aquatic Sciences* 59: 925–929.

Kirksey, S. Eben, and Stefan Helmreich. 2010. "The Emergence of Multispecies Ethnography." *Cultural Anthropology* 25 (4): 545–576.

Latour, Bruno. 2004. *Politics of Nature: How to Bring the Sciences into Democracy*. Trans. Catherine Porter. Cambridge, MA: Harvard University Press.

Latour, Bruno. 2005. *Reassembling the Social: An Introduction to Actor-Network-Theory*. New York: Oxford University Press.

Law, John, and Marianne E. Lien. 2013. "Slippery: Field Notes in Empirical Ontology." *Social Studies of Science* 43 (3): 363–378.

Lien, Marianne E., and John Law. 2011. "'Emergent Aliens': On Salmon, Nature, and Their Enactment." *Ethnos* 76 (1): 65–87.

Lind-Null, Angie, Kim Larsen, and Reg Reisenbichler. 2008. *Characterization of Estuary Use by Nisqually Hatchery Chinook Based on Otolith Analysis*. US Geological Survey Open-File Report 2008–1102. https://pubs.usgs.gov/of/2008/1102/.

Longino, Helen E. 1990. *Science as Social Knowledge: Values and Objectivity in Scientific Inquiry*. Princeton, NJ: Princeton University Press.

Malinowski, Bronislaw. 1935. *Coral Gardens and Their Magic*. London: Routledge.

Mathews, Andrew S. 2018. "Landscapes and Throughscapes in Italian Forest Worlds: Thinking Dramatically about the Anthropocene." *Cultural Anthropology* 33 (3): 386–414.

Mol, Annemarie. 2002. *The Body Multiple: Ontology in Medical Practice*. Durham, NC: Duke University Press.

Popper, Arthur N., John Ramcharitar, and Steven E. Campana. 2005. "Why Otoliths? Insights from Inner Ear Physiology and Fisheries Biology." *Marine and Freshwater Research* 56: 497–504.

Raffles, Hugh. 2010. *Insectopedia*. New York: Vintage Books.

Rappaport, Roy A. 1968. *Pigs for the Ancestors: Ritual in the Ecology of a New Guinea People*. New Haven, CT: Yale University Press.

Smuts, Barbara. 2001. "Encounters with Animal Minds." *Journal of Consciousness Studies* 8 (5–7): 293–309.

Strum, Shirley C., and Linda M. Fedigan, eds. 2000. *Primate Encounters: Models of Science, Gender, and Society*. Chicago: University of Chicago Press.

Tanner, Nancy, and Adrienne Zihlman. 1976. "Women in Evolution. Part I: Innovation and Selection in Human Origins." *Signs* 1 (3): 585–608.

Tsing, Anna. 2012. "Unruly Edges: Mushrooms as Companion Species." *Environmental Humanities* 1 (1): 141–154.

Tsing, Anna. 2014. "More-than-Human Sociality: A Call for Critical Description." In *Anthropology and Nature*, ed. Kirsten Hastrup, 27–42. New York: Routledge.

Viveiros de Castro, Eduardo. 2004. "Perspectival Anthropology and the Method of Controlled Equivocation." *Tipití* 2 (1): 3–22.

Weber, Peter K., Ian D. Hutcheon, Keven D. McKeegan, and B. Lynn Ingram. 2002. "Otolith Sulfur Isotope Method to Reconstruct Salmon (*Oncorhynchus tshawytscha*) Life History." *Canadian Journal of Fisheries and Aquatic Sciences* 59 (4): 587–591.

Chapter 6

A Theory of 'Animal Borders'

Thoughts and Practices toward Non-human Animals
among the G|ui Hunter-Gatherers

Kazuyoshi Sugawara

The purpose of this chapter is to outline a theory of 'animal borders' based on
ethnographic materials I have collected over the past two decades among the
G|ui Bushmen living in the Central Kalahari Desert, Botswana, in Southern
Africa. First, I locate my theoretical standpoint in the 'phenomenological positivism' proposed by Maurice Merleau-Ponty and explicate the dual meaning of
the term 'animal border'. I then offer a general description of the subjects of my
ethnographic research, G|ui Bushmen. In order to surmount the human-animal
dualism, I next criticize the representational view of culture that has been
prevalent in anthropology (Csordas 1994). My general aim is to demonstrate
that our concept of human-animal relationships has to be based on worldly,
corporeal existence. Guided by the notion of 'communicative expectation', the

References for this chapter begin on page 115.

theoretical origin of which is found in the 'relevance theory' proposed by Dan Sperber and Deirdre Wilson (1986), the following text throws light on some essential characteristics of interactions between the G|ui and animals. After outlining G|ui 'folk knowledge' of the metamorphosis from one animal species to another, I show that G|ui intercorporeality is open to the potential for transformation into animals. Finally, drawing on the concepts of *devenir* and *ritornello* proposed by Deleuze and Guattari ([1980] 1994), I argue that the thought and practices of Junichiro Itani, a Japanese primatologist and ecological anthropologist, can be seen as a precursor of the contemporary movement to overcome the human-animal dualism.

The Dual Meaning of 'Animal Border'

Following Merleau-Ponty's ([1945] 2002) *Phenomenology of Perception*, I like to designate my basic methodology as phenomenological positivism. My analysis of ethnographic material, especially oral discourse, is phenomenological in that it sets aside (or 'brackets off', in Husserlian terms) any objective judgment, based on scientific knowledge, concerning the truth value of statements. At the same time, my comprehension of the habitual sense lived by the G|ui people always flows back to my own life-world, where, furthermore, it illuminates the continuity between their immediate experience and mine. At the same time, my methodology is empirical and positivistic in endeavoring to construct an ethnographic description that rigidly relies on direct observations, including systematic transcription of conversations and narratives.

My key term 'animal borders' has a double meaning. The first is of course the boundary between human and non-human animals. As a point of departure, I refer to Peter Singer's ([1975] 2009) controversial *Animal Liberation*. In its preface, Singer expresses dissatisfaction with the limitations of English, where the term 'animal' usually refers to non-humans, implying that we are somehow not animals. Yet anyone who has taken an elementary course in biology knows this to be false.

The statement that human beings are also animals is often found in articles that investigate the human-animal relationship. However, in everyday language, in English and in Japanese and also in G|ui, the human is *not* an animal. Singer's dissatisfaction thus immediately commits us to a particular theory, that is, evolutionary theory, which is indeed the most predominant of all ideas about the human-animal relationship in modern industrial societies. Yet it might be questioned whether this commitment is epistemologically rational.

In *Philosophy in the Flesh*, George Lakoff and Mark Johnson (1999: 4) declare: "The discovery that reason is evolutionary utterly changes our relation to other animals and changes our conception of human beings as uniquely rational." However, they never offer any examples of such an utter change. In contrast, Singer's claim that we must not eat any animal meat deserves to be examined because it proposes a clear agenda for a radical change of the relation of humans to other animals. Yet I have doubts about his simple strategy of reducing the continuity between human and animal existence to the experience of pain. In my view, the best definition of animal behavior is proposed by Merleau-Ponty ([1942] 1983: 125–126) in his early work *The Structure of Behavior*: "The gestures of behavior, the intentions which it traces in the space around the animal, are not directed to the true world or pure being, but to being-for-the-animal, that is, to a certain milieu characteristic of the species." In sum, any consideration of animals needs to comprehend animal existence as inseparable from the structure of the environmental world to which it belongs.

John Knight's (2003) *Waiting for Wolves in Japan* inspires us to further elaborate the concept of 'animal borders'. Imagine, he writes "the feelings of the farmer who, over the year, puts everything into growing his crop, only then to have it eaten up and destroyed [by the wild boars], so that he is left standing, shocked and paralysed in front of fields he can no longer harvest" (ibid.: 58). The farmer would probably cry out, "Let the wild boars be extinguished!" or would regard those conservationists who prioritize the life of animals as enemies. The second meaning of 'animal borders' thus denotes the boundary demarcated by the intentional stance that a human agent, or a group of agents, assumes toward some animal actor(s). For instance, no sooner is the habitual thought of hunter-gatherers toward animals labeled as 'animism' than a sharp-cut distinction separates 'them' from an 'us' who might be Buddhist, Christian, scientific rationalist, and so on (cf. Bird-David 1999).

The thought, imagination, and practice toward animals among the G|ui hunter-gatherers in the Central Kalahari inspire fundamental reflection on these two meanings of 'animal borders'. This reflection is guided by the notion of 'corporeal schema' that was originally proposed by Merleau-Ponty ([1945] 2002), but without a clear definition. I define 'corporeal schema' as a bundle of manifold intentionality toward the surroundings that is united with the physical properties of the body. Assuming that corporeal schema not only is common to all human beings but also is shared, at least in part, with animals, we can establish a bridgehead for striding across the 'animal borders' in the above two senses.

The G|ui Bushmen

The G|ui and G||ana are closely related dialect groups of Khoe-speaking people who have adapted to the harsh dry environment of the Kalahari Desert (Tanaka 1980). The anthropological investigation of the G|ui was pioneered by George Silberbauer (1981) in the 1950s. Silberbauer contributed to the establishment of the Central Kalahari Game Reserve (CKGR) that was demarcated in 1963. In 1966, Jirō Tanaka (1980) began a study of ecological anthropology, primarily in the Xade area, located in the mid-western part of the CKGR. In 1979, the Botswana government started to make the people living in this area settle around the !Oi!om borehole. In 1997, the government carried out a relocation program so that all the residents of the Xade settlement, including G|ui, G||ana, and Bakgalagadi agro-pastoralists, migrated to Qχ'ôēsàkene (New Xade), a new settlement outside the CKGR about 70 kilometers away from Xade (Tanaka 1987). The ethnographic materials referred to in the following analysis were collected between 1992 and 2013 (see also Sugawara 2018a).

The G|ui phonology and grammar have been systematically explicated by my collaborator, the linguist Hiroshi Nakagawa (1996), although he later revised his original orthography (see Nakagawa 2006). The notation system in the present chapter principally follows the revised one. In G|ui, 4 types of click influx and 13 types of click accompaniments are distinguished. The order of words basically follows the subject + object + verb structure. Nakagawa's participation in the research drastically enlightened the non-linguists' obscure understanding of G|ui phonology and syntax.

The Corporeal Basis of Mythical and Magical Imagination

In the cultural relativist tradition, the mythical world, as well as cosmology more generally, has been regarded as an enormous assemblage of representations, each of which is arbitrarily constructed on the basis of local environments (Ingold 2000). Although the following analysis will make use of the model and inferential structure developed in cognitive anthropology, its ultimate aim is to demonstrate that the G|ui mythical and magical imagination is fundamentally based on their corporeal or immediate experience of encountering the natural world rather than on representation.

Dan Sperber's (1975, 1982) cognitive theory of symbolism offers a relentless criticism of relativist and hermeneutic interpretations. When an object, or an instance, is perceived by a human subject, this 'input' is sent to a 'conceptual device' that in turn designates its identity. Having processed this input, the conceptual device convocates from the mnemonic device a set of information pertinent to its identity. Conversely, when the conceptual device fails to designate the identity of a particular input, this input is sent to a 'symbolic device' that searches an indefinite range of passive memories. Thus, some symbolic effect is 'evoked' from the mnemonic device. Evidently, Sperber's theory is characterized by the dualism of conceptual-symbolic devices. Although I share with Sperberian theory an anti-relativist stance, my emphasis on corporeal schema entails a monistic integration of conceptual convocation (i.e., 'deictic cognition' in my terms) and symbolic evocation that is essentially coupled with affective arousal. An argument that is similar to Sperberian dualism can be found in an article by Blurton Jones and Konner (1976) on the ethological knowledge of the !Kung (more recently designated as Ju|'hoan) in the northwestern area of Botswana. Blurton Jones and Konner come to a strikingly dualist conclusion about non-rational beliefs: "They seem to exist in *a domain of the mind quite separate from ethno-ethological knowledge*" (ibid.: 342; emphasis added). Much of the evidence presented below will counter this view.

The first set of evidence has been obtained from ethno-ornithological observations. I identified 81 biological species of birds and collected 75 vernacular names. I also collected various descriptions, discourses, and songs on the subject of birds (Sugawara 2001). Here, I focus on two tales, both of which include a particular species, the black korhaan, as a principal character.

The black korhaan competed with the red-crested korhaan

A long time ago, a red-crested korhaan (g!àī), talking with a black korhaan (‖àà), boasted of his skill: "I am good at falling down head first like a stone." The latter did not believe it. So the g!àī gave a performance, but, immediately before hitting the ground, he turned round to land on his feet. However, the ‖àà did not see this trick. So, encouraged by the g!àī he attempted to do the same thing but crushed his head on the ground. Thus, the head of the ‖àà is still large today.

A popular field guide to Southern African birds describes the behavior of the red-crested korhaan as follows: "In summer [the] male flies steeply upwards to about 30 m and then tumbles as though shot" (Newman 1989: 88). Just like the G|ui people, the Western ornithologist identifies this behavior as a conspicuous feature of that species. This kind of cognition instantiates an identity designation that enables the conceptual device to operate. At the same time, the image of a hard blow on the head so acutely arouses our own corporeal schema that the association of a skull fracture with the flat shape of the male black korhaan's head induces loud laughter at the poor and stupid animal.

A calamity befell the black korhaan

Two women, a guinea fowl (|χane) and a black korhaan (‖àà), and their husbands were living together in a camp. The husbands went hunting and were killed by two 'man-eaters' (mythical beings). They skinned the victims and respectively wore these skins to disguise themselves as ‖àà's and |χane's husbands. The man-eaters went to the camp, and each sat beside one of the wives. One wife, |χane, noticed that this man was not her husband, while the other wife, ‖àà, did not notice and ate the meat of her husband that the man-eater gave her. At night, |χane pretended to take her children to the toilet, calling on ‖àà to go together, but ‖àà came leaving her children in her hut. When she was told of the true character of their seeming husbands, ‖àà was so upset that she ran back to her hut to recover her children. However, the man-eater shot her with an arrow, and she died. All of her children were also killed. |χane and her children took refuge in a camp where kin of both |χane and ‖àà were living. Listening to this news, |χane's aunt boasted and sang: "Oh, as I'm smart, she is smart! *táʔtārārá, táʔtārārá.*" On the other hand, ‖àà's mother cried and sang: "Alas, as I'm stupid, she is stupid! *tòrā̃, tòrā̃.*"

A few days after I was told this tale, the Japanese researchers heard the noisy call of a bird in the evening. My colleagues could not identify the bird. However, I noticed that it sounded very boastful and therefore claimed that it had to be a guinea fowl, to the disbelief of my colleagues. The next evening, we heard the same call while a local research assistant was still present. I asked him: "What is that bird?" He replied: "It's |χane [guinea fowl]."

Elsewhere, I have proposed a simple distinction between deictic and indirect cognition (Sugawara 2001). Deictic cognition refers to any kind of cognition that is produced by the direct perception of objects in the surrounding world. On the other hand, the birdmen (or -women) characters and their acts in the myths described above are obviously not amenable to direct perception. As a contrast to deictic cognition, I have used the term 'indirect cognition' to indicate cognition that is oriented toward features existing only in representation. The point is that deictic and indirect cognition reinforce each other. To notice the conspicuous behavior of a bird reminds one of a relevant tale or myth, while holding a cultural representation relevant to the interpretation of such a behavior may sharpen observational ability.

I now turn to ethno-immunology observations in order to throw light on the continuity of the G|ui corporeal schema with the schema that is lived by 'us' in the modern industrial societies.

The smell of leopards made a woman sick (September 1992)
A middle-aged woman, Ho, about 50 years old, had been sick and could not eat food. Her eldest son, CR, asked a G||ana man to hold a curing ritual. The doctor cut with a razor the skin on the right side of her belly, above the liver. He put his mouth on the wound, sucked out the blood, and vomited it on the sand. He repeated this procedure five times. The doctor put the paste made from the burnt and ground body of a bat on the wound. Afterward, the doctor told the researcher that he had discerned the cause of the illness: the smell of leopards. When Ho was in an extra-marital love relationship in 1987, her 'younger brother' (parallel cousin) killed a leopard, and sold its skin to a rich Kgalagadi man. The latter employed Ho's lover to rub the skin and rewarded him with a bag of maize flour for his labor. When he gifted it to his lover, the smell of the leopard entered her body for the first time. Five years later, in early 1992, Ho participated in a trip to gather berries. Near the bush camp, several young men caught two female leopards, a mother and daughter, in wired snares. When they boiled the meat, Ho was sitting so near that "the smell of the two leopards made the old one recur." She died two weeks after the curing ritual.

Although about 30 percent of adult men eat leopard meat, it is strongly abhorred by women. When I heard the witch doctor's diagnosis, it came to my mind that this interpretation offered something like an ethno-immunology. Any immunological consideration requires an encounter between two or more tokens of a type of experience that are ordered in a temporal relationship of precedence and succession. Both the narrative of allergy in industrial societies and this witch doctor's interpretation are comprehended as an attempt to reorganize the continuity of a person's experience over long periods. Three years earlier I had encountered the following story.

A father worried about his newborn baby's health (October 1989)
In the early period of the rainy season, I went to check snares with two research assistants, CR and TB. CR had married a G||ana girl in 1988, the

previous year, and their first daughter had been born several months ago. In those days, CR was worrying about the newborn baby's bad health. Finding no animals caught in the snares, we arrived at the !Q'are pan, 12 kilometers east of the settlement, and encountered a hunting team consisting of three G||ana men. They were taking a break after butchering a gemsbok they had killed with spears a little while earlier. CR eagerly asked them where they had butchered the game and ran to the spot. He came back with the gemsbok's feces in his hand: "I'm afraid that if I eat this gemsbok meat, my daughter will suffer from serious diarrhea. So, before eating, I'll rub these feces on my daughter's belly. If I do, she will not become sick."

The next case derives from a long discourse recently narrated by an old woman, TS, TB's mother-in-law:

The wildcat killed a man (August 2013)
Because you have eaten that wildcat (!qórù) without knowing what it was, he makes you sick. Then he goes toward your liver. You have a pain every day. Then, if there is a witch doctor, he would cut you with a razor and would say: "Last night, the wildcat killed a man. I smell his odor. So, isn't there the wildcat's fur?" If there is the fur, he would pick up a piece of it and cut [you] with a razor. [He would rub the fur into the wound.] You would recover.

In order to comprehend these cases, it is useful to recall Lakoff and Johnson's (1999: 343) emphasis on "the unconscious inferential structure" of argumentation—that which "is not overtly and consciously discussed in the text, but rather ... must be unconsciously taken for granted in order to make sense of the text." As the inferential structure is essentially deductive, it does not depend on time. On the other hand, like Lakoff's (1987) prototype scenario of anger, the cognitive schema of ethno-immunology has a temporal organization. Accordingly, I designate this schema as a 'scenario' rather than as an inferential structure. Here we can notice that our medical theory concerning allergy and the G|ui ethno-immunology instantiated by "The smell of leopards" narrative have similar features that can be abstracted in scenario α.

Scenario α
(1) As some material X invades a healthy body B, B is transformed into B', which embraces the potentiality of illness.
(2) As the same material X enters B', that potentiality is transmuted into actuality so that B' becomes a sick body ᗺ.

The inversion of this etiological scenario brings about a pragmatic scenario for prophylaxis or curing. Scenario β can be abstracted from the "A father worried about" narrative:

Scenario β
(i) Premise: The father's body B and his child's body b are congruent.
(ii) The invasion of X into B entails that it also invades b, so that b is transformed into a sick body ᖯ.

(iii) If a little bit of x, which is congruent with (or adjacent to) X, is put into b, b will be transformed into b', which is immune to X.

(iv) Then, although X's invasion into B also entails its invasion into b', b' would not change.

Furthermore, scenario γ can be formulated from "The wildcat killed " narrative:

Scenario γ
(I) As X invades B, B becomes a sick body B̶.
(II) Put a little bit of x, which is congruent with (or adjacent to) X, into B̶.
(III) Then, B̶ will become a healthy body, B.

As suggested above, scenario α is homologous to the modern medical theory of allergy. On the other hand, scenario β is identical with a medical theory that supports modern epidemiological practice (i.e., inoculation or vaccination). Although scenario γ has the simplest structure, its inference embodies a logic inverse to our immunological theory. Even so, this scenario is similar to medical practices for curing some diseases (e.g. the allergy shock caused by a tick bite) by injecting the serum into the client's body (as is indeed practiced at the clinic in New Xade).

I noted that the pragmatic scenario of prophylaxis or curing is produced by inverting the etiological scenario α. Notice, however, that this inversion lacks the logical symmetry that structuralism would demand or expect. The point is that although the G|ui lack any concept that corresponds to our 'immunity', they practically grasp proposition (iii) in scenario β: if a little bit of x is put into b, b would become immune to X. When I came across the following incident, I was astonished by this tiny discovery.

"Daddy made this" (13 February 2004)
I visited a G|ui camp located in the peripheral area of the relocated village, New Xade. The eldest resident, AE, was quite an eloquent and intelligent man. I sat in front of AE's hut and exchanged greetings with him and his first wife. After a little while, his son SO, several years older than me, came to sit beside me. In the midst of the rainy season it was so hot that he was naked from the waist up. Showing a round scar of about one centimeter in diameter on his left upper arm, he said: "This is a mark from curing χòrētá [smallpox]." I asked: "Did the white man make it like this?" He replied: "No, Daddy did it. When a co-resident man, who had suffered from χòrētá, was recovering, Daddy picked up 'the rotten one' [pus] from a wound [blister] that was about to heal, mixed it with some medicine, and rubbed it into both me and my elder brother. Therefore, we survived without being attacked by χòrētá." I turned to AE and asked: "Had ǂébè [the Bakagalagadi agro-pastoralists] taught you this treatment?" Smiling pleasantly at me, he replied: "No, I thought of it by myself."

According to a reconstruction of the modern history of the Central Kalahari, the smallpox epidemic was rampant in Bechuanaland, the former British

Reserve, in 1950 and 1951 (Osaki 2001). AE was probably in his early thirties, while SO was six or seven years old. At this time, AE gave a kind of vaccination that he had invented to his sons and saved them from death. Without any knowledge about invisible agents such as allergens or antibodies, some sense of corporeality led him to an attempt to negotiate with the demonic force raging within human bodies. This attempt can be assumed to be guided by the following implicit inferential structure:

(a) χòrētá kills people. But while many people died of χòrētá, other people survived. The χòrētá that had invaded into the latter people should be weaker than what had killed the former.
(b) The force of χòrētá that makes people sick or die should lodge in the blisters.
(c) Let me pick up the weak force of the weak χòrētá from a blister and put it into my sons.
(d) Then, even though the strong χòrētá enters my sons' bodies, the weak one, already having stayed there, would say: "I've been here!" Thus, being deceived, the strong χòrētá would turn back.

It is plausible to assume that in hellish circumstances, where bodies that could not be buried were lying around, one might acquire insights like propositions (a) and (b). However, direction (c) could never been induced merely from the accumulation of empirical observations. Even though assumption (d) provides the reason that prompts one to follow direction (c), I might be accused of fabricating an interpretation of indigenous thought.

Let me therefore return to "The smell of leopards." After the treatment of bloodletting, the witch doctor gave an oracle as follows:

If she does not heal even after this treatment, go to the store, pick up a piece of fur from the lion's skin lying there, and bring it here. [The previous year, a male lion was caught in a steel trap, and its skin had been exhibited at a store in the center of the Xade settlement.] Mix it with a g‖àwã-ìi [the name of a shrub; g‖àwã and ìi respectively denote 'dead spirit' and 'tree'] and burn them near her head. The lion and the leopard are brothers. This is the illness caused by the younger. If the elder enters [her body], it will say: "Hey, my younger brother, are you there? My odor will go there. Don't you trouble this person." Then the younger one will surely hide himself.

The assumption (d) and the inferential structure organizing the witch doctor's oracle are analogous. Neither proposition (iii) of scenario β (if a little bit of x is put into b, b would become immune from X), nor the assumption that two kinds of agents can have a dialogue within the patient's body, is a disembodied representation that emerges arbitrarily. Rather, the G|ui ethno-immunological insights originate from their peculiar sense of the corporeal continuity between human beings, animals, and the material world.

Interaction, Communication, and Metamorphosis between Humans and Animals

Now let us examine the semantic field of a transitive verb ŋ!àrē, which is tentatively translated as 'to sense', 'to have a presentiment', or 'to be affected by'.

(1) The simplest usage of this verb is kʰārī-mà ŋ!àrē: 'to be intoxicated by alcohol'. Not only humans but also animals may be drunk. A steenbok wandering around in a moonlit night is interpreted as 'being intoxicated with the moon'.

(2) A peculiar situation where this verb is used concerns food taboo. In G|ui, the transitive verb ŋ!āā means that its object will cause a disease if the subject person eats it. When the derivative morpheme χò, meaning 'thing', follows this verb, a noun, ŋ!āā-χò, is produced, which means the things that cause disease if consumed or, more simply, things not to be eaten. The category of ŋ!āā-χò, called 'sumo', is the most important. Only elders and infants are allowed to eat sumo. Typical members of this category are the pangolin, kori bustard, black korhaan, leopard tortoise, and Kalahari tent tortoise. Adolescent men always seek a chance to eat these forbidden meats while averting the danger of disease. Suppose that two adolescent men of close kin, P and Q, are sitting near a pot of their common ŋ!āā-χò. P, deciding to eat, will hastily consume it and then upset the pot, orienting its mouth toward Q. By doing so, P will not suffer from sickness while Q will be attacked by diarrhea— because Q's body is 'affected by' (ŋ!àrē) the fact that P ate their ŋ!āā-χò.

(3) Similarly, when one's belly rumbles, this incident is expressed as 'my intestine anticipates [something]' (cíkà |àbē-bì ŋ!àrē) interpreting it as a hunch that, for example, a kinsman will come back with game meat caught in a snare.

(4) When butchering the carcass of a gemsbok, the hunter must not allow his dogs to eat its heart, because next time they go hunting, other gemsboks will 'sense' the dogs that have eaten their conspecific animal.

Thus, we see that the semantic field centered around the verb ŋ!àrē represents invisible networks of various influences that affect not only the human social world but also the world of animals.

The second clue for comprehending the contiguity of the G|ui corporeal schema with that of animals is gained by examining a number of imaginative practices that serve to introduce animal agents into the area of human communication. The clue for the following analysis draws on the relevance theory proposed by Sperber and Wilson (1986). This theory considers the essence of communication as 'ostension', defined as a combination of informative intention and communicative intention. 'Informative intention', in turn, is defined as presenting a set of assumptions to an audience. The point of this definition is to exclude an act of merely showing an informative intention from the 'ostensive communication'. However, loosening Sperber and Wilson's rigid definition of communication, I define a 'communicative expectation' as an expectation that one's informative intention is to be understood by the other. A 'communicative area' can be further specified as an indefinite virtual domain covering all those to whom one's communicative expectation is ascribed (Sugawara 2005).

The G|ui often ascribe communicative expectations toward animals. For example, the G|ui have several songs and dances addressed to birds. When encountering certain birds, people sing a song to them, or even dance for them. The following song is addressed to the lilac-breasted roller: "Charcoal of g!õõ firewood has popped into your back! Charcoal of ‖árà firewood has popped into your back [g!õõ |ʔee ŋǂõm̄ tsà ŋǂúrõ wà ǂāā, ‖árà |ʔee ŋǂõm̄ tsà ŋǂúrõ wà ǂāa]!" Both g!õõ and ‖árà are names of *Acacia* trees. The lilac-breasted roller has a brown back that is likened to a scald in this song. It often emits a hoarse sound, with its shoulders swaying as if it were in pain.

The song of a crowned plover is likened to the noise of filing a knife. It is interpreted as telling a man: "A game animal is caught in your snare. File your knife and cut the animal with it!" Moreover, the songs of many bird species are likened to G|ui phrases or sentences. Thus, the caws of the pied crow are likened to the menacing talk of a sorcerer: "You [male, plural] will know me [my magical power] [ʔǐ‖àò qχ'awa cìà !ʔaa]."

Again, the song of the female red-crested korhaan tells that vultures are flying in the sky. Hearing her song, a man looks up and sees the vultures. Going in their direction, he may find the carcass of a game animal. The reason for this bird's keen sense of vultures goes back to her bitter experience in ancient times. A long time ago, g!àĩ used to lay eggs in the trees. Vultures found them easily and ate them up. A ground agama lizard advised the g!àĩ to lay her eggs in the sand and cover them with grass. Following this advice, the eggs were no longer eaten. Even to this day, however, the female utters a cry of warning at the sight of a vulture.

The ethno-ornithological analysis above reveals that in the G|ui mythical imagination, corporeal schema lived by animals is essentially identical with that of human beings. This homogeneity between animal and human corporeal schemata ultimately entails the potential for metamorphosis.

The kori bustard (gǂeu), a large bird like the crane, is undoubtedly the prototype of sumo meat for elders (Sugawara 2008). In a film I made in 2006, I was eager to ascertain the meaning of a quite difficult indigenous concept, cìmā, which I assumed to relate either to magical power specific to women or to the violation of the food taboo. I asked my two research assistants and principal informant the following question: "When a person violates the food taboo, doesn't this make cìmā?" All three confidently replied "Yes!" in one voice. One declared that the person "would become mad (dzùāzúrā)." The other two then related a story in which a young man who had dared to eat the meat of the kori bustard began to cry and flap his arms, as if he had been transformed into this bird. The highlight was a scene in which my research assistants, one after another, re-enacted the cry, flapping, and gliding gesture of the kori bustard (see fig. 1). In the G|ui life-world, the continuity between human and non-human agents is comprehended in a pre-linguistic way. This understanding may influence their sense of intercorporeality, which is open to the potential of transformation or metamorphosis into an animal body.

FIGURE 6.1 Two research assistants imitate the flying gestures of the kori bustard: (a) GB is flapping, (b) GB is gliding, (c) CR is flapping, (d) CR is gliding

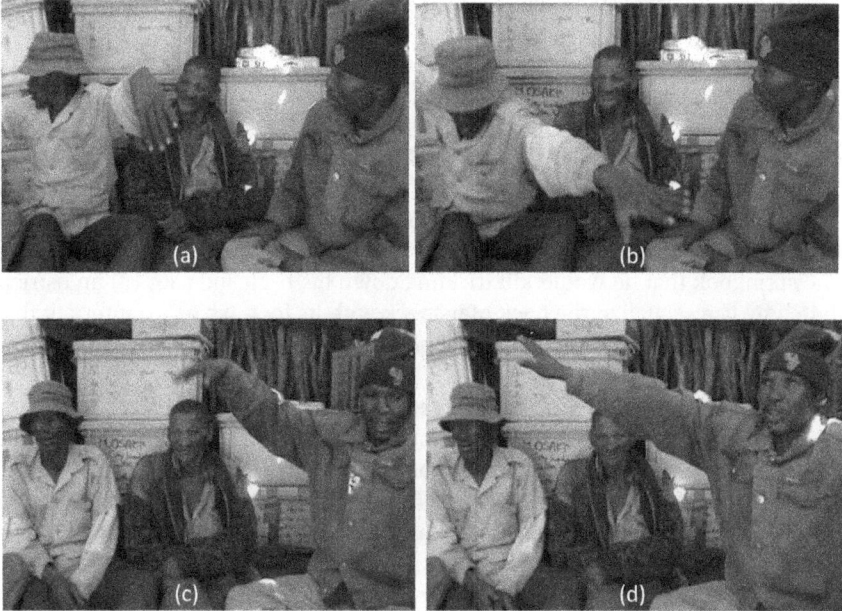

Photographs © Kazuyoshi Sugawara

As a final piece of ethnographic evidence in support of the G|ui belief in metamorphosis, I shall cite some 'folk knowledge' concerning the transformation of one arthropod species into another and about the life cycle of amphibians (Nonaka 1996).

(1) During the final period of the dry season, we often hear the chirps of cicadas. They disappear soon and are transformed into the edible jewel beetles, g‖ōāχàm̀kútsúrō, which appear in the mid-rainy season. People collect and eat them after roasting them with hot ash.

(2) The scorpion |qχ'árì, after digging itself into the sand, is transformed into the edible caterpillar ǂú̀ùŋ!ò̄ō, the larva of the convolvulus hawk moth, which feeds on fresh leaves of Legiminosae trees in the rainy season.

(3) After heavy downpours during the rainy season, small pools form for up to a week in depressions in the bottom of pans. In these pools appear giant frogs and tadpoles. While the frogs are valued as food, the G|ui laughed at my claim that the tadpoles will be transformed into frogs. All tadpoles, they insisted, will die out as soon as the ponds dry up. On the other hand, small frogs drop from the sky with the downpours and grow up to become giant adults.

Below I focus on this third example as providing the clearest clue to under-standing how the G|ui corporeal schema is contiguous with the schema shared by animals, regardless of whether they are prey (game animals), predators (lions and leopards), or 'useless things' (e.g., little birds).

Metamorphosis as the Potential for Intercorporeality

In *Crowds and Power,* Elias Canetti ([1960] 1984) remarked on some Bushmen folklore that was published in the early twentieth century: (1) a man told his children that their grandfather would come soon because he felt his father's old wound in the same part of his body; (2) before hunting, a man felt the blood of the springbok that he would kill trickling down his back and calf; (3) an ostrich bitten by lice scratched the back of its neck with its foot, while a hunter felt this in the same part of his neck and had a presentiment that he would soon encoun-ter it. Canetti referred to these cases as examples of 'metamorphosis'. The folklore Canetti cited had been collected by Bleek and Lloyd (1911) from |Xam bushmen who were imprisoned in South Africa in the late nineteenth century (see also Biesele 1993). The |Xam inhabited the Cape Province and were already on the verge of extinction at that time (Barnard 1992). It is surprising that two studies, Bleek and Lloyd's and mine, carried out independently at intervals one century and 800 kilometers apart, reveal a common corporeal sense that might be specific to the hunting and gathering way of life in the Kalahari savanna.

The notion of corporeal schema, the axis of this investigation, has an affin-ity with Viveiros de Castro's (1998: 478) formulation of 'the body' as a bundle of "affects, dispositions or capacities." In his influential article, Viveiros de Castro argues that for Amerindians the soul, shared by humans and animals, functions as the 'cosmological deixis' in that it always implies a contextual reference point for the first-person pronoun. While his 'multi-naturalism' is not defined as a general alternative to the monistic naturalism of modern science, but rather as a reinterpretation of Amerindian ethnographies, it is nevertheless possible for us to take extreme multi-naturalism at 'face value' in order to try to radically undermine nature-culture dualism. Contrary to the picture of cultural relativism depicted by Ingold (2000), this position refuses the presumption that a uniform plane of nature covers all over the earth, admitting that multiple natures exist, each of which strictly coincides with an indigenous ontology. However, this thought experiment leads to a logical contradiction.

Returning to my own life-world, the proposition that tadpoles become frogs is so firmly based on my immediate experience that I never doubt its truth value. Thus, we can formulate two propositions that are antithetical to each other:

P : Tadpoles become frogs / ~P : Tadpoles never become frogs

The truth values for the above two propositions are inversed depending on the place where we make a statement: in Japan, P is true and ~P is false, while in the Central Kalahari, P is false and ~P is true. If there were two different natural worlds, each permeated with their respective ontology, we should be able to ascertain a boundary that demarcates these two worlds. If there were such a boundary, we could bring a tadpole that had been born in Japan across this boundary into the Central Kalahari. Yet this tadpole is ontologically against the law of excluded middle because it must become a frog in the place where it will never become a frog.

Deleuze and Guattari's ([1980] 1994) *Mille Plateaux* (A Thousand Plateaus) contains resources for reconsidering the apparent contradiction deduced from taking 'multi-naturalism at face value'. Like the snares among the G|ui, their huge volume is organized along the intention of 'anti-communication' and provokes the reader into escaping from institutionalized forms of thinking such as deductive inferences or even phenomenological description. Letting myself be seduced by the snare they had set, I was moved by their argument that the potential for a human to become an animal offers rich possibilities for those who attempt to break through the intellectual impasse under the capitalist regime. Relying on the potential of *devenir* (becoming), we are thus tempted to reconsider the above logical contradiction.

It deserves note that I have never attempted to carry out any experiment designed to prove that the tadpoles caught from a pool in a pan transform into frogs, or to persuade my stubborn research assistants to believe that the tadpoles are indeed the larvae of frogs. In fact, I am absolutely unwilling to commit myself to such an enlightenment project, for I have *become* G|ui to some degree. There is no discrete boundary between the two worlds: rather, my body continuously transfers from one world to another. Once it dwells in either of them, it gets embedded in the relatedness that is specific to the local contexts, either of the Kalahari or of Japan.

I find Deleuze and Guattari's emphasis on the *ritornello* (refrains) with which nature is filled so inspiring that I have been prompted to listen carefully to the crow's cawing or tit's chirp. One morning I noticed that during an interval between a crow's caws, other caws were faintly heard in response. Another morning, hearing the refrain of chirps of an unknown bird, I remembered an old question that I had long forgotten. When I was 14 years old, I read a short English novel translated into Japanese in which a novelist, bothered with his slow writing, felt as if the birds' chirps were laughing at him. I could not understand why. Eureka! The answer came to me: those birds were singing "literature, literature"! In that moment, I also understood that the G|ui interpretation of the caw of the pied crow as "ʔí‖àò qχ'awa cìà !ʔaa" (you [male plural] will know me) was not merely an analogy but conveyed the reality of the sorcerer who was incarnated into the crow. Thus, we are always on the way of *becoming* another existence.

More than half a century ago, in 1950, a young man of 24 was absorbed in the *ritornello* of the voices of Japanese macaques, walking and sometimes running around in a mountain called Takasaki-yama. He was the late Junichiro Itani, a distinguished pioneer of primatology and ecological anthropology. Fascinated by the striking variety of the monkeys' vocal sounds, he decided to note each of them down as accurately as possible. He quietly approached the troop, tracked its nomadic movements all day long, listed a huge repertoire of vocal sounds, and repeatedly reconstructed the theoretical models that could illuminate the internal organization of the macaque troop. Then one day in the early summer, he decided to put into action a plan that he had devised.

As Itani ([1954] 2007: 124–125) explained it: "To make the strongest impact I can on the troop ... I wanted to throw the troop into total chaos ... to see how they recover their order" (in Japanese; my translation). Carefully hiding himself in the forest, he stalked to the edge of a range where the scattered monkeys were calmly feeding and suddenly dashed into the midst of the group. Running at full speed along a monkey trail through the bush, he noticed out of the corner of his eye that panicked big male monkeys were running parallel to him. Merely witnessing the scene, we would have to believe that Itani was crazy. However, it is not quite right to say that he had become monkey. Even in bed, he kept thinking about those Others. "At night, as soon as I closed my eyes, many monkeys appeared ... To get away from these illusionary monkeys, I took up my notebook again. I considered a theory that enables the phenomenon [I have observed] to be settled in *my system*" (ibid.: 86; emphasis added).

Itani never became monkey, but he did keep running along the 'animal border' between human and monkey. His endeavor was firmly supported by the belief that the Japanese macaque must have a unique society, the structure of which could be revealed. Honored with the Huxley Memorial Medal in 1984, Itani tried in his later works to demonstrate that the egalitarianism most typically found in extant hunting-gathering societies was deeply rooted in the legacy from pre-hominid and proto-hominid ancestors (see, e.g., Itani 1988). He never expressed any sympathy with Darwinian evolution theory based on natural selection and the survival of the fittest.

Thus, Itani's 'naturalist' stance was as distant as we can imagine from objectivist naturalism (Olafson 2001). Instead, his intellectual and corporeal practices were motivated by the radical insight that human beings share their corporeal schema with that of monkeys and apes as existences immanently belonging to their own society. Thus, Itani's naturalism opened the way to an interspecies corporeality that drastically extends the intercorporeality (*intercorporéité*) described by Merleau-Ponty (1964: 183) in his later years.

Over the last half-century, most cultural anthropologists in Japan have neglected primatologists' efforts to establish continuity in sociality between human and non-human primates. Indeed, they often emphasize a clear-cut discontinuity. I suspect that their skeptical attitude toward natural history—of either humans or primates—is indicative of submission to various forms of representationalism, whether structural-functional, hermeneutic, or post-structural.

In order to escape from this situation, I dare to commit myself to stand on the 'animal border' along which Itani was running. From this vantage point, how do we see this world in which both we and animals are "fellow participants" (Ingold 2000: 87)? Looking at the animal side, we need to develop the phenomenological tools for describing animal behaviors and societies, positioning animals as 'beings-in-the-world' (Sugawara 2002). Looking at the side of human societies, we have to re-evaluate natural history observations to uncover the immanent structures and schemata of praxis that organize them (cf. Descola 1996). In order to avoid the representationalist bias, we especially need to comprehend human oral discourse as 'genuine gesture' (Merleau-Ponty (1945) 2002: 213). At this point, my methodology of phenomenological positivism has to be transformed into phenomenological naturalism or naturalized phenomenology (Sugawara 2018b). While this approach is quite far from the monistic or mechanistic view of the natural world that underlies modern science, it is resonant with multiple cross-disciplinary approaches that have emerged in recent decades, from anthropology (Descola [1986] 1994; Latour 2005) to sociology (Shilling 2005) and even to the philosophy of science (Hacking 1983, 2002).

Acknowledgments

I wish to express my gratitude to the officials of the Botswana government for their cooperation and hospitality. I am greatly indebted to Dr. Hiroshi Nakagawa for teaching me G|ui phonetics and syntax. I am also grateful to Dr. Jirō Tanaka for his suggestions and encouragement. Lastly, I wish to express my heartfelt thanks to many G|ui and G||ana friends for their generosity and patience.

Kazuyoshi Sugawara is a Professor Emeritus of Anthropology at Kyoto University. His research includes primatological studies of face-to-face interactions among Japanese macaques and the social organization of Ethiopian hybrid baboons, as well as long-term ethnographic research among the G|ui San. His many publications include *Anthropology of Conversation: The Life-World of the Bushman* (1998, in Japanese) and *An Encyclopedia of G|ui and G||ana Culture and Society* (2010, co-edited with Jirō Tanaka).

References

Barnard, Alan. 1992. *Hunters and Herders of Southern Africa: A Comparative Ethnography of the Khoisan Peoples*. Cambridge: Cambridge University Press.
Biesele, Megan. 1993. *Women Like Meat: The Folklore and Foraging Ideology of the Kalahari Ju/'hoan*. Bloomington: Indiana University Press.
Bird-David, Nurit. 1999. "'Animism' Revisited: Personhood, Environment, and Relational Epistemology." *Current Anthropology* 40 (S1): S67–S91.
Bleek, Wilhelm H. I., and Lucy C. Lloyd. 1911. *Specimens of Bushman Folklore*. London: George Allen.
Blurton Jones, Nicholas, and Melvin J. Konner. 1976. "!Kung Knowledge of Animal Behavior (or: The Proper Study of Mankind Is Animals)." In *Kalahari Hunter-Gatherers: Studies of the !Kung San and Their Neighbors*, ed. Richard B. Lee and Irven DeVore, 325–348. Cambridge, MA: Harvard University Press.
Canetti, Elias. (1960) 1984. *Crowds and Power*. Trans. Carol Stewart. New York: Farrar, Straus and Giroux.

Csordas, Thomas J. 1994. "Introduction: The Body as Representation and Being-in-the-World." In *Embodiment and Experience: The Existential Ground of Culture and Self*, ed. Thomas J. Csordas, 1–24. Cambridge: Cambridge University Press.

Deleuze, Gille, and Félix Guattari. (1980) 1994. *Mille Plateaux: Capitalisme et schizo-phrénie*. Paris: Editions de Minuit. Japanese translation by Kuniichi Uno et al., *Sen no Pulatoo*. Tokyo: Kawade Shobo Shin-sha.

Descola, Philippe. (1986) 1994. *In the Society of Nature: A Native Ecology in Amazonia*. Trans. Nora Scott. New York: Cambridge University Press.

Descola, Philippe. 1996. "Constructing Natures: Symbolic Ecology and Social Practice." In *Nature and Society: Anthropological Perspectives*, ed. Philippe Descola and Gísli Pálsson, 82–102. London: Routledge.

Hacking, Ian. 1983. *Representing and Intervening: Introductory Topics in the Philosophy of Natural Science*. Cambridge: Cambridge University Press.

Hacking, Ian. 2002. *Historical Ontology*. Cambridge, MA: Harvard University Press.

Ingold, Tim. 2000. *The Perception of the Environment: Essays on Livelihood, Dwelling and Skill*. London: Routledge.

Itani, Junichiro. (1954) 2007. "The Monkeys at Mt. Takasaki-yama." [In Japanese.] In *The Works of Junichiro Itani, Volume 1*, 39–262. Tokyo: Heibon-sha.

Itani, Junichiro. 1988. "The Origin of Human Equality." In *Social Fabrics of the Mind*, ed. Michael R. A. Chance, 137–156. London: Lawrence Erlbaum Associates.

Knight, John. 2003. *Waiting for Wolves in Japan: An Anthropological Study of People-Wildlife Relations*. Oxford: Oxford University Press.

Lakoff, George. 1987. *Women, Fire, and Dangerous Things: What Categories Reveal about the Mind*. Chicago: University of Chicago Press.

Lakoff, George, and Mark Johnson. 1999. *Philosophy in the Flesh: The Embodied Mind and Its Challenge to Western Thought*. New York: Basic Books.

Latour, Bruno. 2005. *Reassembling the Social: An Introduction to Actor-Network-Theory*. Oxford: Oxford University Press.

Merleau-Ponty, Maurice. (1942) 1983. *The Structure of Behavior*. Trans. Alden L. Fisher. Pittsburgh: Duquesne University Press.

Merleau-Ponty, Maurice. (1945) 2002. *Phenomenology of Perception*. Trans. Colin Smith. London: Routledge.

Merleau-Ponty, Maurice. 1964. *Le visible et l'invisible*. Ed. Claude Lefort. Paris: Gallimard.

Nakagawa, Hiroshi. 1996. "An Outline of |Gui Phonology." *African Study Monographs* S22: 101–124.

Nakagawa, Hiroshi. 2006. "Aspects of the Phonetic and Phonological Structure of the G|ui Languages." PhD diss., Witwatersland University, Johannesburg.

Newman, Kenneth. 1989. *Birds of Botswana*. Cape Town: Southern Book Publishers.

Nonaka, Kenichi. 1996. "Ethnoentomology of the Central Kalahari San." *African Study Monographs* S22: 29–46.

Olafson, Frederick A. 2001. *Naturalism and the Human Condition: Against Scientism*. London: Routledge.

Osaki, Masakazu. 2001. "Reconstructing the Recent History of the G/ui and G//ana Bushmen." *African Study Monographs* S26: 27–39.

Shilling, Chris. 2005. *The Body in Culture, Technology and Society*. London: Sage.

Silberbauer, George B. 1981. *Hunter and Habitat in the Central Kalahari Desert*. Cambridge: Cambridge University Press.

Singer, Peter. (1975) 2009. *Animal Liberation*. New York: HarperCollins. Japanese translation by Kiyoshi Toda, *Dobutsu no Kaihou*. Kyoto: Jinbun Shoin.

Sperber, Dan. 1975. *Rethinking Symbolism*. Cambridge: Cambridge University Press.

Sperber, Dan. 1982. *Le savoir des anthropologues: Trois essais*. Paris: Hermann.

Sperber, Dan, and Deirdre Wilson. 1986. *Relevance: Communication and Cognition.* Oxford: Basil Blackwell.

Sugawara, Kazuyoshi. 2001. "Cognitive Space Concerning Habitual Thought and Practice toward Animals among the Central San (|Gui and ||Gana): Deictic/Indirect Cognition and Prospective/Retrospective Intention." *African Study Monographs* S27: 61–98.

Sugawara, Kazuyoshi. 2002. *Kanjou no En = Jin* [Emotional ape-man]. Tokyo: Kobundo.

Sugawara, Kazuyoshi. 2005. "Body Configuration as Resource in the Experience of 'the Hunter and the Hunted': Narratives of the |Gui Bushmen." In *Construction and Distribution of Body Resources: Correlations between Ecological, Symbolic, and Medical Systems*, ed. Kazuyoshi Sugawara, 56–78. Tokyo: RILCAA, Tokyo University of Foreign Studies.

Sugawara, Kazuyoshi. 2008. "How Is the Memory of Ritual Articulated with 'Now-and-Here' Context? A Reconstruction of the Lost Initiation Ceremony of Male |Gui Bushmen." In *Multiplicity of Meaning and the Interrelationship of the Subject and the Object in Ritual and Body Texts*, ed. Haruka Wazaki, 67–87. Nagoya: Nagoya University.

Sugawara, Kazuyoshi. 2018a. "On the G|ui Experiences of 'Being Hunted': Analysis of Oral Discourses on the Man-Killing by Lions." *Senri Ethnological Studies* 99: 65–82.

Sugawara, Kazuyoshi. 2018b. "The Situationality of Animal Borders: From Phenomenology to Natural History of Evolution." In *The Situationality of Human-Animal Relations: Perspectives from Anthropology and Philosophy*, ed. Thiemo Breyer and Thomas Widlok, 29–49. Bielefeld: Transcript Verlag.

Tanaka, Jirō. 1980. *The San, Hunter-Gatherers of the Kalahari: A Study in Ecological Anthropology*. Tokyo: University of Tokyo Press.

Tanaka, Jirō. 1987. "The Recent Changes in the Life and Society of the Central Kalahari San." *African Study Monographs* 7: 37–51.

Viveiros de Castro, Eduardo. 1998. "Cosmological Deixis and Amerindian Perspectivism." *Journal of Royal Anthropological Institute* 4 (3): 469–488.

Chapter 7

Delta Ontologies
Infrastructural Transformations in the
Chao Phraya Delta, Thailand

Atsuro Morita and Casper Bruun Jensen

As a landform shaped by silt deposited by a river at its estuary, a delta is a meeting place between land and sea, an inherently intermediary space. As conceived by Western science, deltaic landforms are shaped by sedimentation of soil transported by the river and influenced by the sea tide. The interactions of river and sea give rise to complex geomorphological and hydrological features, including a harsh environment and proneness to flooding. The in-between state of deltas also makes it possible for local inhabitants as well as local and foreign 'innovators' to enact deltaic landscapes in radically divergent ways. Here we focus on divergent but co-existing ontologies in the Chao Phraya Delta in Thailand. Characterizing these ontologies entails paying equal attention to processes of infrastructural transformation and cosmological orientation

Notes for this chapter begin on page 131.

(Jensen and Morita 2015). In the Western tradition of geomorphology and land reclamation, deltas are viewed as manifesting the capacity of rivers to shape land. In contrast, the 'galactic polities' (Tambiah 1977) of Southeast Asia conceive of deltas as extensions of the sea into land. Examining these incongruent delta ontologies facilitates an analysis of their ongoing, open-ended dynamics.

Large-Scale Ontologies, Amphibious and Otherwise

Stanley Tambiah (1977: 69) used the notion of 'galactic polity' as a way "to represent the design of traditional Southeast Asian kingdoms, a design that coded in a composite way cosmological, topographical, and politico-economic features." In particular, he suggested that 'galactic' forms of political organization replicated the geometric form of the mandala (a symbol of the universe in Hindu-Buddhist cosmology) as "an arrangement of a center and its surrounding satellites" (ibid.: 73). Thus, the king's court is surrounded by lesser courts, each of which encompasses yet smaller courts. In the following exploration of infrastructures and delta ontologies in Southeast Asia, we are inspired by this integrated account of the cosmological, geometrical, political, and economic organization of galactic polities.

It is worth remarking on the scale of our analysis. As cultural anthropology became increasingly centered on ethnographic specificity and the explication of the minutiae of lived experience, macro-scale analysis and regional comparisons began to fall on hard times. Presently, works such as Karl Wittfogel's (1957) *Oriental Despotism*, which analyzed the general socio-political conditions of 'hydraulic societies', or Sumet[1] and Fuller's (1988) *Naga: Cultural Origins in Siam and the West Pacific*, which explored the emergence of culture out of watery environments, appear eccentric.

In fields related to anthropology, illuminating, large-scale analyses are nevertheless still written. For example, the environmental historian David Biggs (2010) has described the long-term environmental and infrastructural transformation of the Vietnamese Mekong Delta. However, the most relevant comparison for our purposes is James Scott's (2009) *The Art of Not Being Governed*. Scott's analysis focuses on Zomia, "the vast expanse of uplands" in Southeast Asia, "one of the largest remaining nonstate spaces in the world" (ibid.: 13). His 'anarchist' argument encompasses the vast inland territory behind the delta area with which we are concerned. Scott explores "a new genre of 'area' studies, in which the justification for designating the area has nothing to do with national boundaries … or strategic conceptions … but is rather based on certain ecological regularities and structural relationships that do not hesitate to cross national frontiers" (ibid.: 26). In Zomia, Scott tells us, environmental inaccessibility and political detachment go together. His aim is to understand the "fraught dialectical relations" between state centers and "zones of relative autonomy" (ibid.: 2).

While we are not out to develop a general political theory, we take inspiration from the argument that there is a connection between the environments in which people choose (or are forced) to live and their relations with state-making projects. In this regard, the significance of deltas is comparable to the mountain regions of Zomia. Yet while deltas are inhospitable, amphibious environments due to their location at the intersections of large rivers and the sea, this setting can also be ideal for trade and travel and crucial for state-making projects that rely on flows of money, people, and goods.

Below we explore new delta ontologies that emerged in the twentieth-century Thai Chao Phraya Delta due to infrastructure development. In particular, we trace a contrast between terrestrial and amphibious delta ontologies, which originated respectively in Europe and Southeast Asia. As multiple histories of agency—of traveling engineers, scientists and traders, of states and kingdoms, of canals and dikes, and of landscapes—became 'entangled', the Chao Phraya Delta gradually turned into an ontological palimpsest made of complexly layered terrestrial and amphibious infrastructures.

Delta Infrastructures

Between September and December 2011, the Chao Phraya Delta region in central Thailand experienced a devastating flood. The main cause was unusually heavy rainfall, estimated by hydrologists as a once-in-50-years probability (Komori et al. 2012). The flood hit major cities in the delta, including the World Heritage city of Ayutthaya, as well as industrial estates packed with hundreds of factories. Over 800 people died, and the World Bank estimated 1,425 billion baht ($45.7 billion) in economic damages.

The extreme 2011 flooding event revealed the vulnerability of modern infrastructures and the socio-economic development dependent on them (Morita 2015; cf. Mitchell 2002). These novel and distinctly modern forms of vulnerability are often contrasted with the resilience of traditional town planning that involves canals, water transportation, and buildings that are more adaptable to changing flows of water. Thus, the English newspaper the *Guardian* reported:

> In monsoon seasons past, villagers in Pa Mok would quietly embark on their annual vertical migration as the Chao Phraya river swelled and spilled over its banks, inundating rice paddies and neighbourhoods of this low-lying community in central Thailand. They moved to the upper level of their homes, which were built on three-metre high stilts.
>
> Then change rolled into town, around 45 years ago in the forms of cars, roads and a bridge … "Now they park their cars under the house, and they add an extra floor [of living space] under their homes," said Klanarong Chuaboonmee, 69, … "As someone working for the city, I get people asking me, 'Why don't you make it so we don't flood?'"[2]

Similarly, the innovative Thai architect Chutayaves Sinthuphanone reflected on the changes brought about by modernization: "When we look back at the history of settlements of Siam … we see that all of the settlements were situated along the rivers ... How did they cope with flood in the past? The obvious answer was that houses were built on stilts. Another obvious answer was that some of the homes were built as rafts."[3] These explanations point to changes in the design of delta infrastructures over the past 100 years that have dramatically influenced the adaptability of cities to floods. Yet it is not only the built environments that have changed. The 'natural' delta environments have also been transformed due to the extensive construction of water management facilities, such as irrigation dams and canals.

In the early twentieth century, the Dutch engineer J. Homan van der Heide (1903: 3) offered the following description of the delta scenery: "The plain, where not cultivated, is chiefly covered with jungle grass, where herds of elefants [*sic*] feed upon brushwood and bamboo. Extensive forests do not exist. Except in the highest tracts along the rivers, even clumps of trees are scarce, apparently in consequence of occasional floods and want of proper drainage." The difference between the present-day delta, where people live more or less comfortably, and the rough environment described by Homan van der Heide is obvious. In fact, the lower delta remained marshy and relatively unpopulated until the 1957 completion of the Chao Praya River Basin irrigation system, which Homan van der Heide had originally proposed in 1903.

Since the Chao Praya is extremely flat, it is inundated annually during the rainy season. Floods sweep away young trees and keep the plains permanently 'deforested'. In the dry season, the area becomes extremely arid because there are no trees to prevent water from evaporating. Lacking a proper network of canals, sluice gates, and operation centers until the mid-twentieth century, the delta posed severe difficulties for agriculture and was generally inhospitable to human settlements, except on natural levees along the river (Takaya 1987).

Over the past 60 years, the most prominent infrastructural change in the delta area has been the introduction of new irrigation systems and road networks (Morita 2015). Here we are witness to a double infrastructural transformation: a change in urban planning from canal to road centered, and a concomitant change of marshy lowlands into productive paddy fields. Yet it is not the case that 'modernity' has fully replaced 'tradition'. In many cases, new canals and ditches have not eliminated older ones, and the conversion of 'traditional' stilt houses into modern Western ones is not complete. Nor is this very surprising. Since infrastructures consist of a multiplicity of interlocking elements (canals, roads, sluice gates, houses, etc.), it is almost impossible to effect synchronous change. A more fitting image is of infrastructures running in parallel, sometimes entwining, and often taking the form of palimpsest, whereby new systems are added on top of older ones, rather than replacing them. The older forms, now underneath, remain opaquely discernible.

An excavation of Chao Phraya's infrastructural histories allows us to elicit delta ontologies in contrasting forms (cf. Jensen 2015; Jensen and Markussen 2008) and to shed light on the inter-delta networks that gave rise to them. In the following, by paying attention to the interplay between ideas, infrastructures, and deltas, we characterize two ontological 'histories of agency' (Pickering 1994). Western terrestrial ontology, shaped by colonial irrigation projects and techno-scientific expertise, imagined the potential of river deltas in terms of the possibility of land reclamation for agriculture. This led to an infrastructural orientation that focused on drainage and the construction of dikes. In contrast, the amphibious ontology affiliated with Southeast Asian galactic polities did not rely on an agricultural imagination (Brummelhuis 2005). Instead, deltas were primarily perceived and engaged as extensions of the sea, connecting inter-Asian trade networks (Hirosue 2004). This infrastructural orientation centered on water traffic, trade, and architectures capable of adapting to the flows of deltas.

The Land-Shaping Forces of Deltas and Rivers

Of Greek origin, the word 'delta' was adopted based on the similarity of the letter Δ (delta) and the estuary landform of the Nile River. When Herodotus wrote his *History* in the fifth century BCE, it was already used as a proper name. However, the term 'delta' did not acquire its generic meaning until Alexander's invasion of India, where similarly shaped landforms were found at large river mouths. Strabo, the Roman geographer, cited several Greek writers comparing the Nile Delta with the newly visited Indian alluvial areas. Francis Celoria (1966) has argued that the term gradually gained generic meaning through such comparisons. Thus, the Western concept of the delta was deeply embedded in the formation of inter-delta travel routes and encounters between different worlds.

Coining the well-known phrase "Egypt is the gift of the Nile," Herodotus (1890) observed that the mighty river transported soil to the delta, particularly during seasonal inundation. While we would not assume any direct continuity between ancient Greek usage and modern European sciences, it is still interesting to note the commonality between Herodotus's observations and much later views from hydrology and geomorphology (Leopold et al. 1964). What remains stable is a view of rivers as a central force in making landscapes. In fact, however, the modern focus on the power of rivers must be seen as a re-emerging insight, which early modern geology had lost. To bring into view some cosmological underpinnings of this understanding, we examine how agriculturalists and, later, geologists and geomorphologists came to terms with the histories of agency of earth and water.

The idea of creating land by controlling water, particularly through drainage, has long been an important agricultural concern in Western Europe. Wittfogel (1957) noted, with reference to China, that land reclamation by means of hydraulic infrastructures was not limited to Europe. Yet the European interest in reclamation exhibits some unique characteristics that tend to be marginalized in most of Asia. In contrast with China, where the emperor's power was premised on controlling huge irrigation networks spanning the semi-arid inlands, Europeans concentrated on reclaiming fenlands. They were more concerned with removing excessive water than with supplying it to areas of scarcity. This focus is epitomized in the Dutch lowlands, where large tracts of agricultural land were created using windmills and dikes. Originating in the Middle Ages, Dutch technology eventually spread all over Europe and turned the reclamation of swampy land into the core of much European agricultural development (Danner et al. 2005).

Since the early modern era, the power of water to shape landforms also gained significance in the transformation of Western cosmology. The discovery of the force of water, which slowly but relentlessly erodes rocks and removes earth, was important in this regard. While Herodotus observed that rivers transport soil, Ibn Sina (known as Avicenna in Europe) pointed out that landforms are shaped by erosion. His observations left a lasting legacy on European geological thought (Chorley 1969). The study of geological strata and of erosion contributed to the theory of 'uniformitarianism', which argues that mountains and valleys are slowly shaped by continuous geological forces. Geologists came to present the history of their discipline as one in which Enlightenment triumphed over myths, such as the Genesis creation story (Bowker 2005; Rudwick 1985).

However, the importance of rivers in these processes was not understood in detail until the mid-nineteenth century. Sir Charles Lyell, the father of modern geology, saw waves and tides as major forces in making landscapes. He observed that valleys and mountains had been shaped by sea currents at the time when islands and continents were submerged under the oceans. Only decades later, however, did geologists begin to recognize river flows as major land-shaping forces.

In the mid-twentieth century, the geographer Richard Chorley and his colleagues argued that the relatively slowly developing understanding of river forces was due to the 'temperate' environment in which most geologists resided. In such environments, waves are comparatively bigger than in sub-tropical and tropical regions, and their relation to coastal erosion is more plainly visible than that of river flow. In the view of Chorley et al. (1964), the recognition of river forces was prompted by the environmental encounter between colonial European geologists and huge tropical rivers, the cyclical flooding of which attested to their landscape-shaping capacities.

Over time, the major importance of fluvial forces in relation to erosion, transportation, and sedimentation was scientifically established. Furthermore, in the 1960s, geomorphological processes became tightly integrated with hydrological and hydraulic processes at the level of the 'drainage basin': the area drained by a river and its tributaries (Leopold et al. 1964). Geomorphology came to view the drainage basin as the fundamental unit of landform analysis, providing "a clearly defined, unambiguous unit, within which topography, hydrology and hydraulics [can] all be inter-related and studied in a nested systems approach" (Clifford 2011: 505). In the era of computer simulation, the drainage basin also became an important interface between geomorphology and other earth sciences (Morita 2017a; cf. Edwards 2010).

The Western geosciences have thus developed a sophisticated framework for studying the interplay of land and water. In contrast, land formation has not occupied an important place in Southeast Asian cosmologies, which emerged in the string of interconnected deltas situated between the Indian Ocean and the Western Pacific. In the next section, we turn to some relevant contrasts with the galactic polities of Southeast Asia.

River Basins and the Single Ocean

The idea of delta reclamation was not prominent in the vast region stretching from mainland and insular Southeast Asia to Japan. Here, hydraulic agriculture took place in inter-mountain basins located in the upper stream of rivers rather than downstream in the deltas. These basins provided continuous access to water. Networks of ditches designed to distribute water to the fields depended on steep gradients, which allowed farming communities to construct small-scale irrigation systems without massive investment. Zomia's landscape, stretching from northern Burma across northern Thailand and over to Yunnan in southern China, was dotted by principalities of Tai-speaking peoples, whose economic base in rice farming was made possible by such systems (Ishii 1978).

The cultural and economic position of delta communities was very different. Rather than relying on agriculture, their economic base was long-distance trade (Hirosue 2004; Ishii 1978). Referred to as 'port polities', these traditional states prospered by engaging in sea trade with merchants from China, Japan, India, and the Middle East. Rulers gained huge profits by exporting highly valued tropical forest produce collected from their hinterlands (Kathirithamby-Wells and Villiers 1990). Until the mid-nineteenth century, downstream rivers were mostly viewed as extensions of the sea.

John Michael Gullick (1958: 21) described the relation between port polities and rivers as follows: "The territory comprised in a State was related to ... the use of rivers as the main lines of communication and trade. A State was typically the basin of a large river or (less often) of a group of adjacent rivers, forming a block of land extending from the coast inland to the central watershed. The capital of the State was the point at which the main river ran into the sea. At this point the ruler of the State could control the movement of all persons who entered or left his State." In this trading system, rivers were crucial because they connected upstream areas with the sea. The prosperity of coastal port polities depended on their strategic position. Bennet Bronson (1977) and Masashi Hirosue (2004) both developed models of the river basin trading system, according to which the port cities that engaged in overseas trade were usually built at the estuary and thus depended on cities located midstream for the collection and transport of goods that were produced farther upstream. Although the aim of these scholars was to comprehend the flow of goods rather than the flow of water, they shared with hydrologists and geomorphologists an understanding of the river basin as the relevant unit of analysis (Hirosue 2004).

Crucially, delta land was of very limited importance within this system of exchange. In an ecological history of the Chao Phraya Delta, Yoneo Ishii (1978: 28) described the delta as "a belt of mud stretching between the continent and the sea, which, under natural conditions, is unsuitable for inhabitation." Its only conceivable use was as a space for transport. Maintaining this space required digging canals and extending naturally occurring flows of water, and the Ayutthaya and Bangkok dynasties both dug canals with great enthusiasm. In the early nineteenth century, extensive transversal canals connected the Tha Chin, Bang Pakon, and Maeklong rivers running parallel in the Chao Phraya Delta (Takaya 1987). Transversal canals facilitated the transport of sugar and pepper from Chinese-run plantations and enabled the easy dispatch of soldiers to the borderlands.

While trade goods came from upstream, much of the social and cultural life of the port polities was oriented toward the sea. The historian O. W. Wolters (1999: 44) refers to the Southeast Asian Sea as "the single ocean," a "vast expense of water from the coasts of eastern Africa and western Asia to the immensely long coastal line of the Indian subcontinent and on to China." In contrast with the Mediterranean, where seaborne trade was often monopolized by dominant powers, no empire ever succeeded in seizing control over this body of water. Wolters argues that indigenous rulers respected, and even insisted on, "the freedom of the seas" (ibid.: 46). When the Portuguese and the Dutch successively tried to monopolize trade, they met strong resistance from the port polities.

The freedom of the seas gave rise to traditions of hospitality to foreigners and to curiosity about new ideas and knowledge in the cosmopolitan port cities. Because prosperity depended on attracting foreign trade, "suitable port facilities, fair trading practices, and protection from sporadic piracy in local waters" (Wolters 1999: 46) were vitally important to the rulers. Foreigners were often appointed as administrators to provide facilities and services and to supervise trading and the management of the royal warehouses. In Ayutthaya, for example, both a Greek and a Persian held the position of the highest-ranked minister in charge of supervising trade. At lower ranks, Chinese, Portuguese, and Japanese nationals served as sailors on the king of Ayutthaya's merchant fleets, as managers of trading houses and warehouses, and as mercenaries (Ishii 1978).

Materializing the Galactic Polity

Amid this impressive diversity, Hindu-Buddhist cosmology served as a common ground for the political, social, and natural orders (Wolters 1999). Thus, the socio-cosmological form of galactic polity described by Tambiah is of particular interest. According to Tambiah's (1977: 73) influential analysis, Southeast Asian polities are patterned after the mandala and are "employed in multiple contexts to describe, for example: the structure of a pantheon of gods; the deployment spatially of a capital region and its provinces; the arrangement socially of a ruler, princes, nobles, and their respective retinues; and the devolution of graduated power on a scale of decreasing autonomies."

Wolters (1999: 15) argued that this cosmological pattern originated with the region's prehistoric settlements, which were comprised of "numerous networks of relatively isolated but continuously occupied dwelling sites" that depended upon one another for trade. According to his interpretation, the cosmology of galactic polities can be understood as an emergent effect of demography, geography, and trade. Similarly, we view delta ontologies as 'entanglements' of landscapes, cosmology, politics, and infrastructures.

Southeast Asian kingdoms generally assumed "the parallelism between Macrocosmos and Microcosmos, between the universe and the world of men" (Heine-Geldern 1942: 15). According to this scheme of galactic replication, individuals and social groups attain harmony and prosperity by following the given cosmological order. The central role of traditional states and kingships was to maintain this order by organizing city space, rituals and administrative forms. In the galactic polity, the king and his court were surrounded by lesser rulers (loosely corresponding to Bronson's and Hirosue's mid-size riverside towns). According to the principle of cosmological harmony, a king's power "was derived from a single and indivisible divine authority," and each ruler had a "unique claim to 'universal' sovereignty" (Wolters 1999: 27). Thus, rather than conceiving of a trade space in which export goods and water flow from upstream to downstream—as in Bronson's and Hirosue's models—the galactic model has divine authority emanating outward from the capital city and gradually receding with distance from the center.

The mythical location of the holy Mount Meru—surrounded by six rings of continents and seven rings of oceans—emphasizes the importance of the relation between water and land for this cosmology. The same relation reappears in the Thai coronation rite, where sacred water from all over the country is poured onto the king's head to consecrate his divinity. Not coincidentally, most of the rite is performed on a huge decorated raft surrounded by numerous ceremonial boats (Sumet and Fuller 1988).[4] But while the symbolic and political importance of water for the galactic polity can hardly be overestimated, the relation between cosmology and water goes deeper. In the Chao Phraya Delta, the radial flow of divinity also came to take on the form of infrastructure.

The extensive canals built by the Bangkok dynasty exhibit the entangled agencies of galactic polities and delta water flows. The cyclical changes of delta water flow made it possible to dig canals radially in all directions, creating trajectories along which sovereign power could travel. This, however, is also a point at which terrestrial and amphibious ontologies diverge. Indeed, some canals confound Western scientific and engineering expectations, as they neither serve any agricultural purpose nor divert water from upstream to downstream.

The earliest modern canal project in Thailand, the grid-like Rangsit network located northeast of Bangkok, was dug from south to north. The main canal extended northeastward without being connected to any river or canal at its end, thus blatantly disregarding the fundamental features of drainage basins. This strange layout was not 'corrected' until 1924 when new dam and canal constructions were carried out, not incidentally, by a foreigner. Yet from a galactic perspective, the peculiar radial design can be seen as a replication of the kingdom's cosmology at the level of topography. It was made possible by the extremely flat topology of the delta, which allowed the sea tide to influence the water flow far upstream. Galactic polities and delta water flows—two histories of agency that might appear radically disjointed—thus found an unlikely meeting point in amphibious infrastructure development.

Delta Palimpsest

In Thailand, interactions between forms of infrastructure and delta environments have given rise to what Andrew Pickering (1994: 201) has called "complex topological transformations." These transformations have shaped the boundaries between water and land, and between environments and people's modes of knowing, operating in, and transforming them.

The problems that Southeast Asia had with water were quite different from those faced by Europeans. Britain, the master of modern irrigation in the early twentieth century, did not need irrigation at home since rainfall was available year round. British irrigation technology was instead developed in India as part of a colonial effort to reconstruct deteriorated irrigation canals dug during the Mughal Empire (Headrick 1988). Similarly, Dutch technologies were useless in the hills and mountains of Java. After forced sugar cultivation had been introduced, Dutch engineers were required to build paddy field irrigation, which of course had no counterpart in the Netherlands.

In 1902, the government of Thailand, led by King Chulalongkorn (Rama V), invited Homan van der Heide to Bangkok. Due to the declining export of sugar, the Thai economy had become increasingly dependent on rice export (Yamamoto 1998). But although the idea of improving irrigation intrigued the king and a few ministers, it failed to arouse much political support. Indeed, the primary motive behind the king's invitation was that he wanted to introduce modern hydraulics to maintain the transversal canals (Brummelhuis 2005). Because of the delta's slight gradient, the effect of tides could be felt almost 100 kilometers upstream from the coast. The high tide caused stagnation or reversed flows, and this led to silt deposits on the riverbeds. The canals thus grew shallower. At the end of the nineteenth century, many were so silted that they could be traveled only at the highest tide, resulting in massive traffic problems and salt damage. The digging of smaller transportation canals by local people meant that salt water traveled farther inland.

After the submission of his 1903 report, Homan van der Heide was appointed as head of the newly founded Royal Irrigation Department. He drew up an ambitious plan for an irrigation scheme that would connect every existing canal in a coherent system by constructing a huge barrage at the midpoint of the Chao Phraya River. However, his grand ideas about agriculture improvement met with little enthusiasm. While he carefully designed sluice gates, dikes, and ditches in support of terrestrial agriculture, he was mainly allowed to repair, maintain, and upgrade the existing amphibious infrastructure. Rather than simply transforming amphibious infrastructures into terrestrial ones, his legacy was to layer infrastructures, recreating the ontology of the delta as a palimpsest.

In 1957, more than a half-century later, Homan van der Heide's vision finally came to fruition. Since then, the Chao Phraya Dam has diverted water from the main river course into the Noi and Tha Chin rivers as well as into new irrigation canals, which provide water all over the delta (Takaya 1987). In retrospect, his scheme thus did turn out to be an infrastructural turning point. Taking the form of new roads, sluice gates, dikes, and drainage, terrestrialization of the delta landscape has proceeded. The construction of an extensive highway net-work in the delta region since the 1960s, often built on top of waterways, has dramatically altered transportation patterns. Where people mainly used to sail, they now generally drive.

Modern infrastructure development has brought about something akin to a figure-ground reversal in Thai townscapes. Roads had previously been con-structed in parallel with but at some distance from the river. Thus, they faced the backyards of houses, the main entrances of which faced rivers and canals, the major traffic routes. With the increasing dominance of roads, this urban orientation literally turned around. Backyards became front entrances, while the traditional main entrances, facing the riverside boat slips, became back doors.

Meanwhile, the Chao Phraya irrigation system brought water to most parts of the delta. However, the new infrastructural set-up also diverted drainage into lower-lying places and exacerbated flooding there (Takaya 1987). The huge amount of water required for irrigation at the highest altitudes increased inun-dation elsewhere. Farmers responded by returning to traditional floating rice varieties that were able to keep pace with rise of water in the flooding season (Molle et al. 1999).

In his *Ethics*, Spinoza ([1677] 1959: 49) wrote that "bodies are reciprocally distinguished with respect to motion and rest, quickness and slowness, and not with respect to substance." Thus, the bodies of floating rice are distinguished by their ability to keep up with the quickness of rising water (Morita 2017b). In turn, the delta infrastructure dreamed up by a Dutch engineer shaped these flows. Moreover, this infrastructure, too, is a complex set of bodies, distinguished by their capacities to respond to the delta environments. And of course farmers and politicians are also engaged in processes of ongoing and reciprocal adjust-ment to the shifting demands of amphibious and terrestrial delta ontologies.

Despite the rapid development of terrestrial irrigation, however, amphibi-ous forms of agriculture *also* resurfaced in the period up to the 1990s. In places where traditional floating rice varieties are used and that depend on intensive labor for harvesting, dikes around paddy fields keep large amounts of water *within* the fields. Meanwhile, at the upper parts of the irrigation tract, dikes are built to *prevent* floodwater from entering into the paddy. These areas have turned to the use of high-yield short-stem rice varieties developed by the International Rice Research Institute (as part of the Green Revolution) and to mechanized harvesting (Molle et al. 1999).

We Do Not Yet Know What a Delta Can Do

In this chapter we have characterized two contrasting delta ontologies: one terrestrial and one amphibious. Since both were and are composed of incon-gruent relations and comparisons based on travels, this contrast does not correspond to the conventional dichotomy between universal Western science and particular regional cosmologies. According to Wolters (1999), the galactic polity emerged out of complex trading patterns between dispersed settlements that preceded Hindu-Buddhist cosmology. Due to the freedom of the single ocean and frequent travel between the scattered kingdoms of the region, the galactic pattern eventually became a 'regional universal'. Thus, traders and diplomats were able to witness the same political and cosmological order in numerous locations.

At the same time, Western scientific and engineering knowledge depended on travels that allowed for observations of similar landforms all over the world. Thus, the proper name for the Nile Delta became a general noun through comparison with Indian deltas, made possible by Greek military expeditions. Much later, Dutch reclamation efforts traveled across Europe. The delta infrastructures that British and Dutch empires developed in Indian and Java were very different from 'indigenous' European ones.

Homan van der Heide's Chao Phraya irrigation scheme is emblematic of knowledge modified by comparison. Before arriving in Thailand, he had traveled to Egypt, Japan, and Italy to study their systems (Brummelhuis 2005). His assessment of the potentials of the Chao Phraya relied on a constant comparative endeavor drawing on his travel experiences. In his *General Report on Irrigation and Drainage*, Homan van der Heide (1903) cited multiple sources, from William Willcocks's reports on the British modernization of Egyptian irrigation to Tokyo University's *Bulletin of the College of Agriculture*. Meanwhile, King Chulalongkorn read foreign texts on irrigation and canal systems, which led him to invite Homan van der Heide to his court. For both the king and the engineer, delta flows thus operated as what Stefan Helmreich (2011: 132) refers to as "a 'theory machine,' an object in the world that stimulates a theoretical formulation." Or, more precisely, several incongruent ones.

In the context of such entangled histories of agency, Helmreich (2011: 134) urges that attention to incongruent knowledges and practices must "constantly cut across and complicate our descriptive paths." Following this advice, we have described a process of transformation that has simultaneously shaped Western theories and practices of hydrology and geomorphology, Thai farming practices, and galactic cosmologies. Centrally, it has also created the Chao Phraya Delta as an ontological palimpsest, part terrestrial, part amphibious, neither quite nature nor quite culture. Helmreich makes the additional intriguing suggestion that the capacity of water to operate as a theory machine "depends on how quickly one frames it moving, flowing, with respect to 'culture'" (ibid.: 136), a formulation that resonates with Spinoza's argument that bodies are differentiated by motion and rest, quickness and slowness. We would only add that it also depends on which direction bodies like water and land are seen to be moving in. In terms of delta infrastructures it matters a great deal whether land is imagined to extend into the sea or vice versa.

The flow of water is thus not neutral. Nor, of course, is knowledge of it (Strathern 2004). Although Homan van der Heide's Chao Phraya scheme was shaped by unpredictable encounters with several deltas, his fundamentally Western imagination remained intact. While he had no compunction about pushing for irrigation and land reclamation schemes in Thailand, no Thai engineers were invited to the Netherlands to extend the sea into the land. Perhaps, however, as Europe itself becomes increasingly amphibious and prone to flooding, such invitations might yet be forthcoming.

By the turn of the twenty-first century, the Chao Phraya Delta seemed almost fully terrestrial. However, the huge floods of the 2000s made visible their co-existence with half-forgotten amphibious infrastructures. In 2006, the Royal Irrigation Department diverted waters into low-lying tracts in the Ayutthaya province to prevent the flooding of Bangkok. Announcing a call for 'volunteers' who would offer their land to retain excess floodwater, the Department proceeded to divert water to the Western lowlands of Ayutthaya and Suphanburi during the night, leaving farmers on top of their houses in a veritable lake of floodwater (Lebel et al. 2009: 286). Paradoxically, this maneuver simply foregrounded the resilience of supposedly outdated traditional buildings and infrastructures, making clear that the safety of Bangkok's terrestrial infrastructure is entirely dependent on amphibious retention zones. The floods of the 2000s thus brought to light some almost forgotten layers in the Chao Phraya Delta palimpsest, also making visible some rather strange inversions of terrestrial and amphibious infrastructures. Indeed, it is tempting to say that the flooding generated its own infrastructural comparisons (Morita 2014) and found the terrestrial ones wanting.

The occurrence of increasingly severe floods raises important questions about how to 'reconcile' terrestrial and amphibious infrastructure. These are questions about forms of knowledge, culture, and politics, to be sure, but they are mostly about the making of new delta worlds in which water, people, and other beings can find ways of living together. As Spinoza might say, we do not yet know what a delta can do, or what people can do with a delta, but finding out is an issue of increasing urgency.

Acknowledgments

This work was supported by the Japan Society for the Promotion of Science (JSPS) KAKENHI Grant No. 24251017 and No. 15K12957; Open Research Area for the Social Sciences (ORA) co-funded by JSPS, the Economic and Social Research Council (ESRC), the Nederlandse Organisatie voor Wetenschappelijk Onderzoek (NWO), and the Agence nationale de la recherche (ANR); and the Institute for Research in Humanities, Kyoto University.

Atsuro Morita is an Associate Professor of Anthropology at Osaka University. He has done ethnographic research on technology development in Thailand, focusing on how ideas, artifacts, and people travel in and out of Thailand. Together with Casper Bruun Jensen, he currently convenes the Japanese team of the Delta's Dealing with Uncertainty project. He is the author of *Engineering in the Wild* (Sekaishiso-sha, in Japanese) and editor of *Infrastructures and Social Complexity: A Companion* (2016, with Penny Harvey and Casper Bruun Jensen).

Casper Bruun Jensen is Project Associate Professor in the Department of Anthropology, Osaka University. He is the author of *Ontologies for Developing Things: Making Health Care Futures Through Technology* (2010) and *Monitoring Movements in Development Aid: Recursive Partnerships and Infrastructures* (2013, with Brit Ross Winthereik). He is also the editor of *Deleuzian Intersections: Science, Technology, Anthropology* (2009, with Kjetil Rödje) and *Infrastructures and Social Complexity: A Companion* (2016, with Penny Harvey and Atsuro Morita).

Notes

1. Following the convention in Thailand (and in Thai studies), Thai people are cited by first name.
2. "Floating Buildings Could Help Thais Tackle the Flooding Crisis," *Guardian*, 14 February 2012.
3. See http://asitespecificexperiment.wordpress.com/2011/05/12/amphibious-house (accessed 6 March 2017).
4. There are hardly any ceremonies in Thailand that do not involve the symbolic or actual use of water. Parades on water or boat races often pertain to seasonal and Buddhist ceremonies (Sumet and Fuller 1988).

References

Biggs, David A. 2010. *Quagmire: Nation-Building and Nature in the Mekong Delta*. Seattle: University of Washington Press.
Bowker, Geoffrey C. 2005. *Memory Practices in the Sciences*. Cambridge, MA: MIT.
Bronson, Bennet. 1977. "Exchange at the Upstream and Downstream Ends: Notes toward a Functional Model of the Coastal State in Southeast Asia." In *Economic Exchange and Social Interaction in Southeast Asia: Perspectives from Prehistory, History, and Ethnography*, ed. Karl L. Hutterer, 39–52. Ann Arbor: University of Michigan Press.
Brummelhuis, Han ten. 2005. *King of the Waters: Homan Van Der Heide and the Origin of Modern Irrigation in Siam*. Leiden: KITLV Press.
Celoria, Francis. 1966. "Delta as a Geographical Concept in Greek Literature." *Isis* 57 (3): 385–388.
Chorley, Richard J. 1969. "The Drainage Basin as the Fundamental Geomorphic Unit." In *Water, Earth and Man: A Synthesis of Hydrology, Geomorphology and Socio-economic Geography*, ed. Richard J. Chorley, 30–52. London: Methuen.

Chorley, Richard J., Antony J. Dunn, and Robert P. Beckinsale. 1964. *The History of the Study of Landforms: Or the Development of Geomorphology*. Vol. 1: *Geomorphology before Davis*. London: Methuen.

Clifford, Nick. 2011. "Rivers and Drainage Basins." In *The SAGE Handbook of Geographical Knowledge*, ed. John A. Agnew and David N. Livingstone, 502–527. London: Sage.

Danner, Helga S., J. Renes, B. Toussaint, G. P. van de Ven, and Frits D. Zeiler, eds. 2005. *Polder Pioneers: The Influence of Dutch Engineers on Water Management in Europe, 1600–2000*. Utrecht: Koninklijk Nederlands Aardrijkskundig Genootschap.

Edwards, Paul N. 2010. *A Vast Machine: Computer Models, Climate Data, and the Politics of Global Warming*. Cambridge, MA: MIT Press.

Gullick, John Michael. 1958. *Indigenous Political Systems of Western Malaya*. London: Athlone Press.

Headrick, Daniel R. 1988. *The Tentacles of Progress: Technology Transfer in the Age of Imperialism, 1850–1940*. Oxford: Oxford University Press.

Heine-Geldern, Robert. 1942. "Conceptions of State and Kingship in Southeast Asia." *Far Eastern Quarterly* 2 (1): 15–30.

Helmreich, Stefan. 2011. "Nature/Culture/Seawater." *American Anthropologist* 113 (1): 132–144.

Herodotus. 1890. *The History of Herodotus*. 2 vols. Trans. G. C. Macaulay. London: Macmillan.

Hirosue, Masashi. 2004. *Port Cities in Southeast Asia: The Formation of the Region and the World Order*. [In Japanese.] Tokyo: Iwanamishoten.

Homan van der Heide, J. 1903. *General Report on Irrigation and Drainage in the Lower Menam Valley*. Bangkok: Ministry of Agriculture, Kingdom of Siam.

Ishii, Yoneo, ed. 1978. *Thailand: A Rice-Growing Society*. Trans. Peter Hawkes and Stephanie Hawkes. Honolulu: University Press of Hawaii.

Jensen, Casper Bruun. 2015. "Experimenting with Political Materials: Environmental Infrastructures and Ontological Transformations." *Distinktion: Journal of Social Theory* 16 (1): 17–30. Special issue titled "Political Materials: Rethinking Environment, Remaking Theory."

Jensen, Casper Bruun, and Randi Markussen. 2008. "Mårup Church and Politics of Hybridization: On Choice and Becoming." In *The Mangle in Practice: Science, Society and Becoming*, ed. Andrew Pickering and Keith Guzik, 129–163. Durham, NC: Duke University Press.

Jensen, Casper Bruun, and Atsuro Morita. 2015. "Infrastructures as Ontological Experiments." *Engaging Science, Technology, and Society* 1: 81–87.

Kathirithamby-Wells, J., and John Villiers, eds. 1990. *The Southeast Asian Port and Polity: Rise and Demise*. Singapore: Singapore University Press.

Komori, Daisuke, Shinichirou Nakamura, Masashi Kiguchi, Asako Nishijima, Dai Yamazaki, Satoshi Suzuki, Akiyuki Kawasaki, Kazuo Oki, and Taikan Oki. 2012. "Characteristics of the 2011 Chao Phraya River Flood in Central Thailand." *Hydrological Research Letters* 6: 41–46.

Lebel, Louis, Bach Tan Sinh, Po Garden, Suong Seng, Le Anh Tuan, and Duong Van Truc. 2009. "The Promise of Flood Protection: Dikes and Dams, Drains and Diversions." In *Contested Waterscapes in the Mekong Region: Hydropower, Livelihoods and Governance*, ed. François Molle, Tira Foran, and Mira Käkönen, 283–305. London: Routledge.

Leopold, Luna B., M. Gordon Wolman, and John P. Miller. 1964. *Fluvial Processes in Geomorphology*. San Francisco: W. H. Freeman.

Mitchell, Timothy. 2002. *Rule of Experts: Egypt, Techno-Politics, Modernity*. Berkeley: University of California Press.

Molle, François, Sripen Durongdej, Chatchom Chompadist, Alexandre Joannon, and Yuphaa Limsawad. 1999. *Improvement of Rice Cultivation and Water Management in the Flooded Area of the Central Plain of Thailand: A Zoning of Rice Varieties by Using Remote Sensing Imagery.* Bangkok: Kasetsart University, DORAS Center.

Morita, Atsuro. 2014. "The Ethnographic Machine: Experimenting with Context and Comparison in Strathernian Ethnography." *Science, Technology & Human Values* 39 (2): 214–235.

Morita, Atsuro. 2015. "Infrastructuring Amphibious Space: The Interplay of Aquatic and Terrestrial Infrastructures in the Chao Phraya Delta in Thailand." *Science as Culture* 25 (1): 117–140.

Morita, Atsuro. 2017a. "From Gravitational Machine to Universal Habitat: The Drainage Basin and Amphibious Futures in the Chao Phraya Delta." *Engaging Science, Technology, and Society* 3: 259–275.

Morita, Atsuro. 2017b. "Multispecies Infrastructure: Infrastructural Inversion and Involutionary Entanglements in the Chao Phraya Delta, Thailand." *Ethnos* 82 (4): 738–757.

Pickering, Andrew. 1994. "Beyond the Great Divide: Transformations of Science and Its Context in World War II." In *Science and Power: The Historical Foundations of Research Policies in Europe*, ed. Luca Gazetti, 197–206. Brussels: European Commission.

Rudwick, Martin J. S. 1985. *The Great Devonian Controversy: The Shaping of Scientific Knowledge among Gentlemanly Specialists.* Chicago: University of Chicago Press.

Scott, James C. 2009. *The Art of Not Being Governed: An Anarchist History of Upland Southeast Asia.* New Haven, CT: Yale University Press.

Spinoza, Benedictus de. (1677) 1959. *Ethics.* London: J. M. Dent.

Strathern, Marilyn. 2004. "Laudable Aims and Problematic Consequences, or: The 'Flow' of Knowledge Is Not Neutral." *Economy and Society* 33 (4): 550–561.

Sumet Jumsai and R. Buckminster Fuller. 1988. *Naga: Cultural Origins in Siam and the West Pacific.* Oxford: Oxford University Press.

Tang, Alisa. 2012. "Floating Buildings Could Help Thais Tackle the Flooding Crisis." *Guardian*, 14 February 2012.

Takaya, Yoshikazu. 1987. *Agricultural Development of a Tropical Delta: A Study of the Chao Phraya Delta.* Trans. Peter Hawkes. Honolulu: University of Hawaii Press.

Tambiah, Stanley J. 1977. "The Galactic Polity: The Structure of Traditional Kingdoms in Southeast Asia." *Annals of the New York Academy of Sciences* 293 (1): 69–97.

Wittfogel, Karl A. 1957. *Oriental Despotism: A Comparative Study of Total Power.* New Haven, CT: Yale University Press.

Wolters, O. W. 1999. *History, Culture, and Region in Southeast Asian Perspectives.* Ithaca, NY: Southeast Asia Program Publications, Southeast Asia Program, Cornell University.

Yamamoto, Hiroshi. 1998. *A History of the Sugar Industry.* [In Japanese.] Tokyo: Ocanomizushobo.

Chapter 8

THE ONTOLOGICAL TURN
Taking Different Worlds Seriously

Andrew Pickering

> Reality will tolerate alternative descriptions without protest. We may say what we will of it, and it will not disagree.
>
> — Barry Barnes, *Rethinking Objectivity*, 31

> We cannot think first and act afterwards. From the moment of birth we are immersed in action, and can only fitfully guide it by taking thought. We have, therefore, in various spheres of experience to adopt those ideas which seem to work within those spheres.
>
> — Alfred North Whitehead, *Science and the Modern World*, 187

Different worlds—the fact that other social groups understand and act in the world differently from 'us'—have been with us for as long as there has been contact between cultures. They have been a topic of anthropology as long as the

Notes for this chapter begin on page 146.

field has existed. And yet there is something unsettling about them. Surely in the end there is just one world we all inhabit. It seems impossible to make sense of different worlds, even to take the idea of them seriously. During the twentieth century, the response was to not take them seriously. The problematic was defanged academically by adopting a social constructivist or relativist perspective. Following Durkheim's (1995) example, the different accounts of the world offered by this group or that were explained, and effectively explained away, as translations of social attributes of the groups in question. People might talk as if there were different worlds, but in fact the differences reside in us—they are unthreatening differences in social organization and relations, not in the non-human world we all inhabit. There's nothing very disturbing there after all. But in the twenty-first century, the social constructivist consensus has broken down, and both anthropology and science and technology studies (STS) have taken an ontological turn (e.g., Kelly 2014; Woolgar and Lezaun 2013, 2015). Now the aim is to confront different worlds as an unsettling fact rather than something to be explained away. My aim here is to sketch out my own attempt to take different worlds seriously and my own route through some of the issues raised. I begin in STS, because it is the field I know best and because it is where the problem of different worlds can seem most acute. I then tentatively extend the discussion to the anthropological territory of non-scientific worlds.

The theme of different worlds crashed into history and philosophy of science with the publication of Thomas Kuhn's (1962) *The Structure of Scientific Revolutions*. Kuhn's claim was that scientists working in different paradigms act as if they live in different worlds. His argument was that we should take this very seriously, although he conceded he was not sure what to make of it.[1] Instead, the dominant reaction was to shoot the messenger. The idea that scientists have historically inhabited different and 'incommensurable' worlds threatened standard narratives of a certain sort of rationality as the hallmark of science, provoking a rash of philosophical rejections of Kuhn's arguments—he must be just wrong (Hollis and Lukes 1982; Lakatos and Musgrave 1970). Sociologists were less dogmatic. Within the frame of the strong program in the sociology of scientific knowledge, the different worlds thesis could be tolerated, on the understanding, as above, that these worlds were social constructs, projections of the social onto nature (Barnes and MacKenzie 1979). As in anthropology, the twenty-first century has seen an impulse in STS to take different worlds more seriously than that, usually marked by phrases such as 'multiple ontologies' (e.g., Law and Lien 2013; Mol 2002), although the field of examples is less striking and seems less pressing than those offered by Kuhn. In the introductory article of a special 'ontology' issue of *Social Studies of Science*, for instance, Steve Woolgar and Javier Lezaun (2013) focus on 'the wrong bin bag' as a deflationary example of ontological multiplicity.[2]

I have long argued that one can indeed find instances of different worlds—multiple ontologies—in the history of science (e.g., Pickering 1984b), and I want now to examine why this idea is unsettling and to develop a way of thinking about it. I am interested in taking different worlds seriously rather than conjuring them away. The important analytic move, for me, is from what

I call the representational idiom for thinking about science to a performative idiom (Pickering 1995b: 7).

The representational idiom is our usual way of thinking about science, namely, as a set of representations of nature, and this is the way of thinking that makes the idea of different worlds hard to swallow. Representations are sharp-edged things that evoke a sharp-edged nature to go with them. Either our representations are true to nature or they are not; either nature more or less matches our descriptions of it or it does not. Is the world built out of quarks, or have the physicists got it wrong? Different representations cannot all be right, so the idea that different worlds are genuinely to be found in the history of science must be at best an illusion. This line of thought is at the heart of the philosophical rejection of Kuhn's different worlds. Or, of course, at the other extreme, perhaps nature is not really sharp-edged. Maybe it is foggy and amorphous, so the sharpness of our representations comes not from nature but from culture—in which case we arrive back at social constructionism and cultural relativism.[3]

My work in the history of science convinced me that we can never get satisfactorily to grips with scientific research practice in the representational idiom. Instead, we need, in a performative idiom, to think about practice, performance, and agency—doing things—and I want to sketch out briefly how the analysis goes before returning to the question of different worlds. Scientists, I argue, are lively agents in a lively world (Pickering 1995b). We act in the world, and the world acts on us, to and fro, in a dynamic process I call the 'dance of agency', in which all the partners are unpredictably and emergently transformed. This is how scientists genuinely find out about the world. There is nothing mysterious about this. It is just how things go in science and, indeed, everywhere else.

One of my earliest examples concerned Donald Glaser's invention of a new instrument for experimental particle physics, the bubble chamber (Pickering 1993; 1995b: chap. 2). Over a period of a couple of years in the early 1950s, Glaser, as an active human agent, would put together some configuration of apparatus. Then he became passive while the agency of the material object took over, standing back with a movie camera in his hand to see what his latest set-up would do. Switching back, Glaser would react to whatever the machine's performance turned out to be—which was usually not what he wanted (on a scale from inaction to explosion)—and the dance of agency would continue. Its upshot was a new instrument that did new things in a new way, revealing the trajectories of elementary particles as strings of bubbles and winning Glaser a Nobel Prize. At the same time, Glaser was himself transformed: shifting from small science to big science, becoming the leader of a sizable group, becoming famous, changing his ideas about how bubbles form and what bubble chambers should look like, and moving from one sub-field, cosmic ray physics, to another, accelerator-based experiments. A new object and its powers, the bubble chamber, and a new human with new individual and social attributes, Glaser, came into being together and in relation to one another.

This example, like many others, is very straightforward, and I want to generalize from it. The world—humans, non-humans, and whatever—just is an indefinite multiplicity of performative entities endlessly becoming in decentered and emergent dances of agency.[4] This is the ontological picture I want to dwell on. I want first to connect it back to the problematic of different worlds in science before situating it with regard to the ontological turn more generally. I then need to add a new concept—'islands of stability'—which can serve as a pivot from STS to anthropology.

What of different worlds? The point to note is a very simple one: connotations of necessary uniqueness vanish when we move from the representational to the performative idiom (Pickering 1995b: chap. 6). If knowledge demands to be true or false, our performative tracks through history do not. Who knows where dances of agency can take us? We have no clear intuitions about this; we just have to look and find out. And it turns out, for example, that in particle physics in the 1970s, one can document two quite different social, material, and conceptual trajectories of development, which physicists referred to as the old and the new physics. Each had its own distinctive range of machines, instruments, and practices that evoked quite different natural phenomena and spoke to disjoint realms of theory. The old and new physics are thus nice examples of Kuhn's different paradigms as different worlds, different ontologies (Pickering 1984b: chap. 14).[5]

If we remained in the representational idiom, we would have to say that the old and new physics theories described quite different worlds, quite different ways that nature might be, and thus that one or the other (or both) must be wrong. In the performative idiom, in contrast, it seems much less problematic to see the two paradigms as two different 'machinic grips' on nature, the existence of which demonstrates, as an empirical discovery, that there is more than one way to 'tune' ourselves performatively into a lively nature (Fleck 1979; Pickering 1995b). All the puzzlements that attach to the different worlds thesis in the representational idiom are defused, and in the performative idiom it becomes possible to take seriously different worlds in the history of science. Generalizing, the conclusion—the discovery—is that the world just is the sort of place that we can latch onto performatively in many different ways, each of which hangs together with a distinctive story about it (Pickering 2015). That is the key point, which I will return to and elaborate throughout this chapter.

The Ontological Turn

At this point, I should try briefly to situate my analysis with respect to the wider ontological turn in STS and anthropology. Obviously, my perspective is in much the same space as many other non-dualist accounts. This is not the place to go into details, but I hope the following remarks are useful as triangulation.

My ontology is a symmetric one of a multiplicity of reciprocally coupled emergent agents, human and non-human.[6] Clearly, my shift to the performative idiom and my references to the liveliness of the non-human world fit well with approaches that come under headings like the 'new vitalism' or 'new materialism' (e.g., Bennett 2010; DeLanda 2002). What is added to them here is an analysis of how lively human beings are coupled into this lively world—the dance of agency. This moves my analysis into the space of Karen Barad's (2007) relationalism. One difference here might be that my analysis foregrounds the temporal evolution of relational entities. As far as temporality is concerned, there is an affinity between my ontological analysis and Daniel Miller's thinking on dialectical relations between people and things and the co-constitution of both (see, e.g., Miller 2010: chap. 2). In my earlier work I referred to the dance of agency as a dialectic of resistance and accommodation (Pickering 1993, 1995b). Missing from that phrase and perhaps Miller's analysis is a sense of productive latching onto emergent non-human agency (rather than simply friction). Miller's topics and examples (material culture studies) are different from my own (beginning in science studies), and my analyses began from more fine-grained studies than his.

On the other hand, my approach departs markedly from methodological approaches to anthropology that propose to treat things simultaneously as concepts (e.g., Henare et al. 2007: chap. 1; Holbraad 2011). My ontology does not arise from contemplating bubble chambers—or whatever—as somehow both things and concepts. It comes from recognizing them as performative agents, positioned and emergent in engagements with other agents (human scientists). A similar remark applies to all aspects of the ontological turn that center on hybrid terms like 'material-semiotic' and 'nature-culture' (e.g., Haraway 2004).[7] For better or worse, my approach takes off from performances and performative interactions that may, but also may not, include a significant linguistic, semiotic, conceptual component. My analysis gets into focus something more immediate than words.

We could come at this from another angle. The ontological turn of the twenty-first century, at least in STS, grew out of a prior turn to practice from the 1980s onward (Pickering 1992). I once argued that it makes a difference if the word 'practice' has a plural (Pickering 1995b: 4). Studying 'practices' (plural) means looking in detail at particular relatively well-defined ways of doing this or that, in science, math, industry, or whatever. My example was the 'plasmid prep' in molecular biology, explored by Kathleen Jordan and Michael Lynch (1992). By 'practice', in contrast, I meant a generic structure of doing research, which I claimed to have analyzed. The same point can be made about ontology. Studying ontologies (plural) begins with detailed studies of 'found' ontologies, the ontology of this group or that. In anthropology, Viveiros de Castro (2004) takes Amazonian ontologies seriously to reflect back critically on our own ontology, Western dualism. Philippe Descola (2014: 275) offers a four-fold typology of ontologies—animism, totemism, analogism, and naturalism—which he sees as four different organizing principles for both society and nature. Bruno Latour's (1993) typology is even shorter: modern and non-modern. The moderns make a clean dualist split between people and things; the non-moderns do not. In science and technology studies, and harking back to the 'practice turn', one finds an insistence that ontologies are not simply schemes of classification and representation; they are enacted or performed in practice (Law and Lien 2013; Mol 2002).[8]

Much of the ontological turn thus occupies itself with ontologies in the plural: the different worlds that turn up in ethnographic studies.[9] This indeed marks a determination to take different worlds seriously. But a certain puzzlement still remains (to my mind, at least): what sort of world, in the singular, could possibly sustain all these different ontologies, in the plural?[10] And I am thus interested in ontology without a plural, and with questions of what the world is like—what sorts of entities make it up, and how do they relate to one another?—in general and independently of what our informants say about it. My question is, what sort of world could sustain a multiplicity of ontologies in the plural? Even to ask the question might strike many people as ridiculous. It certainly smacks of philosophical hubris, although in fact I think it leads in the opposite direction, to put us in our place. Anterior to Latour's (1987, 2005) thoughts on modern and non-modern ontologies, for example, is actor-network theory (ANT), which is an ontology in the singular, without a plural. The world just is built from networks of human and non-human actors (agents, actants). That is the general ontological conclusion Latour and his ANT colleagues have drawn from their studies. That is the way things everywhere always have been, are, and will be, according to ANT. Non-modern ontologies (in the plural) typically recognize an ANT-style entanglement of the human and the non-human (while dressing it up in all sorts of ways). We moderns are equally entangled, but processes of 'purification' veil this fact from us (Latour 1993). So the ANT ontology (in the singular) puts us in our place—cuts us moderns down to size and situates us on a level with the non-moderns and the non-humans. We are a bit peculiar simply in being unable to recognize the ontological condition we in fact share with everyone and everything else.

My work owes much to ANT, and my thinking here on ontology in the singular (I will drop this qualification from now on) is in much the same space as ANT. It is hard to mark any sharp departures from ANT, not least because of the wide range of territory it has covered and the wide variety of assertions and analyses that have appeared under the ANT banner. I have discussed some points of divergence elsewhere (Pickering 2009). Much of Latour's best known work approaches questions of representation from novel angles, while the ontological picture I am developing here is more determinedly focused on questions of agency, performance, and temporality. Politically, Latour is an admirer of modernity and wants to improve its modes of political representation.[11] I am less enthusiastic, and this correlates with my interest in different worlds (Pickering 2010).[12] In what follows, I return to the performative perspective on different worlds and take it further.

Islands of Stability

Something needs to be added now to my ontology of dances of agency. Science and engineering seek to organize these dances in a peculiar and distinctive way. Scientists like Glaser plunge into dances of human and non-human agency, but always with the object of escaping from them. The telos—the defining objective—of science and engineering is to end them. Glaser wanted to construct a free-standing machine, one that would work independently of him, that he would no longer need to tinker with. That is what he won the Nobel Prize for. In that sense, he succeeded in making the world more dual than he found it. Now it included a new and reliable machine, the bubble chamber, that would predictably obey the will of its human masters—the paradigmatic asymmetric dualist relation imagined by Descartes. That we are, in modernity, surrounded by free-standing machines like that, and that our social worlds are built around them, goes a long way toward explaining the hold that a taken-for-granted dualism has over us. Our made world echoes an asymmetric dualism back to us.[13]

But how can we square the existence of reliable, free-standing machines with my ontology of decentered becoming? I want to say that the success of science and engineering (and all sorts of other practices) shows us that there are what I call islands of stability in the flux of becoming—configurations, socio-material set-ups—where some sort of reliable regularity in our relations with nature is to be found. This, for me, is an ontological discovery. I cannot see that nature had to be that way, but the history of science and technology shows us that it is.

These islands of stability, the ground of our productive engagements with the world, are central to human existence, and they deserve much more attention than I can give them here (see Pickering 2014, 2015). Typically, we take the existence of reliable machines and instruments—bubble chambers, cars, computers—for granted. If we reflect on them at all, we return to the representational idiom and assume that someone somewhere knows how they work and that that knowledge underpins their construction and functioning. But this is a mistake. Arriving at an island of stability is not a once-and-for-all achievement guaranteed by knowledge. These islands remain fragile and uncertain performative accomplishments requiring continual repair and maintenance (Swanton 2013), mini-dances of agency. We are always struggling to stay on them, and sometimes we fall off. Think of the Deepwater Horizon oil spill in the Gulf of Mexico in 2010, or the catastrophic meltdown of the nuclear reactors at Fukushima in 2011, or the massive explosion of stored chemicals in Tianjin in 2015. Such disasters in turn provoke new dances of agency, now seeking to put the genie back in the bottle and to reassert dualist mastery. And our mastery is sometimes, perhaps always, accompanied by a performative excess. Power stations do what we intend them to do (generate energy) but also what we do not intend them to do (generate carbon dioxide and global warming). The flux of becoming never goes away, although we readily forget it.

Returning to my theme, thinking in terms of performative islands of stability is again an antidote to our intuitions of uniqueness. I have no idea how many islands there are, but the divergent histories of the old and the new physics (and many stories like that) make it clear that there are plenty. We can readily imagine an endless number of different worlds founded on different constellations of islands. Here in the West we live on one set of islands; in the Amazon rainforest the Yanomami live on another. The switch to the performative idiom and the ontology of decentered becoming, accompanied by the concept of islands of stability, help us to appreciate this in a non-skeptical fashion, to take it seriously. That the world is such as to support a multiplicity of constellations is indeed something we should wonder at. But in the performative idiom we can grasp how it might be: different worlds no longer appear as a contradiction in terms as they do in the representational idiom.

Shamanism and Science

I now want to leave my home ground of Western science and technology and to venture onto the wider terrain of anthropology in a very tentative discussion of islands of stability in other cultures, including Yanomami shamanism. My ontology is one of endless performative flux and becoming in a space of multiplicity, punctuated by islands of stability. The impulse to find these islands must be quite general. At some level, we all need to find and maintain human-nonhuman configurations that are relatively predictable and dualistic, where we can more or less rely on causes and effects. Even birds and ants build nests. But we could entertain the thought that the telos of finding stability can vary to some extent.

Very crudely, my idea is that the modern West is relatively distinctive in its insistence that its islands of stability are also zones of human mastery where the world performs as a predictable machine. This asymmetric dualism is a hallmark of modernity. In other times and places, the insistence on getting rid of any trace of emergence and unpredictability in nature is less obsessive, and islands of stability can have a different character. Especially, I want to note that stability does not have to entail squeezing all the agency out of the world (or, better, somehow sidelining and then forgetting it) as we do. One thing that ethnographic studies show us is that islands of stability can, in fact, encompass lively non-human worlds that can always surprise us, for better or for worse. The non-human can encompass zones of fear, hope, and magic, non-machine-like worlds that are edited out of modernity.

For example, as I understand it, in everyday life Amazonians are as dualist as the rest of us, in the sense of readily and routinely distinguishing between humans and non-humans, plants and animals, and so on. But this is not a principled Cartesian dualism that marks a difference in kind and an asymmetry of control. Humans and animals are really the same, just clad in different flesh. The animals, like the humans, remain genuine agents in Amerindian cosmologies—unpredictable and dangerous—and the wrong kind of interaction with them can lead to crossovers from the human to the animal realm, becoming animal. So while these people have indeed achieved a stable modus vivendi with their environment, it is not one of dualist mastery. Non-human agency remains ever present, to be feared and continually warded off (Viveiros de Castro 2004).

I can take this line of thought to an extreme by reference to Davi Kopenawa's first-person account of Yanomami shamanism (Kopenawa and Albert 2013). What marks Kopenawa out as a shaman is precisely his access to a different world, a world populated by spirits known as *xapiri*. Kopenawa can see the spirits, communicate and engage with them. They come to live with him, and they instruct and aid him in his life. And the *xapiri* are performative agents—curing and exacting revenge, hunting and gathering fruit, keeping gardens and dealing with the weather. The shaman calls on them, but the *xapiri* do the work that humans alone cannot do.

What can we make of this? In my terms, there is an island of stability here. Kopenawa can reliably and repeatedly access a world populated by *xapiri*. He knows how to do it and what to expect—just like particle physicists when accessing their world of quarks and leptons. We can also speak of a certain duality here. On this island, it is crucial to Kopenawa that the *xapiri* are independent non-human entities, not human beings or aspects of himself. But it is also crucial that the *xapiri* are genuine agents—profound and often dangerous and terrifying ones, easily alienated, unlike controllable and predictable machines such as bubble chambers. Here, then, we have another dualist island of stability, but another kind of island from those of the modern West. It is an island, a world, from which the agency of the non-human world has not been entirely squeezed out and tamed. Within the shamanic assemblage, the liveliness of nature is instead foregrounded, celebrated, feared, and taken advantage of.

This contrast between what we could call the symmetric dualism of Yanomami shamanism and the asymmetric dualism of Western science (and Western common sense) is worth thinking about. On the one hand, we should note that in the representational idiom the spirit world of the shaman is entirely refractory to Western thought. Modern science has no resources for imagining that *xapiri* spirits exist. They can at most be some sort of projections onto nature by the Yanomami. On the other hand, and as above, there is no difficulty in taking the contrast seriously in the performative idiom. Just like the divergent paths taken in particle physics in the 1970s, but in more extreme form, the Yanomami track through the emergent performativity of nature has led them to islands of stability other than ours. From a performative perspective, this is a striking fact, but not ungraspable or self-contradictory.

What this story shows, then, is that the shift to the performative idiom offers us some conceptual elbow room for grasping and taking seriously the possibility of multiple ontologies, not only within science and the modern West, but also across the territory of anthropology. It helps us to comprehend the fact that a single nature might sustain many worlds and to appreciate the possibility of different stances, different ways of being in the flow, that dualize nature in different ways, respectively backgrounding or foregrounding non-human agency. There is nothing mysterious about this, although it is hard not to wonder that we live in such a place.

We might also think about 'progress' here. The standard representationalist position is that modern science is progressive simply in dispelling mistaken beliefs in *xapiri* or whatever. We could reformulate this in the performative idiom by arguing that moving from symmetry to asymmetry is what progress is about. We moderns are better than the rest precisely in getting the upper hand and achieving our own sort of asymmetric duality and machine-like control of nature. Against that, one might argue that modernity needs more fear. We should not overdraw the contrast between 'them' and 'us'. As I noted above, our islands of stability are themselves chancy performative achievements. We might be better off understanding bubble chambers and nuclear power stations as temperamental spirits like the *xapiri*—powerful entities with which we can engage productively but which are always liable to let us down badly. That would help us to get the unpredictable liveliness of nature into focus and to recognize the fragility of our Cartesian islands of stability and the catastrophes and disasters mentioned above that are the dark side of the illusion of mastery. Then we might act differently. That might be the practical politics of ontology in the performative idiom.[14]

Altered States

The discussion of shamanism puts me in a position to emphasize an aspect of the notion of islands of stability that might not yet be sufficiently clear. The temptation is to think of them like real islands that one finds in rivers or seas, entities that are just there, independently of us. Central to my analysis of the dance of agency, however, is that we ourselves are transformed in tuning ourselves into the emergent agency of the world, and that these islands are thus decentered joint products of the human and the non-human. That they sustain a duality of people and things does not efface the coupled transformations that lead up to and away from them. I have tried briefly to express the fact that we are ourselves at stake and liable to transformation in finding these islands by emphasizing the social transformations that Glaser underwent, often reluctantly, en route to the bubble chamber. I think those changes are important to recognize, but they can easily seem unremarkable and not worthy of reflection, akin, say, to finding a new job.

Kopenawa's account of Yanomami shamanism offers us a more striking example to think about. He makes it clear that becoming a shaman entails much more than finding a new job, a new social role. It calls for an intense inner transformation, finding a new self or subject position. As Kopenawa describes in detail, accessing the world of the *xapiri* entails an arduous and multi-dimensional technology of the self, in Foucault's (1988) terms—a regime of abstinence from company, sex, and some or all foods, complex rituals, a hallucinogenic resin (*yakoana*), and near-death experiences.[15] Clearly, then, the strange experiences of the shaman depend on and stabilize an altered state of being, very different from the everyday state of Amazonians or Englishmen. The *xapiri* and the specific altered state of the shaman are two sides of the same coin, collectively constituting this specific sort of symmetric dualist island of stability.

Various comments are appropriate here. I have contrasted physicists and shamans, but now I can qualify the contrast. The *xapiri* are hard to contact, but not many of us can commune with quarks and leptons either. It requires years of training, education, and experience to be in a position to do so.[16] It would be fruitful to take seriously an idea of physicists (and scientists in general) as Western shamans: they are the people who can visit certain sorts of exotic islands of stability for us and report back to us on other worlds. But two differences between science and shamanism remain worth contemplating, both of which concern the anthropological problematic of translation, that is, bringing home other cultures. It is worth emphasizing that neither of these would need discussion in the representational idiom with its focus on words, representations, meanings, and symbolism,[17] but both are pressing if we want to take different worlds seriously as genuine performative engagements of the human and non-human.

On one side, there is a sense in which anyone can see the products of scientific research. Not so long ago, bubble chamber images of particle tracks were on sale as postcards at CERN. As Latour (1987) has argued, scientific research aims to produce immutable mobiles—representations and images that can travel freely. The same cannot be said of shamanism. There are no photographs of *xapiri* to be handed around and examined as part of anthropological scholarship. There are only 'subjective' accounts from shamans like Kopenawa, unverifiable by the non-shamanic anthropologist. And subjective accounts are what scientists seek to exclude from their discourse. So there is a major problem for the anthropologist in bringing home shamanic islands of stability. To take them seriously requires somehow crediting that which should not be credited. The anthropological dilemma is to be trapped between explaining these islands away (as in social constructivism) or leaving the realms of 'objective' science.

From the second angle, the problem is worse. The West is well organized to discredit stories of other worlds, casting them as defective apprehensions, the products of deranged minds—the mad and drug users. Such visions do not correspond to anything that exists, and the seer should be helped to stop seeing them, with anti-psychotic drugs and drug rehabilitation programs. So bringing home shamanic islands of stability requires taking seriously non-modern versions of the self that are devalued and stigmatized in modernity, not least in academia. No doubt, shamanic stories do resonate with many people in the contemporary West, but they are visionaries, mystics, New Agers, recreational drug users and drug addicts, and people verging on one of the many mental illnesses to which modernity is prone—hardly the company one wants in a 'sober' inquiry into ontology and what the world is like.[18] Or, to put it the other way round, taking shamanism seriously as genuine performative engagement with the world (rather than a representational system) would require a reconfiguration of foundational Western hierarchies of approval and disapproval.

There are, then, major problems entailed in taking other ontologies seriously and bringing them back home. Conversely, anthropology might be instrumental in dislodging the taken-for-grantedness of the modern self and the social structures it reinforces.

Beyond the Islands

One final thought on different worlds. So far, the focus has been on the different sorts of islands of stability that characterize different cultures. But we can note that there are cultures that do not center themselves on islands like these at all. In the West, the mainstream sciences taught in school certainly focus on stable machines, stable instruments, and stable knowledge, and stability and reliability are, of course, hallmarks of modern technology and engineering. But the sciences of complexity, for example, foreground emergent, unpredictable processes and help us think about the world more generally as an unpredictably and open-endedly emerging assemblage (Gleick 1987; Kauffman 2002; Waldrop 1992; Wolfram 2002). And I have argued at length that one branch, at least, of cybernetics can be understood as a science of the unknowable, centered on devices that can adapt to the unexpected rather than dominating a world already known (Pickering 2010). These sciences and associated branches of engineering, then, share to some degree the ontology (in the singular) of decentered becoming that this chapter is predicated on (while narrowing it in various ways and then adding to it mathematically).

Many philosophies point in a similar direction. Like cybernetics, Taoism and Zen emphasize graceful adaptation to an emergent world and real-time responses to the moment (Lao Tzu 1963; Watts 1957, 1975; Wilhelm 1967). They also emphasize performance over representation in a way that is echoed by the switch from the representational to the performative idiom. Everyday knowledge and reflection get in the way of the spontaneity valued in Taoism and Zen. Going beyond cybernetics and echoing Kopenawa, they also focus on altered states as integral to their plateau, one might say, of non-stability: meditation as a key technology of the self and, ultimately, enlightenment as the loss, without any replacement, of the everyday self.

This is as far as I can go with this line of thought. I hope to have shown that the switch from a representational to a performative idiom and the concept of islands of stability open up space for an ontology of decentered becoming, in the singular, that can help us to take multiple ontologies seriously, in ways that, in the end, reflect back both critically and constructively—and politically—on our dominant ways of thinking, being, and acting in modernity.

Acknowledgments

I am grateful to an anonymous reader for critical remarks on the first draft of this chapter and to Casper Bruun Jensen for telling me about Kopenawa's book. This work was supported in part by a National Research Foundation of Korea Grant, funded by the Korean Government (NRF-2013S1A3A2053087).

Andrew Pickering is a Professor Emeritus of Sociology and Philosophy at the University of Exeter. His field is science and technology studies, and his current research focuses on art, agency, the environment, and traditional Chinese philosophy. His publications include *The Cybernetic Brain: Sketches of Another Future* (2010), *The Mangle in Practice: Science, Society, and Becoming* (2008), *The Mangle of Practice: Time, Agency, and Science* (1995), *Science as Practice and Culture* (1992), and *Constructing Quarks: A Sociological History of Particle Physics* (1984).

Notes

1. In his later writings Kuhn (e.g., 1991) approached the problematic of different worlds through an analysis of language. He thus remained within the frame of what I call the representational idiom.
2. This deflationary impulse is typical in STS. Sismondo (2015: 441) argues that the "difference between this ontological turn and constructivist work in Science and Technology Studies appears to be a matter of emphases found useful for different purposes." Aspers (2015: 449) likewise argues that "there is no fundamental qualitative difference between the ontological turn and what we know as constructivism." To be clear, my argument here is that taking ontology seriously marks a big and important difference from constructivism.
3. Thus, Shapin's (1979: 139) constructivist analysis of nineteenth-century controversies around phrenology begins with an image of seeing pictures in the clouds from *Hamlet*. Collins (1992: 16) likewise speaks of seeing pictures in the fire in developing his relativist analysis of scientific knowledge.
4. I should emphasize that I do not exclude scientific knowledge from this story. In *The Mangle of Practice* (1995b), I analyze ways that knowledge is bound up and transformed in performative dances of agency. Drawing on detailed case studies in physics and mathematics, I also analyze purely conceptual developments as dances of agency in themselves. In subsequent work, I have extended the analysis to more accessible topics, including major technoscientific transformations in the nineteenth century and World War II (1995a, 2005b), invasive species (2005a), the Mississippi River and painting (2008), and bonsai (2013).
5. The old physics was the dominant mode of doing physics that had evolved since World War II. The new physics became the 'standard model' now taken for granted. To be more specific about technicalities (Pickering 1984b), the switch between the old and new physics entailed (1) a switch between different sorts of machines, from fixed-target particle accelerators to colliding beams; (2) new geometries of experimental particle detectors, singling out rare hard-scattering events from common soft-scattering interactions; and (3) computer filtering of data, rejecting almost all the phenomena of interest in the old physics. These changes at the level of experiment isolated rare phenomena exclusively of theoretical interest in the new physics of quarks, leptons, quantum field theory, and the unification of forces.
6. The symmetry here is at the level of agency as performance: we do consequential things in the world; so do bubble chambers, cats, rocks, and stones. This differs from the humanist identification of 'agency' with will and intention. My argument is that the latter are themselves 'mangled' in dances of agency. They are not independent causes or privileged centers of explanation (Pickering 1995b).
7. Likewise, the central object of my analysis is not the 'entanglement of matter and meaning' (Barad 2007). As noted above, I am happy to include concepts, meanings, and so forth in my analysis of practice, but these occupy no special place in the performative dances of agency I focus on.
8. My early studies of controversies in recent physics can be read as detailed accounts of the enaction of multiple ontologies, although the phrase was not current then. These include charmed quarks (1981c), free quarks (1981b), magnetic monopoles (1981a), weak neutral currents (1984a), and the old and new physics (1984b).
9. In history and philosophy of science, see also Hacking (2002) and Klein and Lefèvre (2007).
10. Salmond (2014) reviews many of the philosophical arguments around multiple ontologies, but the arguments and discussion are framed primarily within the

traditional representational idiom that begins with knowledge, meaning, language, and translation.

11. For a political critique of Latour, see Fortun (2014).
12. Latour's discussions of non-human performance typically circle around his important but relatively undeveloped concept of laboratory 'trials'. His early work focuses on the length of actor-networks: we moderns have long ones, the non-moderns short (Latour 1987). His more recent writing dissects different 'modes of existence' within modernity itself—science, law, religion, and so on—but there is little ontologically puzzling or unsettling about them (Latour 2013).
13. This idea of 'making dual' clearly relates to Latour's concept of 'purification'. However, Latour's discussions of purification are largely epistemological, focusing on the modern impulse to represent the world in a dualistic fashion. I am interested here in a performative split between humans and free-standing machines that obey their will. As usual, one can find traces of this line of thought in Latour's work, too. See, for example, his outline history of the diesel engine in *Science in Action* (Latour 1987).
14. This is where my ontological analysis feeds into a politics that differs from Latour's. On doing things differently, see Pickering (2010). See Kopenawa and Albert (2013) for the contrast between Yanomami and Western relations to the environment.
15. Foucault's (1988) examples of technologies of the self are techniques of self-control. The shamanic techniques described by Kopenawa are better seen as technologies of abandonment, followed by a restabilization of the self in the world of the *xapiri*. Technologies of the self are little discussed in the STS literature. On meditation, see Carvalho (2014a, 2014b). On abandonment among drug users and musicians and music lovers, see Gomart and Hennion (1999).
16. Glaser's dance of agency with the bubble chamber, sketched out earlier, sat on top of and extended that sort of training in an emergent fashion.
17. Eliade (1964) presents a classic representationalist account of shamanism.
18. The Western canon here would include Huxley (1956), Lilly (1972), Laing (1967), and Castaneda (1968).

References

Aspers, Patrik. 2015. "Performing Ontology." *Social Studies of Science* 43 (3): 449–453.

Barad, Karen. 2007. *Meeting the Universe Halfway: Quantum Physics and the Entanglement of Matter and Meaning*. Durham, NC: Duke University Press.

Barnes, Barry. 1994. "How Not to Do the Sociology of Knowledge." In *Rethinking Objectivity*, ed. Allan Megill, 21–35. Durham, NC: Duke University Press.

Barnes, Barry, and Donald MacKenzie. 1979. "Scientific Judgement: The Biometry-Mendelism Controversy." In *Natural Order: Historical Studies of Scientific Culture*, ed. Barry Barnes and Steven Shapin, 191–210. Thousand Oaks, CA: Sage.

Bennett, Jane. 2010. *Vibrant Matter: A Political Ecology of Things*. Durham, NC: Duke University Press.

Carvalho, António. 2014a. "Performing Meditation: Vipassana and Zen as Technologies of the Self." PhD diss., University of Exeter.

Carvalho, António. 2014b. "Subjectivity, Ecology and Meditation: Performing Interconnectedness." *Subjectivity* 7 (2): 131–150.

Castaneda, Carlos. 1968. *The Teachings of Don Juan: A Yaqui Way of Knowledge*. Harmondsworth: Penguin.

Collins, H. M. 1992. *Changing Order: Replication and Induction in Scientific Practice.* Chicago: University of Chicago Press.

DeLanda, Manuel. 2002. *Intensive Science and Virtual Philosophy.* London: Continuum Books:.

Descola, Philippe. 2014. "Modes of Being and Forms of Predication." *HAU: Journal of Ethnographic Theory* 4 (1): 271–280.

Durkheim, Emile. 1995. *The Elementary Forms of Religious Life.* Trans. Karen E. Fields. New York: Free Press.

Eliade, Mircea. 1964. *Shamanism: Archaic Techniques of Ecstasy.* London: Routledge.

Fleck, Ludwik. 1979. *Genesis and Development of a Scientific Fact.* Ed. Thaddeus J. Trenn and Robert K. Merton; trans. Fred Bradley and Thaddeus J. Trenn. Chicago: University of Chicago Press.

Fortun, Kim. 2014. "From Latour to Late Industrialism." *HAU: Journal of Ethnographic Theory.* 4 (1): 309–329.

Foucault, Michel. 1988. *Technologies of the Self: A Seminar with Michel Foucault.* Ed. Luther H. Martin, Huck Gutman, and Patrick H. Hutton. Amherst: University of Massachusetts Press.

Gleick, James. 1987. *Chaos: Making a New Science.* New York: Penguin.

Gomart, Emilie, and Antoine Hennion. 1999. "A Sociology of Attachment: Music Amateurs, Drug Users." In *Actor Network Theory and After*, ed. John Law and John Hassard, 220–247. Oxford: Blackwell.

Hacking, Ian. 2002. *Historical Ontology.* Cambridge, MA: Harvard University Press.

Haraway, Donna. 2004. *The Haraway Reader.* New York: Routledge.

Henare, Amiria, Martin Holbraad and Sari Wastell, eds. 2007. *Thinking Through Things: Theorising Artefacts Ethnographically.* London: Routledge.

Holbraad, Martin. 2011. "Can the Thing Speak?" Open Anthropology Cooperative Press, Working Papers Series #7. http://openanthcoop.net/press/http:/openanthcoop.net/press/wp-content/uploads/2011/01/Holbraad-Can-the-Thing-Speak2.pdf (accessed 6 March 2017).

Hollis, Martin, and Steven Lukes, eds. 1982. *Rationality and Relativism.* Cambridge, MA: MIT Press.

Huxley, Aldous. 1956. *The Doors of Perception; and, Heaven and Hell.* New York: Harper & Row.

Jordan, Kathleen, and Michael Lynch. 1992. "The Sociology of a Genetic Engineering Technique: Ritual and Rationality in the Performance of the 'Plasmid Prep.'" In *The Right Tools for the Job: At Work in Twentieth-Century Life Sciences*, ed. Adele E. Clarke and Joan H. Fujimura, 77–114. Princeton, NJ: Princeton University Press.

Kauffman, Stuart A. 2002. *Investigations.* New York: Oxford University Press.

Kelly, John. 2014. "Introduction: The Ontological Turn in French Philosophical Anthropology." *HAU: Journal of Ethnographic Theory* 4 (1): 259–269. Special section titled "Colloquia: The Ontological French Turn," ed. John Kelly.

Klein, Ursula, and Wolfgang Lefèvre. 2007. *Materials in Eighteenth-Century Science: A Historical Ontology.* Cambridge, MA: MIT Press.

Kopenawa, Davi, and Bruce Albert. 2013. *The Falling Sky: Words of a Yanomami Shaman.* Trans. Nicholas Elliott and Alison Dundy. Cambridge, MA: Harvard University Press.

Kuhn, Thomas S. 1962. *The Structure of Scientific Revolutions.* Chicago: University of Chicago Press.

Kuhn, Thomas S. 1991. "The Road Since Structure." In *PSA 1990: Proceedings of the 1990 Biennial Meeting of the Philosophy of Science Association.* Vol. 2: *Symposia and Invited Papers*, ed. Arthur Fine, Micky Forbes, and Linda Wessels, 2–13. East Lansing, MI: Philosophy of Science Association.

Laing, R. D. 1967. *The Politics of Experience.* New York: Pantheon.
Lakatos, Imre, and Alan Musgrave, eds. 1970. *Criticism and the Growth of Knowledge.* Cambridge: Cambridge University Press.
Lao Tzu. 1963. *Tao Te Ching.* Harmondsworth: Penguin.
Latour, Bruno. 1987. *Science in Action: How to Follow Scientists and Engineers through Society.* Cambridge, MA: Harvard University Press.
Latour, Bruno. 1993. *We Have Never Been Modern.* Cambridge, MA: Harvard University Press.
Latour, Bruno. 2005. *Reassembling the Social: An Introduction to Actor-Network-Theory* Oxford: Oxford University Press.
Latour, Bruno. 2013. *An Inquiry into Modes of Existence: An Anthropology of the Moderns.* Trans. Catherine Porter. Cambridge, MA: Harvard University Press.
Law, John, and Marianne Elisabeth Lien. 2013. "Slippery: Field Notes on Empirical Ontology." *Social Studies of Science*: 363–378.
Lilly, John C. 1972. *The Center of the Cyclone: An Autobiography of Inner Space.* New York: Julian Press.
Miller, Daniel. 2010. *Stuff.* Cambridge: Polity Press.
Mol, Annemarie. 2002. *The Body Multiple: Ontology in Medical Practice.* Durham, NC: Duke University Press.
Pickering, Andrew. 1981a. "Constraints on Controversy: The Case of the Magnetic Monopole." *Social Studies of Science* 11 (1): 63–93.
Pickering, Andrew. 1981b. "The Hunting of the Quark." *Isis* 72 (2): 216–236.
Pickering, Andrew. 1981c. "The Role of Interests in High-Energy Physics: The Choice between Charm and Colour." In *The Social Process of Scientific Investigation*, ed. Karin D. Knorr, Roger Krohn, and Richard Whitley, 107–138. Dordrecht: Reidel.
Pickering, Andrew. 1984a. "Against Putting the Phenomena First: The Discovery of the Weak Neutral Current." *Studies in History and Philosophy of Science* 15 (2): 85–117.
Pickering, Andrew. 1984b. *Constructing Quarks: A Sociological History of Particle Physics.* Chicago: University of Chicago Press.
Pickering, Andrew, ed. 1992. *Science as Practice and Culture.* Chicago: University of Chicago Press.
Pickering, Andrew. 1993. "The Mangle of Practice: Agency and Emergence in the Sociology of Science." *American Journal of Sociology* 99 (3): 559–589.
Pickering, Andrew. 1995a. "Cyborg History and the World War II Regime." *Perspectives on Science* 3 (1): 1–48.
Pickering, Andrew. 1995b. *The Mangle of Practice: Time, Agency, and Science.* Chicago: University of Chicago Press.
Pickering, Andrew. 2005a. "Asian Eels and Global Warming: A Posthumanist Perspective on Society and the Environment." *Ethics and the Environment* 10 (2): 29–43.
Pickering, Andrew. 2005b. "Decentering Sociology: Synthetic Dyes and Social Theory." *Perspectives on Science* 13 (3): 352–405.
Pickering, Andrew. 2008. "New Ontologies." In *The Mangle in Practice: Science, Society, and Becoming*, ed. Andrew Pickering and Keith Guzik, 1–14. Durham, NC: Duke University Press.
Pickering. Andrew. 2009. "The Politics of Theory: Producing Another World, with Some Thoughts on Latour." *Journal of Cultural Economy* 2 (1–2): 197–212.
Pickering. Andrew. 2010. *The Cybernetic Brain: Sketches of Another Future.* Chicago: University of Chicago Press.
Pickering, Andrew. 2013. "Living in the Material World." In *Materiality and Space: Organizations, Artefacts and Practices*, ed. François-Xavier de Vaujany and Nathalie Mitev, 25–40. London: Macmillan.

Pickering, Andrew. 2014. "Reflections on the Dance of Agency: Islands of Stability, Science as Performance." Paper presented at the History of Science Seminar, Uppsala University, Sweden, 3 June.

Pickering, Andrew. 2015. "Science, Contingency, and Ontology." In *Science as It Could Have Been: Discussing the Contingency/Inevitability Problem*, ed. Léna Soler, Emiliano Trizio, and Andrew Pickering, 117–128. Pittsburgh, PA: University of Pittsburgh Press.

Salmond, Amiria J. M. 2014. "Transforming Translations (Part 2): Addressing Ontological Alterity." *HAU: Journal of Ethnographic Theory* 4 (1): 155–187.

Shapin, Steven. 1979. "The Politics of Observation: Cerebral Anatomy and Social Interests in the Edinburgh Phrenology Disputes." In *On the Margins of Science: The Social Construction of Rejected Knowledge*, ed. Roy Wallis, 139–178. Keele: University of Keele.

Sismondo, Sergio. 2015. "Ontological Turns, Turnoffs and Roundabouts." *Social Studies of Science* 45 (3): 441–448.

Swanton, Dan. 2013. "The Steel Plant as Assemblage." *Geoforum* 44: 282–291.

Viveiros de Castro, Eduardo. 2004. "Exchanging Perspectives: The Transformation of Objects into Subjects in Amerindian Ontologies." *Common Knowledge* 10 (3): 463–484.

Waldrop, M. Mitchell. 1992. *Complexity: The Emerging Science at the Edge of Order and Chaos*. New York: Simon & Schuster.

Watts, Alan. 1957. *The Way of Zen*. New York: Pantheon.

Watts, Alan. 1975. *Tao: The Watercourse Way*. New York: Pantheon.

Whitehead, Alfred North. 1926. *Science and the Modern World*. Cambridge: Cambridge University Press.

Wilhelm, Hellmut, ed. 1967. *The I Ching, or, Book of Changes*. Trans. Cary F. Baynes. Princeton, NJ: Princeton University Press.

Wolfram, Stephen. 2002. *A New Kind of Science*. Champaign, IL: Wolfram Media.

Woolgar, Steve, and Javier Lezaun. 2013. "The Wrong Bin Bag: A Turn to Ontology in Science and Technology Studies?" *Social Studies of Science* 43 (3): 321–340. Special issue titled "A Turn to Ontology in Science and Technology Studies?" ed. Steve Woolgar and Javier Lezaun.

Woolgar, Steve, and Javier Lezaun. 2015. "Missing the (Question) Mark? What *Is* a Turn to Ontology?" *Social Studies of Science* 45 (3): 462–467.

INDEX

actor-network theory (ANT)
  defining, 139
  Latour approach to, 139, 147n12
  multispecies anthropology methods in
    relation to, 85, 97n3
  on social relations, 26n2, 66, 74–75
  in STS, 26n2, 66, 73, 74–75
Africa
  initiation ceremonies in, 37
  smallpox epidemic in, 107–108
African bushmen. *See* G‖ana; G|ui
agency
  deltas and histories of, 120, 121–122,
    126, 129
  non-human, 97n3, 138, 141–142,
    146n6
agency, dance of, 143
  case studies including, 146n4
  defining, 3, 138
  in disasters/catastrophes, 140
  performative idiom relation with,
    136–137, 146n6
  in STS, 136, 139–140, 146n4, 147n16
agriculture
  in deltas, 121, 122–123, 124
  human-animal/non-human relations
    in, 102
  in river basins in relation to deltas,
    124
altered states (of being), 143–144, 145
Amazonia
  human-nonhuman relations in,
    141–143
  kinship in, 16–17
  shamanism of, 141–144, 147nn14–15

Viveiros de Castro scholarship on,
  16–17, 61, 138
See also Large-Scale Biosphere-Atmosphere Experiment in Amazonia
Amino Yoshihiko, 7
"Analogic Kinship" (Wagner), 28n24
animal behavior research, 86, 102,
  113–115
'animal borders'
  corporeal schema of, 102, 103–105,
    109, 110, 112, 114
  language role in, 101
  meaning of, 100, 101–102
  See also human-animal/non-human
    dualism; human-animal/non-
    human relations
animal geographers, 87
Animal Liberation (Singer), 101
animal metamorphosis, 101, 111–113
animism, 48, 93, 102, 138
ANT. *See* actor-network theory
Anthropocene, 47, 49, 61, 91
anthropological traditions
  Boas classification approach to, 3
  co-evolving relation between, 10
  diversity of, 1, 3–5, 10, 47–48
  future trajectories for, 1, 12n1
  language in defining, 4
  locality focus in, 8
  minor, 4, 9, 82–83
  mutual influence between minor and
    major, 4, 9
  ontological turn in, 2, 135, 137–139
  socio-ecological approach in, 7–8
  See also specific traditions and topics

historical definitions of, 27n13
kinship in relation to, 17, 20
nature-culture dualism appearance
    with, 19, 27n10
symbiosis and biological view of,
    15–16, 24, 83
Ingold, Tim, 27n11, 89, 112
Inquiry into Modes of Existence, An
    (Latour), 49
intercorporeality, 101, 110, 112–115
interdisciplinarity
    of multispecies anthropology, 11,
        84–85, 86, 94, 95, 97n2, 97n7
    in nature-culture investigation, 9–10
    rise in, 115
International Union of Anthropological and
    Ethnological Sciences (IUAES), 1
irrigation systems, 121–122, 124, 127–129
'islands of stability'
    in altered states of being, 143–144, 145
    for Amazonia shamans, 142, 143, 144
    in becoming, role of, 140, 145
    different worlds understood through,
        11, 137
    disasters/catastrophes reflection on,
        140, 143
    human experience centrality of, 140
    multiplicity of, 140–141
    as performative achievements, 141,
        142
    in STS concept transference, 137,
        144–145
Itani, Junichiro, 101, 114–115
IUAES. *See* International Union of Anthro-
    pological and Ethnological Sciences

Japan
    human-animal/non-human dualism
        in, 114
    modernity in, 8–9
    nationalism and nature relation in, 6, 7
    nature-culture dichotomy approach in,
        5–6
    present-day anthropology origins in,
        4–5
    primatology in, 113–114
    salmon study in, 87–89
    shizen compared to nature in, 5–6
Japanese anthropology
    aesthetico-descriptive style in, 7
    complementary schismogenesis and, 7

equivocations role in, 6, 8–9
at Kyoto School, 7–8, 11
nature-culture multiplicity in, 2
symmetrical schismogenesis and, 8
Western influence in, 6–7, 8
Japanese folklore studies (*minzokugaku*),
    6–7, 9
Japanese language, 101
Japanese Society of Cultural Anthropol-
    ogy (JASCA), 1, 12n1
Johnson, Mark, 101
Jordan, Kathleen, 138

Kafka, Franz, 4
Kalahari hunter-gatherers. *See* G‖ana; G|ui
kinship
    in Amazonia, 16–17
    analogic, 28n24
    'blood' symbolism and interpretations
        with, 22–23, 28nn21–22
    configurations of, 16
    in France, seventeenth-century, 22
    historical interpretations of, 21–22
    individuality in relation to, 17, 20
    internal and external distinctions of,
        17–18, 19, 24–25, 26n3
    linguistic idioms of, 24
    Locke on, 21, 24, 27n14, 27n19
    marriage-as-alliance in, 23
    marriage within, 18–19, 23, 26nn6–7
    'natural' behavior for, 19, 26n8
    naturalism role in identity and, 17–25,
        26n8
    nature-culture dualism role of, 11
    relationality of, obscuring, 23–24
    symbiosis in relation to, 25
    Viveiros de Castro on relativity of,
        16–17, 26n3
    Western thought on, 17
Knight, John, 102
Konner, Melvin J., 103
Kopenawa, Davi, 141–142, 143, 144,
    147nn14–15
Kuhn, Thomas, 76, 135, 136
Kyoto School, Japan, 7–8, 11

Lakoff, George, 101
land reclamation, 119, 122–123, 129
language
    in anthropological traditions charac-
        terization, 4

www.ingramcontent.com/pod-product-compliance
Lightning Source LLC
Chambersburg PA
CBHW070933030426
42336CB00014BA/2659